THE BOOK OF
THE BITCH

A Complete Guide to Understanding and Caring for Bitches

J.M. Evans and Kay White

HOWELL BOOK HOUSE

New York

HOWELL BOOK HOUSE
A Simon & Schuster / Macmillan Company
1633 Broadway
New York, NY 10019

MACMILLAN is a registered trademark of
Macmillan, Inc.

Library of Congress Cataloging-in-Publication data
available on request.

ISBN 0–87605–603–6

Manufactured in Singapore

10 9 8 7 6 5 4 3 2 1

CONTENTS

ILLUSTRATIONS

TABLES

FOREWORD

The Book of the Bitch follows the highly successful formula used in *The Doglopaedia*. The technical information is supplied by a veterinary surgeon with wide experience both in practice and as an advisor to the veterinary pharmaceutical industry; added to this are practical tips, observations and comments from a dog breeder who has owned and bred from many bitches in a long association with the canine world.

The authors hope that between them they are able to fulfil the information needs of both serious breeders and novice owners who want to know more about bitch ownership so that they can get the maximum pleasure from their pet. As the reader will discover, bitches are indeed very different from male dogs.

The book is intended to supply all the technical reference material a bitch owner will need, giving guidance on when to consult the vet and also serving to amplify and explain what was said at the consultation. It is fully indexed and contains a glossary and other listings, so that in effect the book becomes a veterinary dictionary.

The Book of the Bitch is divided into four sections. The first two describe in a straightforward and easy-to-read way the practical aspects of caring for and breeding from your bitch. The third section is more technical and outlines the medical problems specific to bitches. It has been structured for data retrieval at the time of need, although of course can be read through in its entirety. The fourth section covers further useful information and data.

It is hoped that *The Book of the Bitch*, which is both a celebration of and hymn of praise to the bitch, will prove to be of long-term value to all who enjoy the company of the female of the canine species.

INTRODUCTION

This book is the first, we believe, to be devoted entirely to the female of the canine species. There have been books on mating and whelping bitches, but this book goes further in that it deals with all the special attributes of the female, whether bred from or not. It is designed to be read and referred to in conjunction with our best-selling book, *The Doglopaedia*, which provides a comprehensive guide to dog care in general.

The Book of the Bitch commences with the time the new owner is deciding whether to acquire a male or female dog. Advice is given on the special needs of bringing up a bitch puppy, guiding the owner through the bitch's adolescence and first 'heat'. We then follow the bitch through middle age and into old age, with special emphasis on the feminine illnesses which may occur if she has, or has not, been mated.

Should you decide that dog breeding is for you, all the information that you need is here – from finding a stud dog, arranging the mating on the right day, the etiquette of stud dog use, pregnancy diagnosis, to looking after the bitch during pregnancy, arranging whelping quarters, feeding, helping the bitch during the birth and rearing the puppies, and then restoring the bitch to her role as a companion animal.

The anatomical features particular to the bitch are clearly illustrated and the correct terminology is supplied so that the bitch owner need have no diffidence in describing any change from normality to the veterinary surgeon. Alternative methods of contraception for the bitch, and the merits and demerits of breeding one or more litters, are fully discussed.

Both of us have enjoyed the lifelong companionship of a number of bitches in several different breeds and so we seek to celebrate all that is good and beautiful about owning a female dog. We hope that in *The Book of the Bitch* we can show other owners how to make their bitches equally rewarding to own.

J.M. Evans
Kay White

ACKNOWLEDGEMENTS

Writing books in joint authorship is not easy but we both hope that in putting together our combined experience, acquired in our separate roles as veterinary surgeon and as dog breeder/journalist, we have achieved a complication of information which will prove useful to all those who are interested in bitches and puppies.

Inevitably the knowledge which we have acquired has come partly from our own practical experience and partly through the generosity of other people who have, in various ways, shared their expertise with us.

I shall always be grateful to the members of the veterinary profession, both in private practice and in veterinary schools, who have shown such patience and generosity in teaching a layperson.

We are both grateful to the Kennel Club for their help on average litter registrations in the various breeds.

And then there are our bitches. Every one which we have owned has, in her own way, taught us something about the female of the canine species. Dear to the hearts of the Evans family are, from bygone days, the Boxer *Astra*, Bedlington Terriers *Kleine* and *Yo-Yo,* the Dobermanns *Juno* and *Anna.*

My own Duckscottage Boxers have been the cornerstone of a lifetime interest in dogbreeding, so please bear with me if I mention *Tessie* the one who started me on this path. Among many others, I remember with special affection *Jill, Pixie, Panda, Poppet, Dawn* and *Pooka,* as well as the independent and self-sufficient earth mother *Blossom,* her daughter *Berry* and *Holly.* Thank you all, Boxer ladies; you filled my life over many years with your love and your litters.

I would also like to thank the Editor and Editorial Board of the *Kennel Gazette* who inspired me to gather together much of this material for the series 'Musing about Mating'.

Kay White

SECTION ONE:
CARE OF YOUR BITCH

Obtaining a bitch

Bitch management

Educating your bitch

Nutrition and feeding

CHAPTER 1
OBTAINING A BITCH

Why choose a bitch?

Buying a bitch puppy

Adopting an adult bitch

Breeding terms

Choosing for breeding

Choosing for showing

Tips

Why choose a bitch?

The advantages of a female
- She is smaller and lighter than a male.
- She is likely to be more docile and more affectionate than a male to her owner.
- She has a special affinity for children and makes a sympathetic companion.
- She is unlikely to roam or stray from home except when in season.
- She is generally as good as her male counterpart at warning, guarding, retrieving, putting up game, and ratting.
- She is as quick as a male, or quicker, to learn and respond to what is wanted of her.
- She will be easier to house-train than a male and will not usually territory mark in your home, your friends' houses or in hotels.

The disadvantages of a female
- She is subject to mood swings and considerable alteration in disposition during the phases of her oestrous cycle. Allowances should be made for uncharacteristic behaviour at these times. This may still be noticeable to some extent even after she has been spayed.

15

Many bitches will be as eager to seek males during the peak time for mating as the males will be to find them.

There is more competition in bitch classes in dog shows.

An entire bitch may have lengthy periods when she is not in show condition.

She will probably ruin your lawn by scorching the grass with urine patches if you allow her free access.

If you do not have your bitch spayed, or use any contraceptive method, she may make a mess through loss of blood when in season. (See Chapter 2 for advice on managing seasons.)

She may not be able to run as fast as a male nor be as agile.

It is possible that she may need surgery later in life to remove her uterus as uterine diseases are common. This worry will of course be removed if you have her spayed early in life; an action which will also reduce the occurrence of mammary tumours.

A pedigree bitch puppy may well cost more than a male. Breeders tend to keep their best bitches so you may find a female more difficult to buy.

When making your decision, another factor to be taken into account is the sex of the dogs already in your household or those belonging to frequent visitors to your home. If you already own a male dog, either he or the bitch will have to be kennelled while the bitch is in season; it is virtually impossible to keep the two apart in an ordinary home. Bitches and dogs will mate with their closest relations, so you cannot rely on abstinence on their part.

Some consideration should also be given to the sex of dogs belonging to close neighbours. You could cause considerable temperamental upset to their male dogs by exercising an in season bitch on communal territory.

Should you buy two bitches?

This can be a pleasant idea, as sisters are usually good friends all their lives and they are company for each other. They will, however, be marginally more difficult to house-train than single puppies.

If you intend to breed professionally, it is as well to be aware that two bitches are likely to be in season around the same time, even if they are unrelated or are of different ages. This means that you will either have a glut of puppies if you mate both bitches,. or you must mate one bitch at a time. Buying sisters also means that your breeding line has a very small gene pool. You would be better based with unrelated bitches, especially if you mean to keep your own stud dog, and you may well find it more convenient to buy the bitches a few months apart, so that one is partially educated before you begin with the other.

When not to buy

There are occasions when it is not prudent to take on a puppy, particularly a sensitive bitch. Such times may be:
● When a major lifestyle change is imminent. Wait until you are resettled so that you can give maximum attention to the puppy.

- When structural alterations are being made to your property – a danger time for puppies.
- When you expect to take a holiday within the next four months – it is not sensible to board very young puppies in kennels.
- If a new baby is expected. To raise a puppy correctly needs a great deal of time and concentration for the first year.

Buying a puppy

Pedigree bitch puppies

Make a study of the breeds you fancy before you make a commitment to buying.

Many people have an idealized view of the dog they would like to own. Get as much 'hands-on' experience as you can; see what the breed of your choice is like to live with – from puppy days, through adolescence and into old age; in wet weather and in fine; in winter and in summer. See as many of the breed as possible: at dog shows and in the homes of breeders, as well as with friends and acquaintances.

Ask yourself if you could live with this breed in your present home, and with your present and projected work/hobby/family commitments. Never buy on the premise that things will get easier; that the family member who dislikes dogs will 'come round'. Take a hard look at the breeds you favour with regard to grooming requirements; exercise needs; boisterousness; tendency to fight other dogs or to chase livestock; and, of course, consider the maintenance costs.

Consult a veterinary surgeon about hereditary defects in the breeds you are interested in and make a note of what clearance certificates you should ask for when you actually buy. This is important, even if you do not intend to breed from your bitch, for hereditary defects can cause pain and discomfort and even bring about early death, besides possibly being costly to have corrected by a veterinary surgeon.

Always aim to buy your puppy from her place of birth. This should be reasonably easy in most areas, at least for the more popular breeds. Your National Kennel Club will supply you with lists of breeders' and dog magazines carry breeders' advertisements, as do local papers.

See the dam of the litter and ask where you can see the sire, as he may belong to another kennel. Satisfy yourself that the parents meet your requirements and expectations in terms of size, conformation and, most importantly, temperament. Reserve the right to take the puppy back to the breeder if a veterinary surgeon finds her unsatisfactory – do not feel obliged to saddle yourself with an unhealthy puppy. Try to make an appointment to see a vet within an hour or two of purchase so that you have not become 'bonded' with the puppy, and so that she is not away from the breeder's premises for long. If the puppy has to go back to the breeder, it is not kind or helpful to the pup to have kept her in your home for several hours or overnight, and if you have kept her for a few days the breeder would have the right to refuse to refund your money.

If you are seeking to return the puppy because the veterinary examination has shown something to be wrong, make sure you take a signed statement on the vet's headed paper to give to the breeder. Most breeders will take the return of a puppy very seriously and will want to speak to the vet about the fault that was found. If the identified condition is curable, let the breeder have the puppy back until she is in a fit condition for sale. The breeder is the best person to deal with a sick puppy or one that must have surgery – the puppy will get better more quickly if she does not have to adjust to a new home and new owners while not being 100 per cent fit. If you really want the puppy and the veterinary surgeon says the outlook is good, you may agree to wait for her until she is cured.

If you wish to return a puppy to the breeder because she is not right for you, or you find that the actuality rather than the dream causes you too much work and trouble, you are on fragile ground. A full refund of your money is unlikely and you should not expect it. The breeder may offer to take the puppy back and resell her, but you will be charged for her keep, re-advertising, and also for keeping her in isolation, because she may have encountered infection while away from the breeder. Obviously this capricious returning of a puppy is cruel to the pup, giving her a poor start in life, but this situation never need occur if you have done your homework properly.

Never buy a puppy which has already made a long journey from her place of birth as this predisposes her to illness. Some puppy dealers masquerade as breeders, so ask penetrating questions and refuse to be put off by oblique answers. Suspect those who offer more than two or three breeds for sale. If you are in doubt, ask the opinion of veterinary surgeons in the neighbourhood, for they usually know from where the sub-standard puppies come. Failure to make in depth enquiries could cost you dearly later on. Never buy a puppy because you are sorry for her, for you could be letting yourself in for 10 years or more of worry and expense. If a puppy is ill or deformed in some way, the best person to keep her is the breeder. Never be blackmailed into buying, being given, or being sold cheaply a puppy which will otherwise be 'put down'. A puppy which has so little value will not make a good pet, or a breeding bitch, and anything free will usually be costly in vet's fees in the long term.

Mongrel bitch puppies

Realizing that no guarantee can be given for size, temperament, or type of adult coat, and that it will be most unlikely that you will see the father, it pays to follow at least some of the advice given above. A veterinary surgeon may know of a good source of reliable mongrels, or you may obtain a puppy from one of the major animal charity homes. But do choose carefully and sensibly, and don't let your heart rule your head.

Adopting an adult bitch

Taking on an adult bitch is not usually as easy as it may seem. Bitches are creatures of habit and she may find it difficult to make the adjustment to living with you.

You may think at first that you will have no problems with your newly acquired pet, but this may be because you are seeing uncharacteristic behaviour if the bitch is subdued on arrival at strange territory. You may not see her normal behaviour for as long as six to eight weeks. If she has been kennelled for any length of time she may have lost all notion of house-training; she may have acquired habits such as barking and jumping up at gates and fences; she may acutely miss the company of other dogs and bitches or she may have developed a tendency to fight; she may be an incorrigible wanderer if given the opportunity.

You need to give any adult bitch a long trial in your home, at least a month, before you decide whether you are meant for each other.

Find out as much as you can about her past history. Let her tell you her story – if she flinches from men or children, flies in terror from a sweeping broom – and you can draw your own conclusions about how she was treated. Very gradually set about conquering her fears. In the meantime, take the utmost precautions with her until you can read her behaviour in all circumstances. Do not let her off the lead for several weeks, and do not leave her alone with children until you are absolutely sure of her behaviour.

Sometimes the bitches available from breed rescue associations are the 'victims' of divorce or partnership breakup. Such bitches can be in an acute anxiety state if there has been tension in the home or quarrels going on over their heads. The more sensitive and clever the bitch, the more she will have suffered, and she may take a long while to return to normality.

It is not always possible to obtain the history of adult bitches, and sometimes those who seek to dispose of them do not tell the truth. Unless you receive an up-to-date vaccination certificate with the bitch, you will be wise to get her fully vaccinated at once. Take the opportunity also to give her a complete health check, to ensure that any adverse behaviour patterns she shows are not due to pain or illness.

If you take on a bitch which has been kept in a poor way, remember to hasten slowly with feeding. Small amounts of easily digestible food should be given frequently to start with, until she begins to recover. She will also need a course of worm medicine, as advised by your vet.

You may be able to obtain an adult bitch from breed rescue societies, animal charity homes, or from breeders. There are drawbacks to getting an adult bitch if you have breeding in mind, since rescue organizations do not pass on pedigrees with their animals specifically to stop them being exploited for breeding and/or showing. Some rescue organizations stipulate that the bitch is still nominally theirs and they reserve the right to visit your home, initially with a view to checking suitability, and at intervals thereafter. You must decide if you are willing to accept this or if you would regard it as an intrusion. Some adult bitches may already have been spayed, or the rescue organization may get this done for you before you collect the bitch. You will probably be expected to pay the fee incurred.

Breeding kennels sometimes have adult bitches to dispose of, usually those which have failed to breed easily, or which have had several litters and are now considered too old to breed from. It is unlikely that a pedigree will be given. It is sensible to have these bitches spayed very soon after they have settled into your home, for it would be a disaster for such a bitch to become accidentally pregnant.

Pedigree bitches on breeding terms

Sometimes a kennel will have for sale a puppy or a young bitch on breeding terms. This means that you can buy the bitch for less than the normal selling price, but you will have to breed from her under the direction of the original owner and give back some puppies from one or more litters. The arrangements are flexible but, once agreed, they must be adhered to.

Points to consider are:

● When is the breeding to be done?
- Who is to choose the stud dog and who pays the stud fee and travel expenses?
- Who will have the care of bitch and puppies during whelping and after?
- Who pays the costs of veterinary attention?
- Who pays the costs of rearing the puppies?
- What pick will the original owner want (e.g. best puppy and third best, leaving second and fourth for you)?
- At what age will this choice be made?
- At what age will the original owner take his 'picks' away?
- Should the bitch fail to breed or proves unsuitable, what do you have to pay?
- Perhaps your circumstances change and you cannot undertake a litter – do make provisions for this event, as you may have to give the bitch back or pay her full cost, if you cannot fulfil the terms.
- Suppose the bitch does not have enough puppies to take care of the stipulated 'picks' – how many litters must she have to fulfil your obligations?

Remember that the bitch will not belong to you until the breeding terms have been carried out to the satisfaction of your partner, and you have no right to dispose of the bitch, have her spayed, have any other major surgical interference, or have her 'put down' without your partner's agreement and permission.

To have a bitch on breeding terms is not usually a satisfactory arrangement but it may be the only way to make a start in a rare or newly imported breed.

Choosing a bitch for breeding

Take heed of the advice given earlier with regard to hereditary defects. (See also Chapter 7.)

Be prepared to wait for a puppy or put your name down for the choice of an expected litter. Buy from fertile stock on both dam and sire's sides. Infertility, and the ability to produce puppies normally and not by Caesarean, is to a large extent hereditary, as is good, normal maternal behaviour in cleaning and suckling the puppies for a reasonable length of time. Choose from a litter of average size for the breed. Choose a large, rather than a small, bitch puppy, and not the most pushy or forceful of the litter, but not the shyest either.

In a breed where white markings are prized, e.g. Boxers, remember that a bitch with exaggerated white markings mated to a dog of similar coat is likely to produce a high proportion of all-white unsaleable puppies. A bitch with more dark pigmentation may be a better choice as a brood bitch. Buy only from a healthy litter where all the pups are clear-eyed, active, pleasant smelling, and with good clean coats.

Make sure that your puppy is properly registered at your national Kennel Club.

Choosing a bitch to show

Make a definitive study of the breed so that you know just what you should be looking for. See a lot of litters, look at a number of adults in the show ring and assess their progeny, particularly that of stud dogs. When you go to buy make it clear by writing and keeping a copy that you are looking for a bitch to show. No breeder can guarantee that you will get a bitch capable of winning but at least you will have established that you asked for show stock, so you should not be sold a bitch that has an obvious show handicap, such as unacceptable markings. The names of the sire and dam of the bitch you hope to be showing will be printed in the show catalogue, and there is no doubt that the name of illustrious forbears can be important in this context.

It is as well to be aware that you cannot show a spayed bitch in regular competition. There is no restriction on the showing of bitches whose seasons are averted by the use of injectable or oral hormonal contraceptive preparations.

The showing of bitches which are in oestrus at the time, is not banned, but you will find yourself very unpopular both with the judge and the other exhibitors if you shoul do so.

Table 1.1: Tips for owners buying a companion bitch

- Spend time choosing the breed, size, age and type of bitch that suits your lifestyle. Don't be railroaded into buying a bitch you have doubts about. Remember that you are taking on a responsibility for the next 10–15 years.
- Do some research on a local veterinary practice before buying, so you can take the puppy there to be checked right away.
- Buy the puppy from the place where she was born, see the dam and, if possible, the sire and some other relatives as well.
- Enquire how she has been fed. Breeders should provide a diet sheet for you.
- Never buy a puppy because you are sorry for her. A sick or malformed puppy is not your responsibility, so leave her with the breeder to look after.
- Never take two puppies in order to clear the litter, when you know full well that one is going to be as much as you can cope with.
- Don't let someone, however close, buy a puppy for you as a present, or a surprise for the children.
- Remember that you cannot change your pet for a newer or different model. You have her for the rest of her life, so be sure that you can fulfil the commitment for bitch ownership *now* and in the foreseeable future.

Care of your bitch

Table 1.2: Tips for prospective breeders and exhibitors

- Buy from the breeder. You will not find the type of stock you are looking for on dealers' premises or in pet shops.
- Be prepared to wait for the right puppy.
- Make it clear to the seller that you want a bitch for breeding and/or showing. Put this in writing and keep a copy.
- Find out from a vet what hereditary diseases are common in the breed and make sure you see clearance certificates for both parents and the puppy as appropriate, and get copies to keep.
- Buy from sound, fertile, stock, born naturally and not by Caesarean if at all possible.
- Buy a large, rather than a small, bitch for breeding. In some breeds the bitches which are shown are not those which are bred from.
- Have your puppy checked by a vet without delay.
- Avoid breeding terms unless this is your only way into a rare breed.
- If you agree to breeding terms make sure the contract covers all possibilities which may occur.
- Make sure the parents of the puppy are properly registered at the Kennel Club before you buy, and that the puppy's registration is being processed.

CHAPTER 2
BITCH MANAGEMENT

Puppyhood
Adolescence
Adulthood
Old age
Euthanasia

Puppies

Preparation and forethought

Before you collect your bitch puppy from the breeder you will need to make some preparations to welcome her.

● Make an appointment with the veterinary surgeon for her primary vaccinations. Many vets make separate times for puppy clinics to avoid them meeting sick dogs. Take her pedigree and diet sheet with you when you keep the appointment for the veterinary surgeon will want to check her age and may be interested to know from where she was bought. In any case you must know her date of birth, not just that she is 'about seven weeks'.

● Ask the breeder what foods, what type of milk and cereal, etc., you should get in stock. Don't plan to change any element of her feeding for at least two weeks and any subsequent change should take place gradually.

● Provide an easily identifiable small dish for her food (one which is no longer used by humans), and one which does not tip over easily for her water. Don't make the water dish so large that your pup could fall in! You will probably have to replace these dishes for larger ones at least twice in her lifetime.

● Find a cardboard box to serve as her first bed. Cut down the front a little way so that she can climb in and out. Put the box within her crate (see page 26). Create an enclosed living space for her in a corner of the kitchen where she can feel secure, yet see and be seen. Provide some toys, such as a securely lidded tin with a few stones in which she can roll around; a soft toy (remove any glass or plastic eyes); a log of very hard wood; a whole, unsawn marrowbone. Beware of poorly designed squeaky toys which the puppy may destroy to get the squeaker out, because these can be deadly if swallowed.

● Provide some bedding. White polyester fur blankets are ideal – bought from a pet shop or by mail order from addresses given in the canine press. It is a pleasant idea for the breeder to give a small piece of used bedding with the puppy so that she has some scent to relate to her birthplace. If you decide to use old woollen garments, remember to remove all buttons, zips and ornamentation which could be chewed and swallowed.

● Find out from the breeder what grooming equipment you will need. Initially, probably only a small hairbrush and fine comb will be necessary, but it is useful to find out the size of comb (combs are sized by the number of teeth to the inch) and the type of brush she will need as an adult. It is also handy if the breeder demonstrates grooming on one of her adults so that you know what to do when your puppy has more coat. Find out from the breeder what shampoo suits your breed, in case your puppy gets into a mess. Normally, unless you are intent on the show ring, you should not need to bath your pup more than two to three times a year, according to breed. Smooth-coated dogs only need bathing once a year, provided the dust and dead hair is groomed out of their coats regularly.

● Buy a small, soft braid collar and a light lead, but make sure the hook is not a flimsy one and that the collar fastens securely. You will probably need to buy two more collars in successive sizes before your bitch is fully grown.

● Buy a small plastic bucket and foam sponge to use to clean up urine puddles which may be passed on the kitchen floor – keep it handy!

Care of your puppy

Puppies are fed small amounts of food four to five times a day. Make mealtimes regular, and schedule house-training and playtime around them (see Chapter 4). Your new puppy needs to sleep a lot so do not be too ready to show her off to neighbours and friends. She needs rest and long periods of quiet, as well as short intervals of play which should not be of the teasing kind. Keep an eye on her environment – she may not want to be in strong light and she should not be allowed to sleep in a draughty corner.

Your puppy's first night away from her littermates is going to be an ordeal for her. Make it as smooth as you can. If you have a crate, you can take the puppy in that into your sitting-room and into your bedroom, so that with quiet words and a friendly hand you can supply some of the contact she has been used to. You can also carry the puppy outside to be clean if you hear her stirring in the early morning.

If you, as many people do, decide to leave her in the kitchen, provide her with a hooded box and a warm, well-wrapped hot-water bottle or low level electric heating pad which your vet can obtain for you. Feed the puppy last thing at night, take her to be clean, and you should be sure of some hours of peaceful sleep.

While the puppy is young, leave her alone in her enclosure for several periods during the day while you are in other rooms. This will gradually accustom her to going without human company for a while.

Begin teaching good manners from the start, as explained in Chapter 3.

Vaccination

Your veterinary surgeon will advise you on the vaccination programme and when you can start to take her out. (See also p. 168.) Custom is however changing on the need to keep puppies in complete isolation until their vaccinations have been completed. It used to be considered important to confine the puppy until immunity has been established, at around 14 weeks or possibly a week or two later. Modern vaccines are very effective and provide protection quickly, and being able to take your puppy out even in a limited way is most helpful in socializing her. You will not of course want to take her to public parks where lots of dogs are exercised, or to big crowded events such as fairs and fêtes. Let her have a run in a quiet field or a friend's garden. Take her out in the car – don't worry if she vomits for she will probably grow out of car sickness. Generally, very young puppies are less affected by travel sickness than adult dogs and once they are used to car travel you will have no trouble as your puppy grows older. Carry her around a large shop if they allow dogs.

When lead training begins, go out specifically for that purpose. Get the puppy walking as neatly by your side as possible, and if she pulls ahead be prepared to turn and go the other way. Short bouts of training once or twice a day work best. Do not let her approach other dogs you may meet, avoid them tactfully. Do not snatch your puppy up when you see a dog coming, because this may make her aggressive to other animals. Let people speak to her and make a fuss of her. Arrange to pass a school when the children are coming out, and your pup will get all the attention she can handle.

Insurance

Insurance cover for veterinary fees is a relatively new idea that has taken off rapidly in the last 10 years. It is important to realize that pet insurance is not a maintenance contract to cover vaccination and boosters, but it is a safeguard against heavy veterinary bills occurring at an inconvenient time. Veterinary surgeons expect to be paid at the time of treatment and sometimes the accident or illness in your bitch will be when the family exchequer is at its lowest. Statistics show that the first year of a puppy's life is the most vulnerable for accidents, poisoning, allergies and illness. You cannot be watching your puppy all the time, and the very fact of being a joyous adventurous puppy makes her prone to risks of all kinds, from eating poisonous plants to jumping out of windows. Ask your veterinary surgeon about pet insurance and pick up a proposal form at the surgery. (See also p. 165.)

Worming

It is particularly important that your bitch is kept free of worms in puppyhood, especially if you hope to breed from her. The roundworm (*Toxocara canis*), which she harbours now, can encyst in her tissues, only to emerge when she is pregnant to infect her puppies while in the uterus. Buy your wormers from the vet and give them regularly as instructed. Although you will not see any worms expelled when using modern effective wormers, still continue the worming programme your vet prescribes.

Modern wormers do not purge the dog, and for most preparations there is no need to withhold her food. The tablets are not difficult to give and, in any case, you should be training her to take tablets from your hand. *The Doglopaedia* shows how to give tablets to a reluctant dog but you can go one better with your bitch and get her to come when called to take her medicine. Practice with tiny sweets and bits of cheese so you never have a struggle if medication is needed.

Safeguarding your puppy

If this is your first puppy, or the first for some years, you will need to make some adjustments to the habits and routine of your household before she joins you.

Puppy Crates

Remembering that your puppy has to adjust to a totally new world in your home, it is important to provide her with a secure safe area in which she can sleep and also watch and sum up her new 'pack' and its territory. An eight week old puppy will sleep for two to three hours at a time and may be awake for only one hour, this time being used for eating, playing, grooming and house-training. Establish security for your bitch now and it will pay you well later on. These days many people are investing in a folding wire crate which encloses the bitch entirely but allows her to see out (Figure 2.1). The crate is especially useful for the bitch joining a household where there are already other dogs and cats, where only one person is available to look after the puppy or, for instance, if the puppy is going to accompany the owner to the office. The puppy's breeder or a veterinary surgeon will demonstrate and tell you where to buy one, or you will find crates advertised in the canine weekly papers.

Fig. 2.1 **Puppy crate**

Since some people find it convenient to travel with the puppy in the car in a crate, you will find some models made to fit hatchbacks. Get a size suitable for your bitch when she is adult, and block off one end while she is a puppy. Although the crate is an additional expense at this time, you will find it invaluable all through her life and it will have resale value if you ever wish to part with it. A crate simplifies house-training, minimizes damage to your home, and safely encloses the puppy when you are not able to watch her without depriving the puppy of interest and company. The crate will also come into use when the bitch is in season, and in illness when the bitch may need complete rest.

Once the puppy is old enough to have her freedom of your house and garden, the crate can serve as her bed. The door need rarely be shut unless there is some dangerous situation which she must be protected from, for instance, the front door standing open while furniture is moved in, or hot food being dished up in the kitchen. Many new owners find it a little difficult to get adjusted to the use of a crate but dogs, almost without exception, have decided that crates are a very good idea. You should have no trouble at all in getting your bitch to enjoy using hers.

Fencing and gates
Check these before the puppy joins you; it is surprising what a small gap a puppy can get through. Are there warning signs on your gates to encourage people to shut them on leaving? You must check that they are shut *all* the time to be sure.

Garden chemicals
Well before the puppy arrives you must stop using slug bait. Methaldehyde, the substance most commonly used, is not only very attractive to puppies and grown dogs but it is also a deadly poison from which few dogs recover. You can no longer use paraquat as a weedkiller as it is dangerous to dogs, and sodium chlorate should be used only with extreme caution.

Great care is also needed in the positioning of rat or mouse poisons. Make sure they are placed, if you need to use them, within a drain-pipe or something similar where no dog can possibly get at them.

Swimming pools – the biggest risk
The most frequent home accident to puppies and young dogs is drowning in a swimming pool, especially a covered pool. The dog may run across the cover, fall in, and be unable to climb out. Dogs have drowned in this manner within a few minutes, while their owners have been searching for them elsewhere. Make sure it cannot happen in your own garden, and take special care if you take your puppy to visit friends. If you have a pool it is a good idea to accustom your bitch to water from an early age, but even if she can swim it will not protect her from the type of accident which happens in a partially covered pool.

Houseplants
Some of these may be toxic if the puppy chews the leaves. Daffodil bulbs are also a very real danger. Put all indoor plants well out of reach.

Cupboards
If you do not use a crate but leave your puppy loose in the kitchen, there is always the risk that she may learn to open cupboard doors. Fix locks or bolts now and get used to using them.

Make a place for the waste bin well out of the dog's reach. Turning out the rubbish is a favourite occupation for dogs left alone, and some of the contents may be harmful, especially plastic wrappings.

Toys
Impress upon the children that from now on they must be tidy, because they will get the blame if the puppy takes things they have left about. Plastic toys are an especial danger, as a piece of plastic can cause an obstruction in the puppy's intestine which will not even show up on an X-ray, making diagnosis by the vet very difficult.

Adolescence

In some breeds, mainly the larger ones, puppyhood lasts for a long time and puberty and the first heat may be delayed for as long as 18 to 24 months, while the smaller Terriers may be fully grown and have their first oestrus at six months. It follows that even at two years of age, bitches of the larger breeds may not be physically or mentally ready for a litter. The mental state is important, as a bitch which is immature in this way may produce puppies but may not settle with them and/or display good maternal behaviour.

The first heat
The first heat is a major milestone in your bitch's life. You may notice for some days or weeks beforehand that she is showing signs of a temperament change. This will be your first experience of the mood swings which dominate the life of a bitch which is 'cycling regularly'. Cycling is the term applied to regular occurrence of heat in bitches which are not spayed or being given any form of oral or injectable hormonal contraceptive.

Your bitch may seem more excitable under the influence of the hormone changes of oestrus, or she may be more clinging and a little sad. Some bitches can exhibit signs of definite abdominal pain at this time. You will notice an increase in urination, and more deliberate urine marking of her territory, often with one leg half raised in a posture which imitates, as far as she is able, the male urination habits. The scent of her urine will have changed, as she is now exuding animal scents (pheromones) which tell other animals that she will soon be ready for breeding.

Take care, however, that you do not confuse this marking behaviour with the frequent straining and passing of small amounts of urine which may indicate a painful and troublesome cystitis.

Many owners believe that young bitches should be allowed to have one 'natural' season before doing anything about heat control. This serves the purpose of letting the bitch experience her normal adult state and become properly mature and it also allows the owners to see if they can cope with a natural season. As the first heat is not usually as intense as later ones, allowing the first to continue naturally is a useful trial of tolerance. Read our comments on oestrus control and discuss the matter with your veterinary surgeon, with particular reference to your plans for breeding. Many people do not believe in using hormonal contraceptive methods if the bitch is to be bred from at her second or third season, although the evidence is that the modern products do not interfere with future breeding capability.

As the time for the first heat approaches, prudent owners take a look at their fencing to make sure that it is high enough to prevent male dogs jumping over, and secure enough at the base to stop them, or the bitch, digging their way to a meeting.

Physical signs

The physical signs of heat are swelling of the vulva, increased licking of the genital area, and bleeding. The start of vulval bleeding indicates that anoestrus (the quiescent time between heats) has ended and pro-oestrus has begun. Breeders usually time 'the season' from the day on which bleeding starts, but the oestrogen level in the blood has been rising for about two weeks before this, preparing the genital tract for reproduction after its long anoestrus rest. (See also Chapter 8.)

The intervals between seasons vary immensely between individual bitches. Some will have a very regular six monthly cycle almost to the day, others will have an eight or 10 monthly cycle, and some will be entirely variable. Short cycles, with the bitch in season every three to four months, are not a good sign and may be a prelude to some uterine disease. Sometimes a bitch will produce all the signs of coming into heat, including some vulval enlargement and attraction to dogs, and yet will not start to bleed, and the physical signs may regress, only to reappear four to eight weeks later. This is sometimes referred to as a 'split heat'. Presumably in such cases the oestrogen levels she is producing early on are not high enough to bring the bitch properly into season. Your veterinary surgeon may be able to help by giving additional amounts of oestrogen but this is not a good basis on which to breed a litter.

The amount of blood produced by individual bitches varies tremendously. Some will have a copious flow, others very little and some may have no bleeding at all, although the vulva is fully enlarged and the bitch will, at the right stage, allow herself to be mated and produce a litter quite normally. The non-bleeding bitch is described as having a 'colourless season'. Such a bitch may be difficult to mate to an outside stud dog, as there is so little indication of the time for mating, but conversely she may be mated by an unwanted dog. Such an animal is therefore very inconvenient to have as a brood bitch.

An even more difficult type of season is the condition termed as a 'dry season' where there is no bleeding and very little swelling. This is an abnormality which occurs in particular breeds (see Chapter 12) and inevitably puppies in these breeds are not plentiful and they will always be expensive to buy. Conception may only be achieved by letting dog and bitch live together all the time.

Day one of heat

It is important for your bitch's records, and particularly if you mean to mate her, that you are able to pinpoint *day one of heat*. Since many bitches will keep themselves clean, especially at the start of heat, this is best done by testing the vulva with a white tissue twice a day during the run-up time.

Coping with first oestrus

The important thing to remember is that male dogs will be aware that your bitch is in season. None of the tablets or sprays which are alleged to mask a bitch's pheromones does the slightest good, nor does swabbing the bitch's genitals with disinfectants, etc. Furthermore, the latter action could be both painful and harmful.

If you have an entire male dog in the house, either he or the in season bitch will have to be boarded elsewhere, and the preference must be to board

29

the male, as he is likely to be urine marking both inside and outside the house, even after the bitch has gone away.

Your bitch needs maximum supervision during her season. Always know exactly where she is and what she is doing. It follows that she will have to be watched in the garden as there may be a dog waiting for his opportunity, and exercise will have to be on the lead, unless you can take her to a really isolated place *and* you have exceptional control over your bitch. If it is difficult to find a safe exercise place, most bitches will come to no harm without formal exercise for the three weeks or so whilst the season lasts. If she must go out, it is a wise precaution to carry her to the car, so that she is not leaving scent close to your house. Bitch scent, which male dogs can recognize, is emitted even if your bitch does not drop blood or pass urine. It makes no sense at all to walk the bitch adjacent to your home or you will soon have a pack of dogs outside your door. Not only does this cause annoyance to yourself and neighbours, but you may also be attracting other people's pets away from their homes, with the risk that they will be run over, or cause a road accident, while trying to reach your bitch.

Within the home
Your bitch will be discharging a variable quantity of blood for the first 10–14 days of heat which may stain your furnishings and carpets, although stain removers specially designed to cope with blood are now obtainable. However, most bitches will keep themselves very clean. (See Chapter 9, 'What if . . . my bitch makes blood-stains on the carpet and furniture when she is on heat?')

The dangerous time
Your bitch's season will last on average three to four weeks, but it is in the middle of that time that she will ovulate (shed eggs ready for fertilization by the male) and be willing, or even eager, to be mated. There is no positive external indication of this stage, which may occur at 10 to 14 days after the start of bleeding, and may last for several days, or it may start earlier and continue to the end of her season (21 to 23 days). One possible sign is the change in colour of the blood-stained discharge, first to pink and then to colourless, but this cannot be relied upon. The vulva will, at this time, be softened and at its largest expansion. If you run a finger down the bitch's spine, she will often turn her tail to one side as she would to facilitate mating. When the blood-staining has entirely gone it is often taken as an indication of the optimum mating day, but some bitches will continue to bleed for a full three weeks and some may be fertile for nearly the whole of that period. So your defence precautions cannot be relaxed and during the height of the bitch's season you should be wary of putting her into an outlying room or kennel. Dogs have been known to jump through windows to meet bitches which are sleeping far from the rest of the household. If the bitch is no longer bleeding there is, of course, no need to exclude her from your rooms, unless you expect to receive visitors with a male dog in the near future. The scent left by the in season bitch may well trigger bad behaviour in the male to the shame of his owners.

Your best indication that your bitch's active breeding period has finished is the shrinking of the vulva to normal size. It is helpful then, if you live in an urban community, or if you are bringing your own male back from kennels, to bath the bitch to rid her of all lingering odour.

False or phantom pregnancy

All bitches go through the same hormonal changes whether they have been mated or not, so almost all will experience a phantom or false pregnancy to some degree. Some will produce milk and retire to their beds (around 73 days after the start of their season) with some inanimate object which they guard fiercely as if it were an actual puppy. The bitch can show a great deal of physical and mental distress which worries the owner considerably, especially when there is a temporary change in temperament, as this can be frightening to those who have not encountered false pregnancy before. Fortunately, although in the early stages false pregnancy is difficult to distinguish from an actual pregnancy where there are only a few puppies, your bitch should be back to normal in two to three weeks. You can assist a quick return to normality in the following ways.

● Reduce the bitch's water intake and feed less carbohydrate in the diet.
● Remove the toys which she has taken as a substitute and remove her bed during the day. Give the bitch more exercise and do not encourage nesting behaviour or sympathize with her. Take care that small children do not intrude upon her 'nest' as she may be snappy at this time.
● If the signs are really intense and a lot of milk is produced, consult your veterinary surgeon for advice on treatment of this incident and prevention of future episodes, as a bitch which has really vivid false pregnancies will do so again, probably after every heat.

Giving medication to prevent the next breeding cycle, which also helps prevent a false pregnancy, is a matter for discussion with your vet, as is spaying, the ultimate cure for this tiresome condition. Never breed just to satisfy a false pregnancy, if you do that you could be trapped into breeding every six months for the rest of the bitch's life. If she has one litter, her false pregnancy is likely to be even more dramatic next time. There is nothing to support the notion that bitches which have false pregnancies make very good broods; they can very often become irritable with real puppies. In addition, bitches which make a great scene about false pregnancies are equally likely to be difficult at whelping time. (See also Chapter 9.)

To spay or not to spay?

If after reading the remarks made at the beginning of Chapter 5, you decide that breeding is not for you, it would seem that the easiest course would be to have your bitch spayed. Unhappily, the situation is not quite so simple and you are advised to talk over with your veterinary surgeon what the most suitable method of contraception for your bitch would be.

Spaying is the colloquial term for a canine ovariohysterectomy (removal of uterus and ovaries). This is a major operation requiring a full anaesthetic but it is a procedure in which veterinary surgeons are very practised.

Some vets think it is preferable to spay a bitch while she is very young, i.e. before her first season. Others believe it is best to let the bitch become fully developed as an adult and to spay midway between the first and second season. It is not a good idea to spay a bitch immediately before a season, when she is on heat, or while she is having a false pregnancy. Wait until she is in anoestrus, when her genitals and mammary glands are in a quiescent state and not under increased hormonal influence. Bitches can be spayed at any age, but the middle-aged to elderly, overweight bitch is the least favourite proposition with veterinary surgeons and the operation usually

31

costs more for these patients. Your veterinary surgeon will be happy to quote you the approximate cost, tell you when he would like to do the operation, what you should do in advance, and when you can collect your bitch after the operation. Practices vary, so talk it over in advance with the vet or the receptionist so that you know what to expect.

Spaying – The disadvantages

A large percentage of spayed middle-aged to elderly bitches become, to some degree, incontinent of urine. This may happen only periodically while the bitch is asleep and can possibly be linked with hormonal surges at the times when she would have been in season. In other bitches the urine loss is more constant.

Spayed bitches of the Spaniel, Retriever and Collie breeds may show an overgrowth of woolly coat over the back and hind quarters. This hair growth is almost impossible to groom, and the appearance of the bitch is considerably altered and may not please you. Smooth-coated spayed bitches may show some baldness and patches of blackened skin on the flanks, in the armpits and on the abdomen. This again is somewhat unsightly.

Remember that once your bitch has been spayed there is no opportunity to change your mind.

Lastly there is the problem of weight gain. Most veterinary surgeons and breeders agree that spayed bitches do tend to put on weight. This however can be minimized by cutting food intake and giving more exercise.

You should bear all these points in mind when discussing with your veterinary surgeon whether to take any steps to control heat in your bitch so that you can decide what is best for your bitch in your own circumstances. If you have a young healthy bitch and have no intention of breeding from her you should sensibly consider having her spayed. In the great majority of cases there are no adverse side-effects and the benefits associated with spaying far outweigh the possible disadvantages mentioned above.

The spaying operation

You will be asked to sign a form giving your consent to the administration of the anaesthetic and the performance of the operation as a safeguard for the veterinary surgeon. You will also have been asked to withhold all food, and possibly also water, for about 18 hours before the operation. Do take this instruction seriously for it is to prevent your bitch vomiting and choking while under the anaesthetic. It is not always possible to watch bitches all the time and, careful as you are, she may have had the opportunity to eat some food. If you have any suspicion that this has happened, do tell the vet. Don't worry that you will look silly; it has happened many times before with other owners, but your vet would much rather be forewarned and your bitch will be at greater risk if you do not do so. It may be that the operation will proceed with extra precautions taken or it may prove to be wiser to put the surgery off until another day. It is not quite so critical if the bitch has taken a drink of water, as some vets allow water right up to operation time, but it is worth mentioning if she did find a water bowl.

There are two approaches to an ovariohysterectomy, either down the bitch's midline between the mammary glands, or through an incision in the flank. It is usual to let the veterinary surgeon decide which way he prefers, but if you are exhibiting your bitch and do not want the risk of a noticeable scar, this should be discussed well in advance. Many vets like to keep bitches tney have spayed on the surgery premises overnight after the operation just to see that all is well.

Recovery is usually very good and your greatest problem may be to keep the bitch from running and jumping too vigorously for a week or so after the operation. Generally no dressings are put on the incision, which on the whole heals without problems, although you are commonly advised to exercise your bitch gently and on the lead for a week. The sutures are usually removed by the veterinary surgeon at seven to 10 days post-operatively and this service is often included in the cost of the operation.

When you collect your bitch, ask the vet for his advice on aftercare and enquire if there are any particular signs which may indicate that recovery is not proceeding normally. Be sure that you know how to contact him in case you need him out of normal hours. Many veterinary surgeons have printed sheets on which all this information is given.

The advantages of spaying and the pros and cons of chemical controlled heat are discussed in Chapter 9.

The adult bitch

Your adult bitch should be giving you maximum pleasure. She should be well-mannered, companionable and sensible, although it is a good idea to brush up, from time to time, on the things she learnt in her puppy education. Bitches have no menopause, so she will go on coming into season for the whole of her life span, although the anoestrus periods tend to be longer in the elderly bitch.

You and your family will have become used to a routine of grooming, feeding and accommodation. Your bitch will also be used to going into kennels while you are away on holiday.

Don't let attention to your bitch's health be forgotten. Continue with worming at six monthly intervals and do not forget her annual booster vaccinations. Boosters are especially necessary for bitches living in rural areas which are not often taken to towns and urban parks. Bitches which frequent well-used areas are likely to be building up their natural immunity by mild encounters with disease, but the bitch which lives a secluded life is not able to do this and consequently needs renewal of antibodies by vaccination. Keep a check on your bitch's weight and make any necessary adjustments to diet and the amount of exercise you give her. Be meticulous about your own regular checks of the bitch, especially on the mammary glands. Any nodules which you find, however tiny, mean veterinary advice should be sought without delay. The spread of cancer to the lungs is encouraged if you leave these nodules to 'see what they grow into'. Removal is easiest when they are small.

Similarly, any lumps anywhere on the body should have professional investigation and probably removal to prevent the growth of a tumorous mass requiring an extensive operation. Another important sign of disease in bitches is the drinking of large amounts of water, or drinking more frequently than usual. You will find you do notice if she is at the water bowl more often than usual. Other medical problems specific to bitches are described in Chapter 9, and the general medical conditions are found in full in the relevant chapter of *The Doglopaedia*.

Finally do not forget to keep records of the major incidents in your bitch's life. These can be invaluable, not only to you and your vet, but also to your breed club. See Chapter 11.

The elderly bitch

The elderly bitch may find it difficult to get out of her bed, and walks are not the great pleasure they once were. You may have to tailor your life to suit her, as you did when she was a puppy. You may even decide, before she advances too far into old age, to buy a puppy to live with her. The enjoyment of teaching a youngster can often rejuvenate and bring new excitement into the life of an older bitch. You may find that you have to make alternative arrangements when you go on holiday, as elderly bitches are not best suited to boarding kennels. The noise and the summer heat are hard on them, and they have become creatures of habit, very attached to their own home and garden.

Involuntary urination is probably the greatest problem for both bitch and her owners. She should never be reproached for having a wet bed and, if at all possible, some arrangements should be made so that she can go out into the garden during the night if she needs to. Unhappily, sometimes aged bitches will collapse after urinating and if this is the case with yours, you will not want to risk her lying outside all night, but on the other hand you may not welcome having to get up to let her out. Your veterinary surgeon may be able to help by prescribing medication which will help ensure that more urine is passed during the daylight hours.

Make up a special bed for your incontinent bitch so that she remains dry and comfortable overnight. Bean bags are the beds elderly bitches prefer, as the polystyrene beads are warm and support ageing limbs. Put the bed into a strong plastic bag, then lay on several thick folded newspapers topped with an ample piece of polyester fur; this lets the urine through on to the papers, but allows the bitch to lie on a dry, warm surface. The polyester fur can be washed every day if necessary and, if there are any blood-stained discharges, they will be easy to detect on the white fur but will wash away without stain.

Apart from these adjustments you should continue much as you have done before. Your bitch will not want so much exercise, but she will want interest and some activity in her life. She still needs grooming and, more than ever, to have a place of her own where she can be comfortable and quiet. If her sight is failing, remember not to move the furniture and not to leave hazards, such as wheelbarrows, in her way in the garden. Her teeth may be hurting her a little and your veterinary surgeon can help here. Sometimes the extraction of decayed teeth can renew a bitch's interest in eating. You may have to change the type of biscuit you give her to one which is not so hard to crunch.

Your bitch may be more comfortable wearing a coat of woollen or quilted material at night and even all day too in a draughty house. Make her several, so they can be washed often.

Euthanasia

To have your bitch put painlessly to sleep so that she need not endure a painful disability, illness or indignity right to the end is the last great service we can perform for our bitches. Only you, together with your veterinary surgeon, can decide when the time has come that the bitch's day holds more pain than pleasure. Talk the subject over with your vet long before the necessity arises, so that you can do so unemotionally. It is a good idea, when you are faced with a chronically ill bitch, to set a deadline by saying that if she is no better by such a time you will have her painlessly put to sleep. This has the advantage of curtailing suffering, as day to day decisions based on hope can go on unintentionally for much longer than necessary. Also, a decision made in advance will not leave you wondering whether you acted over-hastily or that your action was based on emotion rather than logic.

Your veterinary surgeon should be frank with you about the body disposal facilities available in your area. There are some private animal crematoria and burial grounds, you may want to bury your pet in your own garden, or you may want the veterinary surgeon to arrange disposal for you. Many veterinary surgeons will be prepared to come to your home or you may prefer to take her to the surgery, where she can be held by a trained assistant whilst she is given a simple injection. Skillfully done, euthanasia is smooth and painless, usually only involving the injection of an overdose of anaesthetic into a vein in the front leg.

Once more the decision is yours. You can in most cases opt to stay with your bitch, talking quietly and cheerfully to her while the injection is given and perhaps helping to hold her or you may feel you would rather hand her over to the vet and his staff. Most owners who have been grateful for all that their bitches have meant to them, will be willing to stay with their bitches to the end.

There will be tears, of course, and the veterinary surgeon and his nurses will understand only too well how you feel. A tip from one who has been through this sad experience all too many times in a long life with dogs – either pay in full in advance for euthanasia and body disposal, or hand over your credit card or a blank cheque beforehand. Going through the rigmarole of paying bills immediately afterwards is an ordeal you can save yourself.

CHAPTER 3
EDUCATING YOUR BITCH

Natural behaviour

Leadership

Beginning the right way

House rules

Growing up

House-training

Biting

Bitch abilities

Tips for success

Introduction

Your bitch puppy has much to learn about living within a human pack, as well as the special rules and routines that apply in your particular household. You will have no trouble in teaching her if you are patient and are prepared to give her your full attention for the first few months she is with you.

Violence, shouting and punishment are unnecessary and counter-productive. Punishment is only appropriate when you know the bitch is aware she is doing wrong but is deliberately testing you to see how far she can go. This phase is one of adolescence and the way to correct bad behaviour at this stage is fully explained in *The Doglopaedia*.

To get the maximum pleasure from your bitch and to ensure that she is socially acceptable, it is essential that you teach her good manners. It will not be difficult if you start early because bitches are very sensitive and they enjoy their owner's approval. All canines respond well to consistent leadership – do not allow her to do something one day and then reprimand her for doing the same thing the following day.

A bitch does not want to be a nuisance and it is up to her owner to see that she is not. It is an essential part of responsible dog ownership to understand how a dog thinks and learns, and how to prevent and, if necessary, cure behaviour which is inappropriate to being a domestic pet.

Natural behaviour patterns

We must not forget that dogs have been, and in many cases still are, bred to perform functions which are useful to man. Hounds are bred to run far and fast, and to follow scent with persistence and concentration; Terriers are meant to kill vermin with a quick snap of the jaws; Spaniels have the ability and instinct to flush out game from hedgerows and woodlands; and the herding dogs find it difficult to curb their rounding-up instinct. Breed clubs are, quite rightly, very keen to perpetuate the working ability of their dogs.

It is unreasonable to expect pet animals to 'switch off' their natural behaviour because we have no need for it. These instinctive behaviours are very difficult to quell entirely, so the owner must learn to read their bitch and anticipate her reactions and she must not be allowed into situations which could lead her into trouble. It is especially necessary to be aware that guarding home and owners never involves biting. Efficient guard dogs threaten but do not bite. Tolerance of biting, even mild mouthing, can lead to tragedy later.

Leadership

Dogs and bitches are naturally conditioned to living in packs in which the members depend on each other for survival. Every pack must have a leader, and probably several sub-leaders who hope to make it to the top one day. Among wild dogs, or in working packs, the pack leader will always be the strongest male. In a domestic/breeding situation, a pack starts with three animals and the leader is very often a bitch, strong-minded but not necessarily physically the strongest. She expresses her domination over other dogs and bitches by hard looks, riveting stares, low growls and body language (the latter term is fully explained in *The Doglopaedia*).

As the bitch's owner, you must always be the alpha-pack leader. You will be responsible for the detailed education of a new addition to the pack but you will find this a lot easier when there is an adult trained bitch to set an example. However, the human pack leader must always retain the ascendancy. The other dogs may do as the leader bitch says but she must do as you say. You can use on her the methods she uses on the rest of the pack – a forbidding facial expression, an upright aggressive stance and a growly voice.

Where there are no established dogs to help in educating the new puppy, the human teacher must spend time ensuring the puppy does the right thing. Work on the principle of not giving the puppy opportunity to do wrong, rather than letting her commit errors and then seeking to correct them. In this context you should confine the puppy to easily-cleaned rooms where you can see her actions, rather than letting her run all over the house and you should keep close observation on what she is doing in the garden.

There should very seldom be any need for physical correction of a bitch. Being able to read your bitch is the main expression of your pack leadership. When we show that we can anticipate what she was thinking of doing, we display to her that we are always one jump ahead, and fully competent to be pack leader.

In educating bitches, especially those which may be bred from, obedience to command and tolerance of handling by owner and veterinary surgeon is most important. A bitch should have complete trust in her owner so that she will respond to commands unhesitatingly when she is in season or taken for mating. She must learn from puppy days to submit to handling and examination of genitals and mammary glands so that she will be easy to assist, if the need arises, at whelping or in illness. The bitch which will not allow her owner to come near her or her newborn puppies is a disaster. This behaviour may be inherited and quickly copied, so the pups will be useless as pets or breeding stock however beautiful they may be.

Beginning the right way

When you initially collect your puppy from the breeder, it is inappropriate to immediately seek to establish your pack leadership.

Your puppy is going through the most traumatic few days of her whole life. You have to win your puppy's trust and affection, and forge a bond which will last all her life. Some bitches will choose the family member to whom they want to belong, and it is not always the one the bitch was bought for. Sometimes the bitch will recognize as pack leader the person who spends most time with her, or the person who provides her education. When a bitch joins an existing dog pack, even of only two others, the pack hierarchy is already established. The solitary bitch puppy has the opportunity to mould her own family pack somewhat to her own wishes. She may not respond to the strongest, or the loudest, of her mentors.

She must, however, be civil to all family and visitors and she must do as she is told by all immediate family. It is not a good idea in these formative days to allow casual visitors to give orders to your bitch, and if they do, you should not insist she obeys. It is up to you to control your bitch.

Her first lesson should be to teach her to come when she is called. If you are kindly and represent a slightly familiar element in an alien world, she will want to come anyway, so you are teaching her by reinforcing her own actions. It is useful to have established the bitch's name even before you bring her home. If the name no longer appeals when in use, it can be changed gradually. Many bitches respond to two or three pet names or diminutives. She will actually be responding to the sound of your voice.

Welcome her with petting for the first few weeks. Later you may want to introduce a small food reward as an incentive. As she grows, a pleasurable game can be developed in which she runs between two or more family members in turn, being welcomed and petted by each. This is also an excellent way to exercise a dog in a confined area. The game can be developed by directing the bitch to run to a family member by name. Eventually she can become a useful messenger about the house and garden.

House rules

Even before the pup comes home, establish some guidelines for her behaviour – is she to be allowed to sit on furniture, to go upstairs, etc.? Once the rules are made, stick by them and severely punish any member of the family who makes a variation of rules in order to win favour with the bitch.

If there are children in the family, although they should rank in the family hierarchy above the dog, it is not helpful if they constantly bully and correct her just for the pleasure of having someone subordinate to them. Admonition given at the wrong time in the wrong way only confuses the puppy.

Growing up

At around four to five months the puppy will have reached maximum activity. Puppy watching is almost a full-time task, as she will sleep little during the day and all her effort will be spent exploring and playing. If you can devote much of your time through this phase, eventually you will have a superb companion animal who needs minimal supervision. If there are other dogs in the house, your new puppy will learn to take her place in the pack and to partake in their own canine life, parallel and compatible with the activities of the human pack.

You will find the most useful word in puppy education is 'No!' (preceded by the puppy's name). Use it from the start whenever you want to curb a behaviour pattern. 'No!' can be taught from six-and-a-half weeks onwards and will work for you until the end of the bitch's life.

Select a word of your choice to indicate that the puppy should pass faeces or urine. Further useful commands are, 'Sit', 'Stand', 'Stay' and 'Roll over'.

House-training

It is usually quicker to house-train bitches than males so long as you are willing to devote some concentration to the task. Understand your puppy's signals. Identify her signs of needing to pass urine. Go into the garden with her and stay with her until she has done what is required. Shutting her out alone is worse than useless. Be patient if her attention is distracted, draw her back to the site she has used before and when she performs be lavish with your praise.

It may be too ambitious at first to get the puppy to perform on the area of ground you have designated. Compromise by being very pleased when she performs outside at all, and when she has perfected that, make your next lesson performing on the lawn, rough area or whatever you choose. It follows that when she makes a mistake in the house it is your fault because you did not read the signals correctly. Say nothing to the puppy, except to growl quietly while you clear up the mess. Do clean very thoroughly but do not use products with an ammonia content. If you leave any trace of the urine scent, that patch becomes 'the place to do it' in the puppy's mind. See the 'What if' section in *The Doglopaedia* for advice.

Grooming

Your bitch puppy must be groomed every day, even if she has not enough coat to warrant it. You are teaching her to be passive while she is handled.

At first it is more convenient to groom a tiny puppy on your lap, but as soon as you can, teach her to stand and to lie on a table. Set up a mock veterinary examination frequently so that she is used to the procedure. Gently pull down her lower eyelids, look into her ears, at her pads, and under her tail. Stretch out each leg in turn, and roll her over to look at her mammary glands. If you intend to show the puppy she will have to be bathed frequently. Let her hear and feel a hair drier on her coat, if only for a moment. Those with coats which will have to be clipped later should also get used to the sound of electric clippers.

Biting

At three to four months old your bitch may be in pain while she is cutting her second, permanent, teeth. She may at this time have a compulsive need to gnaw everything, even people's hands if she gets the opportunity. She must be told 'No!' and the object taken out of reach, but she should not be punished. Give her a safe gnawing object instead.

Biting at hands at this stage is not a sign she will be savage later – this behaviour pattern does pass. Snapping in anger when being picked up is another matter altogether. This merits a growl and a snap on your part, copying the mode of punishment an adult dog would give her. A sharp shake is an extreme lesson, but sometimes necessary when the puppy gets over-excited as she will on occasion until she learns her limits. Putting the puppy in her crate to be quiet for a while, with growls and 'No!' from you, serves to emphasize that her behaviour is quite unacceptable.

When the second teeth are completely through and the gums no longer hurt, it is a good thing to make a routine of cleaning your bitch's teeth. Your veterinary surgeon or nurse will show you how and can probably sell you a long handled toothbrush and meat flavoured dog toothpaste. Do not use pastes made for humans, since they are unsuitable.

Teach your puppy to take tablets without struggle or fuss. Many canine medications, such as vitamin/mineral supplements and worm tablets, are now made in a palatable formula which a puppy will enjoy taking. Make some of her normal food into little pellets which you can 'give' by mouth with ease. Your bitch will soon respond to the command 'Open your mouth' and this gives you one-upmanship when you are at the vet's.

Bitch abilities

Your bitch will soon be able to run and dodge much better than you can, so do not get into such contests unless in play. If your bitch does not come when you call, never go after her. Instead, continue to attract her to you, perhaps by getting down to her level and clapping your hands. When she does come to you, reward her by petting and giving a titbit which you need to have readily at hand. Rewards must always be instant, so that they are associated with the behaviour just performed.

Your bitch can probably see further than you can. She sees moving objects best, so if you want to attract her attention from a distance wave or walk around. She can hear sounds that you are unaware are being made, and she can distinguish between similar sounds very clearly. Her sense of smell is 10 times more powerful than a human's: she finds her way about through scent and sound. Use these factors to make the most of her. The more you teach her, the better companion she will be.

Table 3.1: Educating your bitch – tips for success

- Ensure that your bitch regards you as the pack leader – if necessary carry out the dominance exercises described in *The Doglopaedia*.
- Bitches learn by trial and error. If a behaviour brings a pleasurable reward it will be repeated; if it results in punishment, pain or disapproval the action will not be taken readily again. If the bitch gets no response from the owner the behaviour will be forgotten (extinguished).
- Dogs can only link the action they have taken and the consequence if they occur within *half a second* of each other. Thus it is very often necessary to pre-plan situations so that punishment or reward can be given *as the behaviour takes place*.
- A vocabulary of 25 or even 30 words is well within the ability of most bitches but they must be used consistently and rehearsed periodically to avoid them being forgotten. It is a good idea to undertake such training at a set period each day or week as appropriate. It can be counter-productive to train dogs piecemeal and certainly when there are other things going on to distract them.
- Contrary to popular belief simple training can start from eight to 12 weeks of age. There is no need to wait until adolescence has been reached.
- The best reward is undoubtedly a coveted titbit. Failing that lavish praise and petting will bring instant satisfaction to most bitches.
- If punishment is used it must be strong enough to disrupt the undesirable behaviour but not cause suffering – hitting or slapping may be confused with play by big dogs and thus should be avoided. Shy and nervous bitches should never be punished and punishment should not be used in puppies aged between seven and 14 weeks. Thrown objects can be very effective, especially in a set-up situation, as they give immediate punishment which can be administered whilst the 'crime' is being committed.
- Puppies go through a critical period of socialization between three and 12 weeks of age. During this time it is essential, if they are to be properly adjusted later in life, that they encounter as great a variety of noises, people and situations as possible. Buy your puppy early and take her home between six to eight weeks of age so that you have the maximum possible time to socialize her. This has to be balanced against the need to avoid the risk of infection; your veterinary surgeon will advise, but it obviously makes sense to avoid going to places frequented by lots of dogs or where dogs are crowded together in a confined space. It is particularly important that bitches intended for breeding are properly socialized with other dogs so that they will not react badly when taken for mating.
- The critical period for sensitivity in puppies is from eight to 12 weeks of age. Any experience which causes acute fear during this time may make a bitch anxious, shy or very fearful of similar situations for the rest of her life, especially if there is already a tendency to nervousness. Try to ensure that your bitch is protected from possible frightening situations during this time.
- Make rules – decide what your bitch will be allowed to do and what is forbidden or frowned upon and ensure that you and your family stick to them consistently. Reward good behaviour, punish unacceptable acts – but get it right. If you are in doubt about what to do it is better to ignore the incident.
- Finally, exercise your dog's mind; play games like hide-and-seek with her, and set her problems to solve to make her think. You will get maximum pleasure and reward from your bitch if she has an active mind and body.

CHAPTER 4
NUTRITION AND FEEDING

Nutrient requirements

Types of food

Practical feeding –

   Adult bitches

   Breeding bitches

   Puppies

   Ageing bitches

Obesity

Introduction

Correct feeding is essential to maintain health and to allow growth and breeding in bitches. Many different foods and feeding regimes can be used, but the food or combination of foods chosen must provide all the essential nutrients and energy that the bitch requires. These nutrients must be present in the diet and not be bound in such a manner as to prevent their digestion and absorption. The diet must be palatable, the most nutritious diet in the world is of no use if the bitch refuses to eat it! Safety is also an important consideration and the diet should be free of any toxins, bacteria or parasites that could harm the bitch or be passed on to her owners.

The concentration of the diet should also be considered. If the diet is not sufficiently concentrated, the bitch may be unable to take in enough food to provide all the nutrients that she requires and this can become critical during times of high nutrient demand such as growth, lactation or the latter part of pregnancy.

Nutrient requirements

The diet must supply a number of essential nutrients to keep the bitch healthy – protein, fat, minerals, vitamins and water. All of these must be present in the diet and in the correct proportions for the diet to be both complete and balanced. As with any diet the absence of any one nutrient, even a vitamin needed in tiny amounts, will render the diet inadequate. Contrary to popular belief carbohydrate is not an essential nutrient in the diet of the bitch, although it is generally well-digested and is frequently included as a source of energy.

The amount of each of the essential nutrients that the bitch requires depends on her physiological status, e.g. whether she is a growing pup, an adult, or perhaps lactating. Detailed information about the requirements for individual nutrients can be found in the books listed under 'Further Reading' at the end of this chapter.

Energy

Apart from the specific nutrients which are later discussed in more detail, the bitch also requires energy (calories) from her food. Three components of the food combine to provide these calories – fat, protein and carbohydrate. The amount of each of these present in a food will determine its energy content. Fat is the richest source of energy containing more than twice as many calories per gram as carbohydrate or protein. Energy is required for exercise, for work, for maintenance of body temperature and for a variety of other essential metabolic processes.

The amount of energy required by the bitch is dependent on a number of factors including her body weight (Figure 4.1), the amount of exercise that she takes, the environmental temperature and physiological processes such as growth or reproduction.

If more energy is taken in than the bitch needs, the excess is deposited in the tissues as fat. To have a certain amount of body fat is quite normal, but an excessive accumulation can have serious consequences for the health of the bitch (see also the section on obesity).

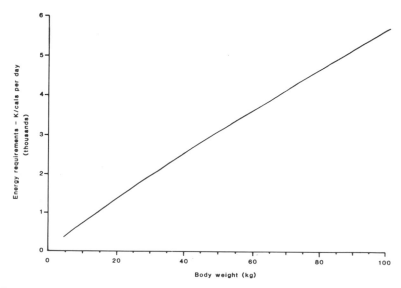

Fig. 4.1 **Energy requirements – adult dogs**

Fat

In addition to providing energy in the diet, fat also acts as a source of essential fatty acids and as a carrier for the fat soluble vitamins A, D, E and K. Essential fatty acids are compounds which the bitch is unable to produce herself and therefore requires in the diet. Deficiency can lead to a dry coat, dandruff, skin lesions and reproductive failure.

Protein

Protein is required by bitches at all stages of their lives and is important both for maintenance and growth of tissues and in the regulation of metabolism. Protein requirements during growth and reproduction are higher than those of non-reproducing adult bitches because of the need for protein for production of milk and new tissues.

It is important to consider the quality of a protein when selecting a protein source. High quality proteins contain all the necessary building blocks (amino-acids); lower quality proteins may be deficient in one or two of these amino-acids. In general terms, the highest quality protein comes from eggs and milk, followed by meats, fish and cheese, and finally cereal proteins. This does not mean that only meat and eggs should be fed, but that selection needs to be made more carefully if vegetable protein sources are being used. Prepared foods are carefully formulated to take account of the quality of different protein sources, to ensure that the dog's amino-acid requirements are met.

Carbohydrate

Carbohydrate is not an essential nutrient for the bitch, but it is a good source of energy and frequently forms a part of many diets, either as biscuit or meal. Sugars, starch and dietary fibre are all different forms of carbohydrate. Sugars are generally easily digested by bitches, but large quantities of milk sugar (lactose) may lead to diarrhoea. Starch, which is composed of chains of simple sugars, is present in many cereals. It requires degrading by cooking or crushing before it can be readily digested by bitches.

Dietary fibre is not digested by bitches and passes through the gut relatively unchanged. The consumption of fibre has been described as being beneficial in a number of diseases in man, but these diseases are not common in the dog. However, dietary fibre does affect the speed at which ingested material passes through the digestive tract and it has an influence on the water content of faeces. These effects enable dietary fibre to be used as an aid to the management of diarrhoea and constipation.

Vitamins

A detailed discussion of the role of vitamins and minerals is beyond the scope of this chapter, and further information should be sought from the sources listed in the 'Further Reading' section of this chapter.

Briefly, vitamins are organic compounds required in minute amounts in the diet. They are essential in the regulation of many metabolic processes. They divide into two groups – water-soluble (B group vitamins) and fat-soluble (vitamins A, D, E and K). An important consequence of this difference is that the fat-soluble vitamins are stored in the body and can accumulate if fed in excess.

If a diet contains the minimum amount of each vitamin required by the bitch, additional supplementation will give no further benefit and may even do harm. **In normal healthy bitches there is no need to supplement an already balanced diet, even if it is to be fed to giant breeds or to bitches during growth, pregnancy or lactation.** Particular care must be taken if supplements rich in fat-soluble vitamins (e.g. cod-liver oil) are being given, as overdosage can have very serious effects.

Minerals

Twelve minerals are required in the bitch's diet and these are involved in a variety of essential processes including, for example, transport of oxygen by the blood (iron) and in the structure of bones (calcium and phosphorus).

Whilst care should be taken with diet formulation to avoid mineral deficiencies, unnecessary supplementation should be avoided as minerals can be toxic with repeated overdosage.

Water

Water should be considered as an essential nutrient. Indeed, a lack of water will lead to illness and death more rapidly than a deficiency of any other dietary component. Water is lost from the body in urine, in faeces, by evaporation from the lungs, and in milk if the bitch is lactating. Water is gained from drinking, from food and from some of the processes occurring during metabolism. The daily requirement of a bitch will depend on the interactions between these factors and therefore a plentiful supply of fresh, clean water should always be available.

Types of food

Foods that may be used can be divided into two broad categories, prepared pet foods and home-prepared diets.

Prepared pet foods

These fall into four basic categories which are listed in Table 4.1. The major

Table 4.1: Types of prepared pet foods

Type of food	Feeding guide
Dog mixer biscuit/meal	Complementary – to be mixed with fresh meat or canned food
Dry complete foods	May be fed alone, only water required
Semi-moist foods	May be fed alone, only water required
Wet Foods Canned	Some are complete, but mostly such foods are complementary – they need to be fed in conjunction with biscuit or meal
Frozen	Generally complementary – they need to be fed in conjunction with biscuit or meal, and may need additional supplementation
Chub packs	Generally complementary – they need to be fed in conjunction with biscuit or meal

benefits of prepared pet foods are guaranteed nutrient content and balance, palatability, digestibility, safety and convenience. These factors make correct feeding with prepared foods very much simpler than with home-made diets, particularly during times of high nutrient demand such as lactation. Different recipes of prepared foods have been developed specially to cover various parts of the life cycle of the bitch, the labels specify the intended role as well as providing guidelines for the amounts to be fed.

Home-prepared diets

These can certainly meet the necessary nutritional criteria, but preparing such a diet can be both time-consuming and complicated, requiring considerable knowledge of the nutritional adequacy of the ingredients used. Although meat is thought by many people to be the natural diet for dogs, in the wild dogs usually eat the whole of their prey including the skeleton, skin and gut contents from which they can obtain all nutrients essential to them. In the domestic environment, however, meat alone does not form an adequate diet as it is deficient in several minerals and vitamins, and a combination of foods must therefore be used in preparing a complete diet. A number of commonly-used foods are listed in Table 4.2, together with information about their nutrient content and any major deficiencies.

A further complication that may be experienced with home-prepared diets is the variability of raw materials. For example, the fat content of meat may vary considerably from one purchase to another. This will obviously have a significant effect on the energy content of the diet and thus the quantities of all the other nutrients required in it.

Cooking of most components of home-prepared diets is advisable to help kill any bacteria and parasites, but over-cooking should be avoided because it may destroy some of the vitamins.

Household scraps

Dogs are frequently fed the remains of dishes served at the table or scraps from human-food preparation and many seem to appreciate these treats. This is not generally harmful, provided that some selection is practised and that the quantity is not too great. For example, highly-spiced or exotic dishes are probably best avoided as they may cause digestive upsets, and particular care must be taken with any food that might contain bones.

The major problem likely to be encountered with scraps is overfeeding, possibly leading to obesity. The feeding guides supplied with prepared pet foods assume that they are being used as the sole source of food when fed as directed, thus reductions in amount will have to be made if large quantities of scraps are fed.

Finally, remember that scraps are not nutritionally balanced and if fed in large quantities the balance of an otherwise adequate diet could be upset.

Feeding adult bitches

The amount of food needed to maintain an adult bitch in good, healthy condition is dependent on a number of factors, the most important being her body weight. The relationship between body weight and energy require-ments is shown in Figure 4.1. The energy requirements are also affected by such variables as the amount of exercise, the environmental temperature and age.

Table 4.2: Fresh foods

Food	Source of	Seriously deficient in	Comment
Meat (e.g. lean chopped beef, chicken, lamb, rabbit)	Protein, fat, some B vitamins, some minerals	Calcium, phosphorus, iodine, copper, fat-soluble vitamins, biotin (a B group vitamin)	The fat content of meat, particularly chopped beef, may be very variable from one purchase to another. Cooking can reduce B vitamin content
Tripe	Protein, fat	Calcium, phosphorus, many trace minerals, most vitamins	Should be cooked prior to being fed
Liver	Protein, fat, fat-soluble vitamins, B vitamins	Calcium, phosphorus, other minerals	Excessive amounts of liver may lead to disease. Cooking can reduce B vitamin content
Milk	Most nutrients	Iron	Some dogs cannot digest the lactose in milk
Eggs	Most nutrients	Calcium	Large quantities of raw egg-white may lead to biotin deficiency
Bones	Calcium, phosphorus, magnesium, protein	Fat, vitamins, some minerals, essential fatty acids	Only feed large, uncooked bones, not small or splintery ones
Bread/cereals	Carbohydrate, some protein, some minerals and vitamins	Fat, essential fatty acids, fat-soluble vitamins	High levels of phytate (a phosphorus-containing compound) may restrict absorption of minerals
Fresh fish	Protein, some B vitamins	Minerals, vitamins	Thiaminase, an enzyme found in some types of fish, will reduce vitamin B content of diet unless cooked
Canned fish	Protein, fat	Minerals, vitamins	

Exercise does increase energy requirements, but the amount by which it does so is often over-estimated, leading to unnecessary increases in the amount of food offered. Older bitches tend to be less active than young ones and are thus more prone to obesity. Similarly, a decrease in the environmental temperature increases the amount of energy needed by bitches that are housed outside, for example in a moderate winter about 25 per cent more calories would be needed to maintain weight.

Some examples of diets for a bitch are given in Table 4.3 and this data together with Figure 4.1 may be used to estimate the food requirements of bitches of different weights. It is sensible to use the bitch herself as a guide, taking into account the factors considered above. **Just sufficient food should be fed to allow her to maintain a steady body weight and stay healthy and active.**

Many different food types may be successfully fed to adult bitches including dry foods, home-made diets of fresh meat and biscuit, canned foods etc. but sudden changes of diet should be avoided as they may lead to digestive upsets. If dietary changes are made, they should be done gradually and the new food mixed with the existing diet for a number of days before the new food is fed alone.

Some individual bitches may not be able to tolerate certain foods or food components and feeding these will result in diarrhoea. With individuals like this it is necessary to try different types or brands of food to identify the ones that the bitch is able to tolerate.

The daily food allowance may be given as one or two meals, with the majority of the food usually being given in the afternoon or early evening. The remaining food can be given as a small breakfast. Feeding at specified times is essential with fresh or canned foods which will dry out if left all day, but alternative feeding patterns may be used with other types of food. For example, dry foods can be left out all day for the bitch to help herself, but care must be taken with greedy bitches to ensure that they do not overeat. There is no preferred system and the feeding regime chosen will depend on the type of food used and the preferences of the individual owner and bitch.

Please note: 1 Kilogram = 2.2lb (100g = 3^{1}/$_{2}$oz)

Table 4.3: Examples of daily diets for an adult Beagle bitch weighing 13.5 kg

Method 1	Complete Dry Food – 285 g	Method 3	Tripe – 370 g Mixer Biscuit – 185 g + vitamin and mineral supplements
Method 2	Canned Food – 480 g Mixer Biscuit – 160 g	Method 4	Canned Food – 405 g Mixer Biscuit – 135 g Egg – one Poached Cod – 100 g + vitamin and mineral supplements

Notes
- Fresh water must always be available.
- One large can of dog food contains approximately 400 g.
- The recommended ratio in Method 2 is approximately equivalent to equal volumes.

Feeding breeding bitches

Mating

There are no special nutritional requirements for a bitch at the time of mating over those of a normal bitch. If necessary, however, food intake should be adjusted before mating to ensure that the bitch is healthy, in good condition and not overweight. It is useful to record the weight of the bitch from the time of mating and through pregnancy and lactation.

Pregnancy

Correct feeding forms an important part of management during pregnancy and helps to ensure successful breeding and rearing of the litter. It does, however, demand some understanding of the underlying processes. The majority of foetal growth does not occur until the last-third of pregnancy and this is the time when food intake should be increased. Thus, contrary to some popular opinions bitches do not need increased amounts of food throughout the whole pregnancy. In fact this could result in a very overweight bitch and contribute to problems at whelping. Even in late pregnancy, increases in food allowance should not be excessive and should be made gradually. For example, a 10 per cent increase per week from the sixth week of pregnancy leading to an intake of approximately 50 per cent more than the maintenance allowance at the time of whelping has been shown to be quite satisfactory.

The rapidly enlarging uterus takes up much of the space in the bitch's abdomen, so to enable her to eat the increased amount of food, the daily allowance should be divided into several small meals.

Many owners like to supplement the diet with vitamins and minerals during pregnancy, but providing that the normal diet of the bitch is properly balanced there is no need for any additional supplementation. The increased demands for these nutrients will in fact be automatically met by the increased level of food intake.

Lactation

Lactation is the most nutritionally demanding part of the life cycle, because the bitch has to provide enough milk to satisfy all the nutrient requirements of the growing puppies until weaning commences. The amount of food required will depend on the litter size, but most bitches will need to eat up to three to four times their maintenance allowance in the third and fourth week after whelping, which is the peak of lactation. Table 4.4 shows the energy intake of a Labrador bitch during gestation and lactation. To allow the bitch to eat this increased amount, frequent feeding is necessary and food will have to be available during the night as well as during the day. Where food intake does present a problem, the use of concentrated foods such as puppy foods, dry or semi-moist complete foods will help in achieving these high levels of intake.

Vitamin and mineral supplementation is once again unnecessary provided that the chosen diet is properly balanced and that the intake of the bitch is adequate.

The bitch requires a lot of fluid at this time to allow for milk production, so it is essential that a plentiful supply of fresh drinking-water is available

Table 4.4: Typical energy intake in gestation and lactation by a Labrador bitch

Gestation		Lactation	
Week	Energy intake (K cal per day)	Week	Energy intake (K cal per day)
1	2200	1	3900
2	2200	2	6400
3	2200	3	7300
4	2200	4	6400
5	2200	5	6000
6	2530	6	4200[2]
7	2860		
8	3300		
9	3600[1]		

Notes
[1] Energy intake may be variable at this stage of pregnancy, with reductions occurring in the last few days up to whelping.
[2] Energy intake should be reduced to maintenance levels in the last two to three days prior to weaning to help dry up the bitch's milk.

night and day. Milk may be used as a part of this fluid supply, provided that two factors are borne in mind:
● some bitches are unable to adequately digest large quantities of lactose (milk sugar) resulting in diarrhoea;
● milk is not a balanced diet and therefore should only form a small part of the total food allowance for the bitch.

Feeding puppies

During weaning
During weaning two major changes are experienced by the puppies:
1. a change from a liquid to a solid diet;
2. a change from total dependence on the bitch to an independent life.

This means that weaning can be a very stressful time for puppies, but careful management and feeding will help to minimize this.

Weaning usually starts at between two to four weeks of age and should be completed by about six or eight weeks, but the exact timing will depend on the size of the litter, the milk supply of the bitch and the preference of the individual breeder.

Foods that are suitable for weaning puppies will be soft, highly nutritious and palatable. A wide variety of foods may be used including proprietary puppy foods, mince and cereals. If non-proprietary foods are used, a mixture of different food types should be fed so that all the puppies' nutrient requirements are met. The food should be offered to the puppies in shallow bowls. Strict hygiene is important, as the puppies tend to climb into the bowls and possibly urinate and defecate in them. Puppies may need encouragement to eat in the early stages, for example, by letting them lick food from your fingers, but providing that the food is sufficiently palatable most will quickly learn to feed from the bowl. Use identical bowls for each member of the litter.

The amount of food offered can be gradually increased and several meals should be fed each day. The bitch's milk should, however, remain as the major source of food until the puppies are at least three weeks old. After this time the bitch should be separated from her puppies for progressively increasing periods of time during weaning to allow her milk supply to dry up and to allow the puppies to adapt gradually to the new source of food. This process will enable most puppies to be fully weaned at six to eight weeks.

After weaning has been completed, the food intake of the bitch can be adjusted to correct any changes in body weight or condition that have occurred during pregnancy and lactation. If feeding has been correct little adjustment should be necessary as only small changes in body weight will have taken place.

Growing puppies

Growth is a period of considerable nutritional stress and whilst there are probably almost as many regimes for rearing puppies as there are breeders of dogs, two basic factors need to be remembered when selecting a system.
1. Puppies require larger amounts of food relative to their body weight than adults, as the food has to provide for growth as well as for maintenance and exercise.
2. Puppies have small stomachs in relation to their food requirements.

Knowledge of these factors enable several basic recommendations to be made:

It is very important to divide the total daily food allowance into several small meals. At eight weeks of age three to four meals should be given each day and this number may be reduced progressively as the puppy gets older. The age at which the number of meals is reduced will depend on the breed of dog. For most dogs the number of meals can be reduced to two daily by six months, but very large breeds should continue to receive three meals a day until they are nine to 12 months of age because they have a longer growing period.

Meals should be spread as evenly as possible throughout the day, starting early in the morning and finishing late at night.

The diet should contain all essential nutrients in a balanced and highly-digestible form. Protein and mineral content is especially important at this time.

The diet should be in a concentrated form to minimize the bulk that has to be eaten by the puppy to provide all the nutrients that it needs.

The diet should be very palatable to ensure that the puppy is prepared to eat enough of the diet to satisfy its demands. The most nutritious diet in the world is of no use if the puppy refuses to eat it.

It is just as important to avoid over-supplementation with vitamins and minerals as it is to avoid nutritional deficiencies. Supplementation of an already balanced diet is at best wasteful and can actually be harmful.

Sudden changes of diet should be avoided, as they can lead to digestive upsets.

Many different diets and feeding regimes can satisfy these criteria and breeders often supply detailed diet sheets to the new owners of puppies. An alternative and often simpler approach is to use proprietary puppy foods, which have been shown to be effective in raising puppies of many breeds of dogs, including giant breeds.

Puppies are individuals and it is difficult to give precise recommendations about the amounts of food that they should be given. Ideally, however, they should be fed enough to allow a good growth-rate for the particular breed, whilst avoiding both over- and under-feeding which are likely to cause problems.

As a general guide, growing puppies should be fed twice as many calories per unit of body weight as would be given to an adult of the same breed. When 40 per cent of adult weight is achieved, 60 per cent more food should be fed to growing puppies than to an adult of equal size, and when 80 per cent of adult weight is reached 20 per cent more food will be needed.

Examples of diets that could be used for puppies are given in Table 4.5. Specialist books, breeders and veterinary surgeons will be able to give advice on the growth rates to be expected and if any particular animal is not achieving these, then veterinary help should be sought earlier rather than later.

Feeding ageing bitches

As bitches get older they are more likely to suffer from a variety of medical conditions, some of which require special dietary therapy. Fortunately the majority remain in good health and, provided that the points suggested below are borne in mind, they should continue to receive their normal diet. Where specific conditions do exist, a veterinary surgeon will be able to advise on the best form of management.

Chronic kidney disease is one example of a common condition where dietary modification forms an important part of management. In bitches with this condition, protein intake needs to be restricted to prevent the build-up of waste products from protein breakdown. Diets prepared for bitches with this condition should therefore contain small quantities of high-quality protein. In addition to this, they should have restricted levels of phosphorus, which tends to accumulate in kidney failure, and increased levels of water-soluble vitamins to compensate for possible losses from the damaged kidneys. Several proprietary diets are available to assist in the management of chronic kidney disease. Consult your veterinary surgeon for further advice.

A few general points concerning feeding of ageing bitches can be made. Obesity tends to be more common in the older bitch than in the young one, probably because of a decrease in physical activity. It is therefore particularly important to monitor body weight and to regulate food intake carefully to avoid this problem.

Other elderly bitches suffer from poor appetite and hence loss of weight. Warming the food to blood-heat, but not beyond, helps to increase palatability and may tempt some bitches to eat. Where intake of food is poor, vitamin and mineral supplements may be carefully added to help maintain intake. A greater total daily food intake may often be obtained by dividing the food allowance into several small meals, rather than by giving all the food as one meal.

Obesity

Obesity is a very common problem in bitches and is actually much more common than diseases associated with nutritional deficiencies. Obesity is linked with a number of serious health problems and therefore its

Table 4.5: Examples of daily diets for a growing Beagle puppy

	At 8 weeks (approximate weight 3.1 kg 7 lb)	At 18 weeks (approximate weight 9.1 kg 20 lb)	At 32 weeks (approximate weight 11.5 kg 25 lb)
Method 1	Canned puppy food 570 g	Canned puppy food 1100 g	Canned puppy food 1090 g
Method 2	Canned puppy food − 425 g + one egg + 100 g poached cod + vitamin and mineral supplement	Canned puppy food − 960 g + one egg + 100 g poached cod + vitamin and mineral supplement	Canned puppy food − 950 g + one egg + 100 g poached cod + vitamin and mineral supplement
Method 3	Canned puppy food − 280 g + mixer biscuit − 95 g	Canned puppy food 540 g + mixer biscuit − 180 g	Canned puppy food 535 g + mixer biscuit − 180 g
Method 4	Canned puppy food − 210 g + mixer biscuit − 70 g + one egg + 100 g poached cod + vitamin and mineral supplement	Canned puppy food − 475 g + mixer biscuit − 160 g + one egg + 100 g poached cod + vitamin and mineral supplement	Canned puppy food − 465 g + mixer biscuit − 155 g + one egg + 100 g poached cod + vitamin and mineral supplement
Method 5	Tripe − 255 g + mixer biscuit − 125 g + vitamin and mineral supplement	Tripe − 490 g + mixer biscuit − 245 g + vitamin and mineral supplement	Tripe − 485 g + mixer biscuit − 245 g + vitamin and mineral supplement

Notes

- Fresh water should be available at all times
- The recommended ratio in Method 3 is approximately equivalent to equal volumes
- 'Egg' refers to raw, not cooked, egg

prevention or management is very important. Any bitch can become overweight through a combination of overfeeding and under-exercise, but the condition is seen more often in spayed bitches and in older bitches.

Successful management of obesity requires very careful regulation of calorie intake. This requires considerable determination on behalf of the owner and all who come into contact with the bitch. A weight reduction programme is best followed under veterinary supervision and may utilize either a home-prepared diet or, preferably, one of the specially formulated commercial diets available for weight reduction.

Obesity may be avoided by careful husbandry. A simple approach to this is to weigh the bitch regularly; small changes will become apparent from weighing long before they are noted by eye. Ideally, weighing should take place at the same time of day on each occasion and on the same scales. This will help to reduce small fluctuations in weight caused by factors such as feeding and enable changing trends in body weight to be observed early on. The food intake of the bitch can then be adjusted, with the aim of maintaining a constant body weight. For example, if a small upward trend is observed, a reduction of 10 per cent in total food allowance could be made.

Your veterinary surgeon or knowledgeable breeder will be able to give you advice on the optimum weight for your particular bitch.

Further reading

Doglopaedia, J.M. Evans and Kay White (Howell, USA, Ringpress Books, UK)

Acknowledgement
The authors would like to thank Peter Markwell, BSc, BVetMed, MRCVS and Derek Booles of The Waltham Centre for Pet Nutrition for providing the text for this chapter.

SECTION TWO:
BREEDING FROM YOUR BITCH

Forward planning

Pregnancy and whelping

Care of your newly-whelped bitch and puppies

CHAPTER 5
FORWARD PLANNING

Forward planning

Genetics

Management before
mating

The stud dog

Getting your bitch mated

The mating process

The breeding process

Introduction

Many people who own bitches unfortunately fall into the trap of not thinking ahead before they decide to breed from their pet. Make sure you do not get ensnared in this way, as it may not only be costly in time, money and inconvenience but it could also bring a great deal of anxiety and unhappiness.

Breeding from your bitch means adding to the enormous surplus of dogs we already have, so you must have very convincing reasons before you plan a litter. Around 150,000 healthy dogs are destroyed every year because they are unwanted, and up to 250,000 dogs, both pedigree and cross-bred, are in rescue kennels waiting for a new owner. The dog in rescue kennels is on a downward spiral, for the longer they are kennelled, the less their chances are of getting a good home.

You may feel, especially if you have not bred a litter before, that such a fate could not happen to your puppies, but the chances are that some will end up this way, especially if you are interested in the popular and prolific breeds. Experienced breeders will tell you that clients who make firm promises of homes often back out when the puppy is ready. The most carefully screened families sometimes turn out to be bad owners, and all too often the lives of your best clients change direction soon after the purchase of a puppy and they want you to take it back. Morally you should do so, as you were responsible for originating the litter.

You have to keep your litter until all the puppies are sold; this may be as long as 12 to 16 weeks, or even six months. Welfare societies and breed rescue schemes are not established for the purpose of taking puppies off breeders when it is inconvenient to keep them any longer.

Many people fail to realize that they may have to face having the puppies they have reared humanely destroyed when only a few months old simply because they cannot be found homes. Puppies should never be given away or sold cheaply in order to get rid of them, because most people agree that anyone taking on a puppy must want it enough to pay the asking price for it. The new owner must also be able to financially maintain the dog with regard to food, veterinary attention, boarding for holidays, etc.

Pedigree dog breeding on a small scale is not a paying hobby and deliberately breeding mongrels is extremely foolish.

There is never a medical reason for breeding from a bitch. The idea that it is good for a bitch to have one litter has been proved to be untrue. Having a litter does nothing to preserve your bitch's health and may even bring about disease, so do not be led into breeding a litter for these reasons.

If you are determined to breed a litter, for whatever purpose, resolve that this will be the healthiest and best socialized litter ever to be offered as companion animals. Even if you are trying to breed a superb show specimen to keep, it is as well to acknowledge that 75 per cent of your litter, and every litter ever bred, are destined for the pet market. You can do a lot to help your litter make successful pets by early conditioning to the life they will have to lead.

Forward planning

There are a number of questions which you should ask yourself before deciding to breed from your bitch. You should only proceed if you can answer them all satisfactorily.

Do you have the space?

Consider the requirements of breeding a litter in terms of space. You must have a secluded, heated room for whelping. This room must be capable of being darkened and, ideally, it should be fitted with a wash basin and it must have handy electric points. The bitch and her puppies will remain in this room until the pups are about three weeks old. The breeder will spend a lot of time here too, probably several nights as well as a considerable part of the day especially during the early stages.

The location should not be near a front door or where there may be sudden alarming noises, nor should it be accessible to other dogs or cats. On the other hand the bitch should not feel her whelping location is one totally alien to her. To put her in the garage, for instance, or a kennel newly-provided at this time, may indicate to her banishment from her familiar home, and she may hold up her whelping dangerously if she does not feel comfortable in her situation.

It is not wise to count on using a glass-roofed house extension at any stage of whelping or rearing puppies as these rooms heat up too quickly and also lose heat very rapidly in colder weather and at night. Temperature of the environment is a highly critical factor in rearing puppies. Many people find a spare bedroom ideal to convert to a whelping room.

In contrast, when the puppies are about three weeks old, they must have an entirely different environment. They need to be in a 'busy' place with their dam, where they can see and be seen. A partitioned-off corner of the kitchen often fills the need ideally. The puppies require a 'little house' to retreat into (this could be a large cardboard carton on its side). The 'house' should be placed within a playpen which can be expanded by adding extra panels to accommodate the puppies' increasing activity. In addition, there must be a separate bed for the dam, within the same room but where the pups cannot get at her, so that she can get some much deserved and needed peace. If you have a medium to large breed, you will find that several puppies of eight weeks plus can scarcely be accommodated in the average kitchen. Yet it is vitally necessary to make plans for keeping pups of this age which may not have been sold. Such pups need space, and they need socializing. It may prove possible to make an enclosed area of the garden containing a rain- and sun-proof shelter in which these growing pups can spend at least part of each day.

You will also need a room in which to interview buyers and show them the puppies.

Experience shows that each customer needs to visit at least twice, sometimes more often. Buyers tend to come in family groups at week-ends and they will stay a long while, maybe for as long as two or three hours. This is necessary because you will want to talk in depth to them to check their suitability, and the buyers will want to take a long while choosing their puppy, since this is, for them, a very important buy. Because other members of your family may not take kindly to having their living-room or kitchen occupied continuously over the week-end, it is as well to have another room available in which to see your customers. There should be a small playpen set up in which you can put the puppies which are available for their choice.

You should have all the paperwork (pedigrees, photographs, feeding charts etc.) to hand as well as books on your breed. It is unwise to leave unfamiliar people alone with your puppies for long, as the pups may be mishandled by children and adults who are unused to holding wriggling puppies.

Have you the time?

Looking after a whelping bitch, rearing and selling puppies involves a long term commitment, perhaps four months of fairly continual work when the bitch and her family must have first consideration.

Around the time of mating there is need for a week of flexible time, when you are able to take the bitch to the dog on the day the bitch shows that she is ready. Many stud owners will want the mating to take place during the daytime. Around the time of whelping, on average two months or so after mating, the bitch will need constant observation for several days. For a week after whelping, your presence is constantly required until good maternal behaviour is established and the puppies can be seen to be thriving. If your bitch is doing her job well your workload will lighten for two weeks, but once weaning starts, feeding the puppies (up to five times a day) and cleaning up after them (almost continually), as well as socializing them for several hours a day, is an 18 hour a day job for one person with a sizeable litter.

This routine goes on with increasing intensity until the last puppy is sold. Dog breeding is labour-intensive work.

Have you the temperament

Baskets full of pretty puppies on a birthday card are one thing – bringing those puppies into the world and looking after them is quite another.

Almost inevitably, in•your litter there will be some puppies born dead, some which may die later on, some which are congenitally deformed, and probably some which are surplus to the number you can hope to sell to the right home. Will you grieve for the dead and dying? Are you clear-thinking enough to decide that the greatest kindness is to have some puppies put down at birth? If *you* can cope with these decisions, will *your children* be able to take them in their stride? Many people want to produce a litter from their bitch in order to give the children experience of seeing mating and birth, but for some, the total package of deformity, death or elective culling may be too much to handle.

Have you the money?

Having a litter involves a considerable outlay of money before you see any return on puppy sales. To begin with you will have to pay a stud fee, which can be considerable for a good dog, veterinary fees, travel to the stud, extra food for bitch and puppies (your bitch requires more during the latter part of her pregnancy and at the peak of lactation), some equipment, extra heating and lighting, washing powder and cleaners, telephone and stationary, Kennel Club registrations, puppy insurance, advertising, photographs etc. In addition, if you are improvizing whelping accommodation within your house, you must allow for a certain amount of wear and tear on carpets, furnishings and paintwork. This is inevitable if you allow, as you probably must, growing puppies to run around for exercise.

You may eventually get some or all of this money back from puppy sales, but if disaster occurs you could lose quite a lot or even all of it especially if the bitch has to have a Caesarean and the puppies eventually die. At any rate, you will see no return for four to five months after the mating, until the puppies are ready to sell. Most pet owners who take one litter from their bitch find themselves out of pocket in the end, especially if other paid work is given up in order to look after the litter.

Have you the market?

If there are a several established breeders in your area producing puppies in your breed, the outlook for selling your litter is not good. There is no greater panic-inducing situation than having several eight to 12-week old puppies on your hands and no buyers forthcoming.

It is unrealistic to think that other breeders will send you customers; they would rather, quite understandably, persuade these buyers to wait until they have their next litter. The only help you are likely to get with sales is if you have used a well-known stud dog whose progeny are in great demand.

In general, new owners want puppies up to eight weeks old, especially in medium to large breeds, and they are quite correct in making this preference. If you have not sold your puppies by that time the only way you can make them appeal is to house-car-lead-train them and have them fully vaccinated and socialized. Unfortunately, the selling price of puppies goes down the older they get, so the cost of your time is unlikely to be repaid.

The time of year, the scarcity or abundance of puppies locally at the time, the colour and sex available, the show wins and the breeding of the stock involved, as well as the hard-won reputation of the breeder, all have a major effect on sales.

Breeding plans

Most bitches start their breeding career at their third heat, or when they are about two years old. Your forward planning must allow for at least five months of intensive care and attention of your bitch and her puppies, as it is not wise to board her during pregnancy and lactation.

There are times when puppy selling is difficult – mid-summer (from June to early-September) and during very hard weather in January and February – so avoid having puppies ready to sell at these times. You may have to keep them a long while at the stage when they should be socializing in their new homes, when they are beginning to cost a lot to feed and vaccinate, and when they will be doing, as a group, a tremendous amount of damage to your house and garden. If you are a novice, it can be a bad mistake to arrange to have your bitch mated by a friend's pet dog, however charming he may be. You will be missing out on the expertise and the sales contacts that an established breeder may be able to help you with. Contact the breeder who supplied your bitch. Breeders are always interested in the progression of their own line, and can give invaluable advice on the selection of a stud dog.

If you are no longer in touch with the breeder, join your local canine society and find other people interested in your breed, or go to a big dog show and find your fancy there.

Genetics

You will find that knowledgeable breeders talk about in-breeding, line breeding, and outcrossing.

Put very simply, in-breeding means mating the bitch to a very close relative, perhaps her half-brother or her grandfather. This was a formula very popular 15–20 years ago when many champions bred in this way were made up in certain breeds. It can be a successful breeding method to fix good characteristics quickly and there may be, if you are fortunate, one puppy in the litter in which all the good things have come to the surface. But in-breeding doubles up on the unwanted features too and it is probable that many of the adverse inherited conditions such as hip dysplasia and progressive retinal atrophy, which we are now trying to eradicate, were in fact established, or at least aggravated, through in-breeding.

Line breeding involves mating your bitch to a dog of the same family, with common ancestors four to five generations back. This can be a better breeding policy but for true instant success you need to have actually known the dogs whose names appear on the pedigree, so that you can evaluate their virtues, know how long they lived and how they died etc. Such knowledge is almost impossible to come by for the newcomer to breeding.

Outcrossing means breeding your bitch to a dog which is, as far as you can see, totally unrelated to her. Remember that in many breeds, particularly those which have had a rapid population explosion, all the dogs on the pedigree go back to a very few animals. If you have put in a lot of study beforehand you will know that because dogs bear the same kennel prefix it does not necessarily mean they are related; many big kennels run two or three breeding lines. On the other hand, dogs which are closely related may bear entirely different kennel prefixes if one was sold to another kennel as a puppy. You can obtain an extended pedigree for a fee from the Kennel Club which will show you more generations of your bitch's ancestors and also those of the prospective stud dog.

Genetics means the study of genes, the unique individual patterns all animals carry in the cells of their bodies. Each individual carries, at the moment of conception, the genes which determine what he/she will look like, and also the genes which will influence the way he/she will behave. Genes are carried in a composite way within the body on strings known as chromosomes. Dogs have 39 pairs of chromosomes, each pair taking one chromosone from the dam and one from the sire. These genes are present in the sperm and in the egg, and they combine differently in each of the fertilized embryos. The combination is totally random, which is why you do not get all that is beautiful and good in even one of your puppies. The feature which you are trying to improve, such as head type, may involve many genes so making it very hard to alter.

However not all genes are equal. There are dominant and recessive genes. Put simply, dominant genes show in the dog or bitch, recessive genes are hidden only to surface when they meet at mating with a dog or bitch which also carries that gene as a recessive.

Two more words come into the vocabulary here. Phenotype, which describes those characteristics of the way an individual dog looks, and genotype, for the combination of genes he has for that feature. If a dog (or bitch) carries two dominant genes for a feature, e.g. very dark eyes, all the progeny inherit this feature. But although the dog may have dark eyes himself he may carry a recessive gene for light eyes, and if he is mated to a bitch with a similar recessive gene for that feature, you will have a proportion of pups with light eyes. Many people regard light eyes as a very unattractive feature, except, of course, in those breeds such as Weimaraners, where light eyes are accepted as normal. So how do you know what kind of genes your bitch and the prospective stud dog carry? The answer is, you don't, and you cannot except by checking on your bitch's siblings, taking note of the characteristics they show, and by checking on the progeny of the stud dog you propose to use.

Now you see why it is best to take advice from a person with long experience in your breed. Such a person will also point out the features in which your bitch fails in the beauty stakes, so that you may choose a dog which is likely to improve on these points for your puppies.

Most dog breeding, even by experienced breeders, is experimental. Breeders will try one stud on their bitch, and at the next breeding period try another. While a breeding match may look good on paper, it does not always work out in actuality any more than humans can predict what their offspring will be like. There is no formula for producing a good-looking, good-tempered litter, but experienced breeders can help you lower the odds against disaster.

A newly imported breed or a very scarce breed has a small gene pool; that is, because there are so few individuals capable of being mated together, in-breeding is inevitable, and the stock is weakened because no 'fresh' blood is available.

Mongrels are mongrels because of the very wide assortment of genes they carry. This means that the size, colour, temperament, and coat are relatively unpredictable, and so are the inherited diseases the pups may carry. Mongrels do have hip dysplasia and hereditary deformities but we tend to hear less about them.

Many of the deleterious deformities and diseases which we would like to see eliminated from dogs are carried on recessive genes. Eye conditions, cleft palates, wrong coloration, wrong type of coat, dwarfism, bad tooth placement, poor ear carriage, etc. are all thought to be brought about by recessive genes. Stud dog owners may boast that their stud dog never produced a pup with, for instance, a kinked tail. It may be that his genes do not allow him to produce kinked tails, or it may be that he has never been mated to a bitch who carried the gene for kinked tails. Fate may decree that he only meets such a bitch at the end of his stud career and then it becomes known that he was carrying and passing on the gene for kinked tails, so that all his progeny will be capable of producing kinked tails too. The example is for a feature which is comparatively trivial but there are many other recessive genes which produce features and conditions which are far more harmful. These features may not show until the litter are mature animals, maybe until they have been bred from themselves. Some of the eye conditions which cause pain and blindness may not develop until five years of age or even older.

Many breeds now advocate examining all breeding stock for a number of inherited diseases and malformations so that two dogs which are badly affected are not bred together. These conditions are mainly hip dysplasia and several eye defects, but some breeds have their own particular scourge for which dogs and bitches are screened. Don't take it for granted that your bitch does not have the condition because you have seen no sign of it – she could be a carrier. In any case, reputable stud owners will not allow their dogs to be used by unscreened bitches.

Ask your breeder or your veterinary surgeon about the conditions in your breed and where to get screening. Checking for eye conditions is often done at eye clinics, arranged at shows or at private houses. You will find the details given in the canine press.

One deleterious condition for which there is no official screening is demodectic mange. If your bitch had this skin condition as a puppy, she should not be bred from at all, as she is very likely to pass it to her puppies, even though the mange has apparently cleared up. Demodectic mange is a skin condition caused by infestation with the mite *Demodex canis* but it does seem that a basic inherited defect in the immune system is probably responsible for the naturally occurring disease and that this is why the condition is more common in certain breeds, e.g. Dachshunds, Boxers and Dobermanns.

Bitch management before mating

Get your bitch absolutely fit before you think of breeding from her. She should be in lean, hard condition when she goes to be mated so work towards this state by providing a properly balanced diet in the correct amount, lots of exercise and extra grooming.

Where bitches are fed on a bulky complete diet, they may find it difficult to consume the volume of food which they need during later pregnancy and lactation. You may want, in the run-up to mating time, to make a gradual change to meat and biscuit feeding which supplies animal protein in a more compact form.

You should also clear up any disease conditions in your bitch, such as any ear or skin problems, and it can be a good idea to have her teeth checked because dental and oral disease may pass on bacteria to the puppies when the dam licks them, especially around the severed umbilical cord. A veterinary check-up at this time will not go amiss.

In relatively recent times it has been discovered that the pups' vaccination regime is easier to handle if they do not obtain too much antibody to disease from the dam. The current opinion is that the best vaccine state for the bitch at mating time is to be about halfway through her vaccine year, i.e. about six months after a booster dose has been given. Many veterinary surgeons do not now, in the light of up-to-date information on canine parvovirus infection, favour giving booster doses just before mating or during pregnancy. However, the timing of vaccination of bitches and puppies will be dictated by local disease conditions and you should always seek the advice of *your* veterinary surgeon.

The stud dog

Male dogs have to be allowed a small space in *The Book of the Bitch* because without them we should have no new generation.

If you intend to take up dog breeding, should you keep your own stud dog? These are the arguments for and against:

In favour
- Your own dog is the only one on which you will have complete information about character and health.
- Your bitches may be easier to mate because they have had experience of living with a male. Some bitches have never even encountered a male dog until they are taken for mating.
- If you wish to exhibit, you have an entrant for the dog classes.
- Your dog may get some outside stud work which adds interest, income and also broadens your breeding line – but will you find it easy to cope with visiting in-season bitches?

Against
- Your dog will soon be of limited use to you, as you come to breeding from his daughters.
- Having a dog in the house where there are in-season bitches can make life exceedingly difficult, but so can banishing the dog to a kennel in the garden.

● You can use the best, and most suitable stud dogs in your breed for far less than it would cost to keep a male of your own for limited use.

For many novice breeders, keeping a castrated male proves to be a successful compromise.

Selecting a stud

When making your choice of stud dog, take into consideration the fact that you will have to take the bitch to him on the day *she* decides she is ready, and probably on another day about 48 hours later – can you be sure of doing so on any day of the week, in any weather? Your choice may be influenced by transport problems. Few people now have the capacity to board an in-season bitch and few owners will want to let her stay away at this sensitive time. Furthermore, most people like to be there to see the mating take place.

Some stud owners will visit bitches with their dogs but you will have to pay their transport costs in addition to the stud fee and many dogs do not work so well away from home.

Getting your bitch mated

Select your stud dog, with perhaps another as back-up choice, well ahead of your bitch coming into season. See the dogs at shows, ask the owners for stud cards or copy pedigrees to study. If you are not able to get to shows, the secretary of your local Canine Society, or your veterinary surgery, may be able to help. Beware of persuading the owners of pet dogs to allow them to be used at stud, a very occasional use of a male dog can upset his whole life and alter his character and suitability as a pet. Use a professional stud dog which has a regular supply of bitches coming to him, but never use, no matter how big a winner he may be, a dog which is a unilateral cryptorchid, i.e. has only one testicle descended into the scrotum. This condition is hereditary and so will be passed on to his offspring; it is not just a cosmetic fault since retained testicles can give rise to a particularly unpleasant form of cancer which affects the coat, the metabolism and the whole body of the dog. Many veterinary surgeons advise that an undescended testicle should be removed, whether it is giving trouble or not, when the dog is about 18 months old. Your veterinary surgeon can give an informed opinion about the likelihood of undescended testicles when the puppy is eight weeks old. If a breeder has deliberately introduced this fault into your line, the customers may look to the breeder to pay for the operation.

Also check the dog's hip dysplasia and eye clearance certificates as appropriate. Each country has its own scheme, and the age when dog's are tested may vary. Consult your National Kennel Club for further information.

Will the dog you use on your bitch be fertile? The answer is, of course, neither you nor his owner will know unless a very recent sperm analysis is available. Male fertility depends not only on the readiness of the dog to perform the mating act, but on the quantity of sperm, its motility (the power to reach the uterine tube) and the fact that the sperm is not in any way deformed. Sperm which is abnormal does not produce deformed puppies, it will not fertilise the bitch's eggs. It is as well to realise that the sperm which the dog produces on the day your bitch goes for mating was in fact created several months ago, so the dog's fitness at the moment of mating is no guide to his fertility. Even a completely healthy dog may have a noticeable variation in sperm output for no discernible reason. Treatment with corticosteroids, to subdue inflammation or the itching of a skin problem, can affect sperm being stored in the dog's reproductive system. An illness which causes a very high body temperature will shut down sperm production which will be experienced about two months later. An episode of canine parvovirus infection is a typical example of an illness which will stop sperm production and some males which had this illness as puppies have never been fertile.

Very hot weather, and certainly an experience of being overheated at a show or in a car, can produce a summer sterility which has its effect in the autumn. It is also not uncommon for stud dogs to go into a state of spermatogenic arrest as early as two to three years old, although they have been fertile before this, and this type of sterility seems to be permanent but the cause is not known. Since very few stud dog owners have their dogs assessed until several bitches have missed to them, the bitch owner has no guarantee of being offered a usable stud. In order, then, to have the best chance of your bitch conceiving, it is necessary to have at least two matings, 48 hours apart, and for really optimum conditions, a mating every 48 hours as long as the bitch will stand for the dog.

You may find a reluctance in the stud owner to allow their dog to be used in this way. You may be told that it was such a good mating, that a return visit is not necessary, but remember, high libido (willingness to mate) gives no assurance of a fertile mating. Many bitches are more relaxed about mating on their second visit to the dog. While asking for several matings or even for your bitch to live with the dog may seen unreasonable, two matings always used to be the custom. There is no reason to suppose that the current conception rate is so high that the second mating can be dispensed with.

The mating process

Encourage your bitch to pass urine before you reach the stud dog's premises so that she feels comfortable during the mating. Remember that her urine is loaded with bitch scent, so get her to use an inconspicuous place and not outside the stud owner's home.

Have the bitch on a lead and under control when you arrive since there may be other dogs about. A Halti head collar can be a very useful control during mating.

Dog and bitch should be allowed some play together before they come to the point of mating. The dog then mounts the bitch, penetrates the vulva with his penis, whilst clasping the bitch around her waist level.

The ejaculate of a normal dog consists of three fractions; the first is thought to clear any residual urine from the penis, the second, which is delivered within one minute or so of penetration, contains the sperm. You will see the dog make strong, thrusting motions with his penis. Following this, comes the third fraction, from the prostate gland. This consists of a considerable amount of fluid which is ejaculated intermittently during the tie and helps transport the sperm up to the oviduct. In principle, the sperm should be in the uterine tubes before the eggs are ripe for fertilization.

Then follows the tie, during which the expanded bulbous penis of the dog remains in the bitch's vagina. The tie can last from five minutes to almost an hour. Stud owners will turn the dog so that he no longer rests on the bitch's back, and will steady the dog and bitch so that neither is pulled around

Fig. 5.1 **The stages of coitus**
(a) mounting
(b) the tie

during this close contact which many bitches find very irksome. The tie finally breaks spontaneously.

Some of the prostatic fluid may drain out of the bitch. This does not contain sperm and there is no justification at all of the ancient ritual of holding up the bitch by her hind legs so that the fluid drains back. A fertile mating is possible without a tie taking place, provided the dog's penis has remained within the bitch for a few minutes after ejaculation, but obviously a tie, with an average time of 20 minutes, is more satisfactory.

The stud owner makes the rules at mating time and organizes the proceedings. The only duty of the bitch owner is to steady the bitch and prevent her from sitting down when the male tries to mount her, and also to hold her steady during the tie.

The convention is that you pay the stud fee in full at the conclusion of the first mating. You should then receive the signed pedigree of the stud dog, which should include his Kennel Club registration number, and also a Kennel Club form signed by the stud owner to certify that the mating took place on the date stated, to enable you to register the litter when it arrives. Some stud owners will not give this form until the litter is born. You should also get photocopies of the dog's hip and eye certificates, perhaps a list of his show wins, and it is a good idea to take a photograph of him to show the puppy buyers.

Since old customs are dying, it is perhaps wise to ask if the stud owner believes in giving a free mating at the next season if your bitch should miss. If you wish to claim this privilege, you must remember to notify the stud owner directly the expected whelping date has passed. Since you paid for the services of the dog and not for an actual litter, you cannot expect to get your money back if you no longer wish to mate your bitch or you want to go to a different stud dog next time.

Even more problematical is the right to a 'free' mating if all the pups die at or soon after birth, or if all are an unacceptable colour, such as white or checks in Boxers. While the reason for the former problem is likely to lie with the bitch, the formation of unacceptable colours comes from both sides, so it may be unwise to mate these two animals again, even without charge.

There may be some variables on the payment of stud fees; for instance the owners of a young dog not used at stud before may require payment only when the litter is born.

Some stud owners will ask for 'the pick of the litter' instead of half or even all of the stud fee. This is no bargain for the bitch owner. Not only may the pup you preferred for yourself also be the choice of the stud owner, but you will also be held up in promising any of the litter until the stud owner has made his choice. Also, the selling price of a puppy is often roughly twice the stud fee, so you would be paying dearly for not paying at the time of the mating.

Remember that when you leave the stud dog your bitch is still very much in season, capable of being mated by another dog, and probably less reluctant now than she once was.

If your bitch should be mated by another dog, whether or not of the right breed, all is not now lost. A new process, called genetic fingerprinting, can disclose, through a small blood test, which of the pups in a litter carry the same genes as the dam and sire, and which are the offspring of the dam and another dog, even if the dog is a stray and cannot be found to take part in the test. No longer need dogs appear in show catalogues with dual parentage nor need a litter be sold without a pedigree because another male mated the bitch after or even before the planned mating.

Genetic fingerprinting is also a safegard for substitution of one stud dog for another.

Your veterinary surgeon will be able to help you with more information on genetic fingerprinting.

Table 5.1: Mating – in summary

- Two matings 48 hours apart are the minimum you should accept for your bitch.
- A good mating performance is no guarantee of fertility in the male.
- Expect to pay the stud fee in full after the mating is over.
- Find out what concessions you may be entitled to if the bitch should miss.
- Collect all the relevant paperwork before you leave.

The breeding process

Whether you mean to take only one litter from a pet bitch, or indeed if you have a litter thrust upon you by an accidental mating, or whether you mean to found your own special breeding line, you must understand the reproductive process in the bitch in detail. If you do not take this trouble, you will not be able to help your bitch when she needs you most. The bitch's oestrous cycle is fully described in Chapter 8, but from the breeding aspect the most important point is that under the influence of a hormone, known as luteinizing hormone (LH), an unknown number of follicles rupture to release their eggs into the uterine tube at each heat period. This is called ovulation and it coincides more or less with the days when the bitch is most willing to be mated (around the ninth to 14th day of the season).

The ova are released in an immature state. They mature within the oviduct over four to five days, and only then are they ready to be fertilized by the dog's sperm. Fertilization therefore depends on live active sperm meeting mature eggs at just the right time, and this is why two matings, usually 48 hours apart, are advisable to give optimum chance of ovulation and maturation coinciding with the presence of live sperm. Fortunately sperm from a really fit stud can live in the bitch's reproductive tract for three days, and even up to seven days, so even if she is mated early there is a good chance that the sperm will still be viable.

Normally the head of only one sperm penetrates the softening wall of each egg, although there are probably thousands of sperm waiting from the mating. If more than one sperm fertilizes an egg, the embryo will be abnormal and will die before whelping but this is an unusual occurrence.

After fertilization there are two nuclei in each egg envelope, one from the sire and one from the dam. Each carries half the chromosomes of the parents. When these two nuclei fuse, a whole new entity, carrying the full complement of 78 chromosomes, comes into being. Each puppy is programmed by these chromosomes for all the inherited characteristics it will have. Once fertilized, the egg goes through a process of very rapid cell division.

The fertilized eggs are free in the uterus and uterine tube for up to 20 days after mating, and they are surprisingly safe and immune from any infections etc. which may occur to the bitch. At 20 to 21 days after mating, the embryo begins to change shape and to attach itself to the walls of the uterine horns. The following two weeks are probably the most vital ones for the prospective litter. The body organs and the limbs of the embryo puppies are now being rapidly formed, and the embryos are very susceptible to events which happen to the bitch. If she picks up an infection, is given certain kinds of medication or live vaccination, if she has an accident or is poisoned, or becomes overheated through confinement in a hot car, the development of the organs of the foetus may be arrested or distorted. Deformities such as cleft palates, single eyes, undeveloped limbs, absence of feet or anus, abnormalities of the urinary system and the heart and circulatory system, all occur at this time, although the foetus is only one-and-a-half to two inches long. Foetuses even more badly affected may die and be reabsorbed by the bitch so that you may never know they existed.

It is therefore important to keep the bitch away from any source of infection, including any assembly of dogs at a show or training class during this time (three-and-a-half to five weeks after mating). This period, before

Table 5.2: The development of puppies in the uterus

The pre-attachment stage

Fertilization + 96 hours – The ovum has divided into two cells
+ 120 hours – Four cells
+ 144 hours – Eight cells
+ 192 hours – A mass of cells known as a morula
+ 8 to 9 days – The morula is passing down the uterine tube and then into the uterus

The embryonic stage

Fertilization + 15 days – A blastocyst is formed, the ovum having reshaped into a hollow sphere still floating free in the uterus

+ 17 to 18 days – Placentas begin to develop from the yolk sacs of the ovum

+ 20 to 21 days – Embryos, less than half an inch in diameter begin to attach to the walls of the uterine horns. Ideally they should be evenly spaced, as overcrowding leads to poor development and weak puppies at birth. At this stage the central nervous system is formed

+ 21 to 28 days – The brain and spinal cord are developing, the embryo begins to bend its head forward and curl up in the classic foetal position. All the organs of the body, the limbs, head, eyes and face are being formed

+ 28 days – The embryo is oval in shape and is about one inch in diameter

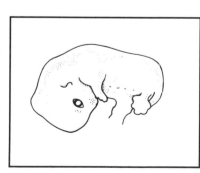

Fig. 5.2 The development of puppies
(a) a late embryo

Table 5.2: (cont.)

The foetal stage

Fertilization	+ 29 to 30 days –	Male and female sexual characteristics show and the eyelids close. Those puppies which are born with no eyes at all under the closed lids had some mishap at this time
	+ 35 to 44 days –	Abdominal enlargement should be noticeable in the bitch if an average size litter is present. Mammary glands develop and 'point'
	+ 45 to 55 days –	Rapid growth of the foetus. Folding of uterine horns, occurs when the bitch is carrying an average or large litter, creating a dramatic change in her outline. This change will not be seen when only two to three puppies are present. In a Beagle bitch of 18 to 20 lb foetuses are now about three and a half inches long. A waxy plug can be expelled from the teats, followed by a watery fluid. Calcification of the bones of the foetuses occurs and they can be seen on X ray
	+ 57 days –	Live full term puppies can be born. The last four weeks within the uterus are used for greater differentiation of the features and establishment of the body systems in relationship to the placenta. Some dramatic changes in these systems still have to occur very quickly at the time of birth

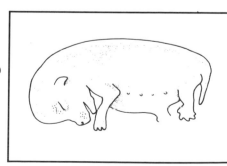

(b) an early foetus

the bitch shows much in the way of positive signs of being in whelp, is a very significant time of pregnancy with regard to producing a healthy litter.

It is useful to keep a very detailed pregnancy diary for your bitch, so that if a deformity occurs in the puppies you may have some incident to which you can attribute it. Although this is no actual help to you with this litter, most breeders find it satisfying to be able to link pre-natal problems to a cause and if you are able to do so, it may be of help in a future litter.

The events described above are summarized in Table 5.2.

The placenta

The placenta, sometimes known as the afterbirth, is attached to the wall of the uterus and joined directly to the embryo by the umbilical cord, which acts as a cable transmitting nourishment and some antibodies. The umbilical cord also transfers hormones and oxygen and removes waste products. The establishment of a good placenta is crucial to a healthy puppy at birth.

Different animals have different types of placenta. The canine race has what is known as a zonary placenta, a structure similar to a broad belt encircling each embryo. As the embryo grows and develops, so does the placenta. A puppy which weighs to 12 to 16 oz at birth may have a placenta weighing 2 to 3 oz.

The edge of the canine placenta has a border of broken-down red blood cells (known as a marginal haematoma), which in the course of their degeneration form a dense green pigment. The broken-down blood emerges from the bitch at whelping time as a dark fluid, which stains practically everything it touches, including the hands and nails of ungloved helpers,

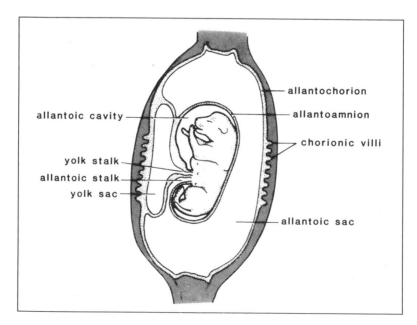

allantochorion

allantoamnion

allantoic cavity

chorionic villi

yolk stalk

allantoic stalk

yolk sac

allantoic sac

Fig. 5.3 **The structure of a foetal unit**

with a bright green stain which can be particularly difficult to remove from towels, overalls and other clothing. However, the stain washes out quite easily from white polyester fur.

The green stain can be a warning sign. If you see it before any puppies are born, it is an indication that something is going badly wrong and you should seek veterinary help at once. After one or more puppies have been born, the green stain is normal as it is released as each placenta separates from the uterine wall.

CHAPTER 6
PREGNANCY AND WHELPING

Pregnancy diagnosis

Psychology during pregnancy and whelping

Care during pregnancy

Preparations for whelping

The whelping process

Whelping lore

Emergency 'what ifs'

Pregnancy diagnosis

For just a few days around three-and-a-half weeks of pregnancy (20 to 30 days after mating) it may be possible for a veterinary surgeon to feel the tiny marble-size foetal units in the uterus, strung out like a bead necklace. The thinner and narrower the bitch is, the more likely an accurate diagnosis can be made. In large broad-bodied bitches it may not be possible.

Once fluids have accumulated in the foetal units, held in their double-walled membrane made up of the allantois, nearest the puppy, and the amnion on the outside, the uterus becomes an even width along its length making it very difficult indeed, if not impossible, to identify the foetuses until much later in pregnancy.

Since the foetuses are at such a critical stage at about 24 to 35 days of pregnancy, it is extremely unwise to let anyone try to feel for the foetuses. If it is vital for you to know whether your bitch is pregnant, let a veterinary surgeon make the diagnosis using some other technique (see later) but even then a negative verdict cannot completely be relied upon and, not uncommonly, a bitch has surprised both her owner and the vet.

The bitch may show very few external signs of pregnancy until about the 35th day of pregnancy. At this time a number of changes are usually visible.

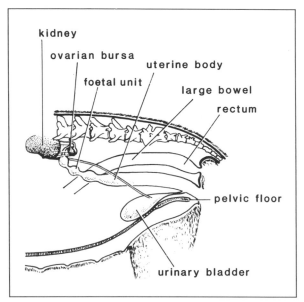

Fig. 6.1 **The uterus** *in situ* **21 to 25 days pregnant**

The teats
The pink colour of the teats deepens, due to increased blood supply, and the teats become enlarged and more erect. Development is always most noticeable in the pair of teats nearest the hind legs, and least prominent in the pair near the front legs which may sometimes not come into use at all. It is of no importance if a bitch does not have her teats evenly paired or if there are more puppies than teats, provided that the milk supply is plentiful.

The mammary glands
The mammary glands begin to enlarge and develop more functional tissue ready for milk production. This engorgement seems to cause some bitches a little discomfort and they may lick or scratch the glands.

Vaginal discharge
From about the 35th day there is likely to be a discharge of opaque or white mucus from the vagina, and this is a fairly reliable indication of pregnancy. Any blood-stained or coloured discharge is a reason to consult the vet.

Morning sickness
Many bitches will vomit a quantity of frothy liquid in the morning and may refuse food until around midday. This is caused by hormonal changes and the pressure from the stretched uterus. No treatment is needed beyond a little sympathy, and the offering of food when she feels ready for it. Morning sickness may be an indication that the bitch should now be given three smaller meals a day.

By the sixth week food should gradually be increased (see Chapter 4). As pregnancy progresses the bitch may need to be fed four or even five times a day – give her smaller quantities when she feels ready for food. Regular meal times need not be adhered to as it will not be unusual for her to refuse food for some part of the day or even miss a day altogether due to discomfort from pressure on her abdominal organs by the enlarging uterus. Many bitches refuse milk at this stage of pregnancy and this does not matter. However, consistent refusal of food over several days, together with other signs of illness, warrant a veterinary consultation.

Abdominal enlargement

In large breeds it is difficult to see any abdominal enlargement until about the six week stage (40 to 42 days). Then the signs of pregnancy sometimes appear suddenly, and very often overnight.

When the uterine horns are becoming very full with developing foetuses there is no longer room in the abdomen for the horns to lie parallel, so they fold back upon themselves and drop lower into the abdomen, making a very noticeable change in the bitch's outline. The weight of the dropped uterus pulls upon the spine, making the vertebrae very prominent.

At this stage, too, the mammary glands begin to differentiate clearly from the smooth line of the abdomen. Where the litter is small, this abdominal shift may not occur and you may still have no clear indication of pregnancy.

Later diagnosis

Puppies may be seen on X-ray from day 45 to 50 of pregnancy (about three weeks before whelping), when the bones of the foetuses have started to become calcified. You may also see foetal movement at this stage when the bitch is lying on her side after a meal, or when she has taken a long drink of water.

Modern ultrasound machines are increasingly available in small animal practices It is possible by means of ultrasound to monitor a difficult pregnancy throughout and to see if the foetuses are distressed. Foetal growth can be measured and scanning has a useful role to play in detecting the number and relative size of the foetuses at the end of pregnancy and thus it can help veterinary surgeons decide whether a Caesarean delivery may be needed. Pregnancy diagnosis is said to be 94 per cent accurate when ultrasound is used, but assessing the number of pups in the litter is not so accurate, especially when there are more than six foetuses.

Recently, a new test has been introduced which can determine the presence of pregnancy from a blood sample taken between 28 and 37 days after mating. This measures the levels of certain plasma proteins which are elevated at this time in pregnant bitches. It is vital to ensure good clinical health before testing since some clinical conditions may lead to false positives in the absence of pregnancy. This test is now available through many veterinary surgeons and gives a good degree of accuracy.

In the later stages of pregnancy it is possible to detect the foetal heartbeats either by using a stethoscope or the modern electronic equivalent. These devices can be useful at the very end of pregnancy and possibly whilst whelping is taking place.

Bitch and human psychology during pregnancy and whelping

The whelping bitch demonstrates canine confusion at its strongest. As an affectionate pet used to her indoor comforts she wants to be close to her owner, but instinct tells her that she should be digging a whelping cave outdoors, so as to have her puppies in a warm, dry, secure place where she can hide them from prying eyes.

She wants to be away from other animals and humans, but since she is strongly attached to her owner and the family, she welcomes their support at whelping time, but help must be discreetly offered.

Many novices at breeding think they cannot manage alone and so will invite a support group for themselves but this will upset the bitch. You can manage alone. You have this book and you have your veterinary surgeon on the end of the telephone; you have common sense and you have sympathy with your bitch. You are better off without any other people present. What you do need is a car and driver at your disposal, day or night, so that your bitch can be taken to the surgery if the veterinary surgeon feels that will be best. Transporting the bitch is a two person job, since she may produce a puppy on the journey.

Your bitch may, because of breed conformation developed by man or because her muscles are slack from lack of exercise, need help at whelping time. She may, through long domestication have become unused to bearing pain and may produce an exaggerated reaction to the discomfort of whelping, which will unduly alarm her owner. Tension is heightened between owner and the bitch who is in this state, and she is capable of voluntarily delaying whelping.

There are many non-maternal bitches which are completely disinterested in their puppies. Unfortunately it is not possible to know this before you have mated the bitch and the litter is born. Working bitches, very masculine bitches, those with strong guarding instincts, and toy breeds can refuse to look after their newly-born pups. If a bitch with a phantom pregnancy is available, she may take on the care of the litter and even produce milk for them, but otherwise the litter is very much the breeder's problem.

Some bitches seem to be almost afraid of their new-born puppies but will feed them if her owner sits beside her and holds the pups to the teats. Some will feed but will not clean their puppies. Some get on such a 'high' during whelping that they cannot seem to settle with their litter when it is over. Some may become so protective and fierce that hardly anyone, maybe no-one, dares approach the bitch. This can happen even in a bitch which is normally very civil, and may be due to an exaggerated instinct to protect the puppies or perhaps a reaction to pain. Yet another type of bitch will be so over-maternal that she will lick her puppies until she has taken all the skin off their abdomens. She may even erode a foot or a whole limb. Some bitches get so confused that they will kill their puppies and eat the bodies so the 'enemy' can find no trace of them. Some heavy bitches are just plain clumsy and will flop down on top of their puppies, quite oblivious to their cries. If the owner is not nearby a puppy can quickly be asphyxiated in this way.

Care of the pregnant bitch

Vitamins and minerals

Every breeder wants to do as much as possible to ensure a healthy litter, and it is understandable that novices may have the urge to give vitamin and mineral supplements in quantity to be sure their bitch lacks for nothing. Unfortunately this is mistaken thinking because as you will see from Chapter 4, if the bitch is already having the correct proportion of vitamins and minerals in her normal food, the increased food requirements of pregnancy and lactation will automatically give her more of these elements.

Resist the temptation to be lavish with supplements because too much or too many can do a great deal of harm. Read the labels of any supplements you buy carefully. You may find that although the brand name of one is different, it may be duplicating the contents of another. There is no evidence that vitamin C is necessary at all for the healthy bitch (and you should not be breeding from her if she is in any other state) nor is vitamin E, or iron supplements. Raspberry leaf tablets are an old gipsy nostrum said to ensure easy birth but there is no scientific evidence that they have any effect on whelping.

As we have seen, the less medication (and all these tablets on general sale are still medication) given during pregnancy the better.

Over-supplementation with calcium and vitamin D can lead to skeletal disorders in the puppies and even in the bitch. Breeders who fear the post-whelping condition, eclampsia, due to an imbalance of calcium in the blood stream, are tempted to give a great deal of calcium as a preventative. Recent knowledge has shown that giving calcium by mouth to the pregnant bitch can even go some way towards inducing eclampsia because the bitch may be inhibited from marshalling her own calcium in a crisis. The one 'medication' which seems helpful and can do no harm is to give the homoeopathic remedy arnica after whelping to ease bruising and promote healing.

Coat

During pregnancy the cyclic growth of the hair coat is altered, so that all the hairs which make up the coat will be in their growth phase at once. As a consequence, after whelping a considerable amount of hair is usually lost.

While the bitch is pregnant and lactating take care to keep the coat free from fleas, ticks, lice etc. by daily brushing and combing. Beware of applying insecticidal baths or sprays because the chemical content can be licked off by the bitch, or may be absorbed through the skin, and so may do harm to the puppies in the uterus.

If your bitch needs to be taken to the veterinary surgeon, do not fail to remind him that she has been mated and may well be pregnant. Do not rely on the condition being obvious or the veterinary surgeon remembering. Some of the medication which may ordinarily be prescribed may be harmful to the pregnant bitch.

Just before whelping is expected, the hair should be carefully trimmed from around the vulva and the nipples.

Exercise

Take the bitch out for exercise every day; steady road walking on the lead is a good idea. However, excessively long expeditions or climbs should not be undertaken and during hot weather exercise should be taken early in the morning or late evening. Towards the end of pregnancy the walk will be a slow one, and the distance should be decided by the bitch.

It is important to avoid the sudden chilling which can occur when a hot dog jumps into a pond. Particular care must be taken that the bitch does not become overheated through being left in the car, or even being driven in the car during very hot spells. Hyperthermia in the dam may bring about deformities in the puppies in the uterus.

If you have other dogs and bitches in the home, watch for interactions with the pregnant bitch. The unfamiliar scent which she gives off may lead to inter-bitch aggression or harassment of the pregnant bitch, and she herself may be more irritable. There may be jealousy, leading to fights, because the pregnant bitch is getting extra meals. Fights are a frequent cause of abortion.

Digging

It is probably better not to suppress your bitch's primitive urge to dig a cave-like structure to whelp in, as this may be part of the natural sequence of whelping. However, you must monitor the site and the progress of the excavation so that she does not get out of your reach in the later stages of pregnancy. Particular care must be taken on sandy ground to ensure that a fall of soil does not trap the bitch. The latter warning also applies to rabbit-hunting bitches who may get down a burrow but be unable, owing to their unaccustomed girth, to turn and get out again.

Urination

When the uterus is full and pressing on the urinary bladder, the bitch will not be able to contain her urine for long periods in her usual manner. If there is an overnight lapse in house-training, no reproaches should be made.

Worming

With modern wormers (vermifuges) it is safe and efficacious to worm your bitch during pregnancy, but ask your veterinary surgeon's advice and get the dose prescribed for your bitch. Worming preparations are available which will go a long way to exterminating encysted *Toxocara canis* larvae in the bitch. These larvae can migrate in the pregnant bitch to infect the puppies in the uterus and via the milk as described in Chapter 9. If you can prevent your puppies having such a heavy worm burden they will be much healthier and will grow and thrive better. Ask your veterinary surgeon about this worming regime which involves giving a worming dose every day over a three week period.

Duration of pregnancy

The length of pregnancy in bitches used to be categorically stated as 63 days from the day of mating. More recent studies have shown that a normal pregnancy can last as little as 54 days, or as long as 72 days, after mating. In fact the duration of pregnancy is the time from fertilization to whelping and is remarkably consistent at around 60 days.

It is the variation in time between mating and fertilization which gives rise to the apparent variation in gestation length. The bitch which ovulates early in her season will have mature eggs waiting to be fertilized on the day of mating, while one which is slow to ovulate will have what seems to be a much longer pregnancy. The average bitch takes 62 days but five per cent of all bitches take 66 days. There is a breed variation too; Pekes average out at 61.4 days, but French Bulldogs have on average a 70 day pregnancy. Considering these are breeds in which Caesareans are common, it is important to know the average length of pregnancy. If a Caesar is undertaken too early, the puppies may be weak and there may be problems with lactation in the bitch. The breeder must therefore be prepared for the whelping at any time from about eight weeks after the day of the first mating.

If the bitch is mated twice in her season, say on the tenth and twelfth day following the start of bleeding, this will not have the effect of creating two bouts of whelping as some breeders fear.

Puppies born from the 56th day of pregnancy onwards are usually viable.

Table 6.1: Looking after your bitch during pregnancy – summary points

- Do not give an excess of vitamins and minerals.
- Get rid of external parasites. Use chemical preparations only under veterinary supervision.
- Exercise should be regular but moderate.
- Allow a controlled amount of digging in late pregnancy.
- Get advice from your veterinary surgeon about worming.
- Free yourself from the notion that canine pregnancy lasts 63 days.

Preparations for whelping

The whelping room

Prepare your whelping room with care – you and your bitch are going to have to spend some time there. Get it ready well ahead of the anticipated whelping day so that the bitch is reasonably familiar with the situation, although she may refuse to spend any time in her whelping box until the births are imminent.

The earliest preparation should be to collect clean newspaper, preferably fresh, unsold copies which have not been contaminated by other animals. Stockpile them – you can't have too many.

Your whelping room should be capable of being heated, but also capable of being cooled in summer. It should be secluded and away from other animals and people. If it is a little-used room in your home, make sure it is draught free at floor level and not damp. Cover the carpet to prevent spoiling.

A cordless telephone is a great help, since you can describe to the vet what is happening to your bitch from right beside the whelping box.

A source of hot and cold water, ideally a handbasin, is a great asset in a whelping room.

An exit to a fenced-in corner of the garden is a luxury for the bitch. Do not allow any other animals near the window or door.

A camp bed or similar is a luxury for the breeder who may have to spend several nights keeping vigil over the bitch and puppies.

Get two very large cardboard cartons to serve as a whelping box for your bitch. The one to form the bed should be long enough to take the bitch lying down on her side. Very large strong boxes can be obtained from shops selling refrigerators, televisions etc. It is preferable to use cardboard boxes as they can be destroyed when soiled and will not carry any lingering infection, whereas wooden boxes can. Create a hood for the bed from the other box, so that the bitch feels, as closely as possible, in the cave which instinct tells her she needs at this time.

Provide a mobile light source which can be very bright when needed for examination of the bitch or a puppy, but which can also be dimmed.

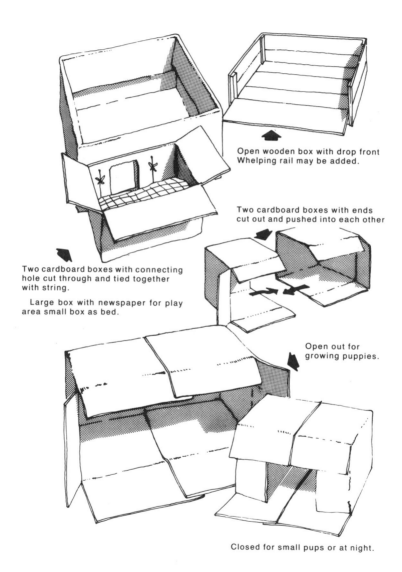

Open wooden box with drop front
Whelping rail may be added.

Two cardboard boxes with ends
cut out and pushed into each other

Two cardboard boxes with connecting
hole cut through and tied together
with string.

Large box with newspaper for play
area small box as bed.

Open out for
growing puppies.

Closed for small pups or at night.

Fig. 6.2 **Whelping boxes**
(a) designs for cardboard whelping boxes

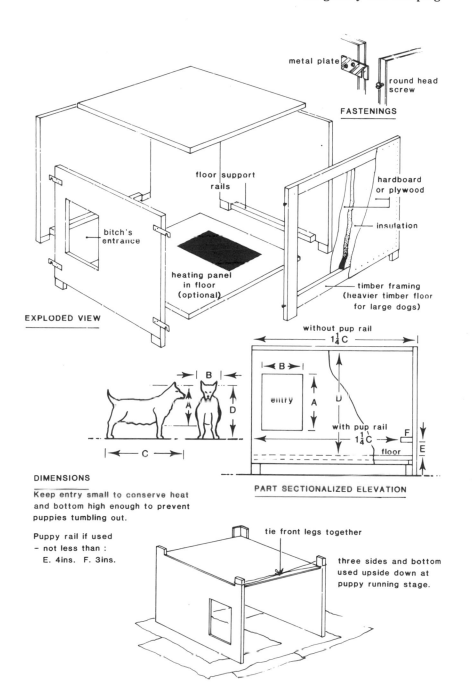

metal plate

round head screw

FASTENINGS

floor support rails

hardboard or plywood

bitch's entrance

insulation

heating panel in floor (optional)

timber framing (heavier timber floor for large dogs)

EXPLODED VIEW

without pup rail
$1\frac{1}{4}$ C

entry

with pup rail
$1\frac{1}{4}$ C

floor

PART SECTIONALIZED ELEVATION

DIMENSIONS

Keep entry small to conserve heat and bottom high enough to prevent puppies tumbling out.

Puppy rail if used
– not less than :
E. 4ins. F. 3ins.

tie front legs together

three sides and bottom used upside down at puppy running stage.

(b) a design for a permanent wooden whelping box

85

Include a sturdy table in case you or the veterinary surgeon need to examine the bitch.

Buy three or, preferably, four pieces of polyester fur to fit the bottom of the whelping bed.

Obtain from your vet an electric heating pad which will occupy one corner only of the whelping bed. The puppies will gravitate to this source of heat during the whelping of further pups, or later on when the bitch is away.

Arrange an electrical power point close to the box, so that the cord from the pad is as short as possible, leading out of a hole in the back of the box straight to the source of electricity.

The following items should also be assembled:

a small box with towelling-covered hot-water bottle to receive the puppies if you have to remove them from the bitch;

a box of fine plastic surgical gloves from your vet;

a tube of KY Jelly to act as a lubricant;

nail-brush, soap and towels;

old, soft towels, which can be discarded, for drying the puppies;

notebook, pen and scales;

glucose and water drink for the bitch (one tablespoon glucose to one pint water);

soft kitchen paper and gauze swabs;

clock;

● powerful flashlight in case bitch goes outside during hours of darkness, (she may deliver a puppy while urinating);

surgical scissors, one blunt-ended pair, one sharp-ended pair, standing in a vessel of antiseptic;

thermometer with stubby end;

A premature baby feeder (it is best to have at least two as they break quite easily), sterilizing solution and bowl, bottle brush, bitch milk replacer;

plastic sacks for soiled paper;

lidded bucket for offensive discards, such as placentas;

another covered container to put outside the door to place any puppies born dead, for examination later;

telephone number of vet;

something for you to do. Whelping can take many hours and it is better for the bitch if you do not concentrate on her too closely, especially in the early stages.

The whelping process

Duration
There is great variation in the time bitches take to produce their puppies. A fit, healthy, young bitch, in perfectly suitable whelping conditions, can produce a whole litter in an hour, while some of the slow-whelping breeds, see Chapter 12, can take 24 to 36 hours or longer, yet still produce perfectly normally without complications.

Stages of whelping

Whelping is described as happening in three stages, but actually there is a preparatory stage during which the levels of progesterone, the hormone which has maintained the pregnancy and prevented the uterus from contracting during the growth of the foetus, in the blood fall, and oestrogen takes over again. The production of prostaglandin is stimulated allowing whelping to begin.

It is thought that these hormonal changes are in fact triggered by the rising cortisol levels produced by the developing puppies in the uterus. During the few days when this is happening, the bitch's body temperature will drop. Many breeders like to take the temperature two or three times each day so that they can pinpoint the drop, which can be as low as 99°F, or even 97°F, for a few hours, as indicative that the bitch will whelp within the next 24 hours.

However, in the last week before whelping the bitch's body temperature is usually lower than normal, so when calculating whether a significant drop has taken place, it is as well to start from a basis of 100°F rather than the true normal of 101.5°F.

The three recognized stages in the whelping process

Stage one

It is the foetuses, and not the dam, which trigger the start of whelping. Towards the end of pregnancy the foetuses become crowded in the uterus and increasingly stressed. This stimulates the immature cardiac and respiratory systems to become ready to make the dramatic changes which will be necessary when the pup is born.

During this stage the bitch will be restless, usually refusing food for as much as 18 to 24 hours, and she may vomit. She will drift into very deep panting which can last for as long as 24 hours during which time the bitch may sleep intermittently. She will also spend a lot of time shredding her bedding (the experienced breeder will provide a pad of newspaper just for this purpose), and generally behaving in a restless manner. This behaviour pattern may last up to 48 hours, or it may be quickly over – if you are very lucky, the first puppy may drop out before you are aware that stage one has even begun. Bitches are capable of infinite variation in behaviour, not only as individuals but also at each whelping. On average stage one of whelping lasts six to 12 hours, but it may be as long as 18 hours.

The bed shredding action is no longer thought to be a primitive impulse to create a whelping nest, but it is more properly interpreted as a reaction to pain, caused when the full uterus presses down on the cervix to induce it to open. Short episodes of bed tearing may be repeated between puppies or even in the days after the birth. Once more, this is thought to be a reaction to slight-to-moderate internal discomfort. Bitches in serious pain do not make these rapid paw and head movements.

Throughout pregnancy there has probably been a slight mucoid discharge from the vulva. Just before whelping this increases in volume, as the mucoid plug which has sealed the cervix dissolves, sometimes appearing as strings of mucus hanging from the vulva.

Stage two

In the first stage of whelping the cervix should have dilated to allow the puppies to pass from the uterus, down the vagina and out into the world. Unless the cervix has dilated, birth by natural means cannot occur, but unfortunately, except in the smallest toy bitches it is impossible to know if the cervix is open by digital exploration. It is this factor which makes the whelping of bitches so difficult – for the bitch, for the breeder and for the veterinary surgeon. In future the development of ultrasound scanning may possibly make things easier.

(i) The journey

The foetuses must rotate from the position in which they lie in the uterus, which is often on their backs (see Figure 6.3) so that ideally they pass through the birth canal head first in order to meet the open cervix centrally. The foetus should still be in its double layered water bag which helps their journey by means of a push, squeeze and relax process of the uterine muscles, which is also assisted by pulsation of the vagina.

Even when a bitch's cervix is fully dilated, there is very little room for an average-sized puppy of the breed to get through and, obviously, in those man-made breeds which have large heads and shoulders the problems of normal birth are even more exaggerated.

There is recent evidence that foetuses are born alternately from each uterine horn. If a foetus presents at the cervix in an awkward fashion, with head flexed and the shoulder attempting to lead the way, or if the foetus bypasses the cervix and starts moving up the opposite horn, the bitch and foetus are immediately in trouble.

One foetus which holds up the whelping in this way, or one grossly oversized or dead puppy, can prejudice the birth of those following it, since once the placenta has separated from the uterine walls, it is urgent that the foetus is born as soon as possible. It is also vital for their survival that when they get into the outside world the puppies should take their first independent breath as soon as possible.

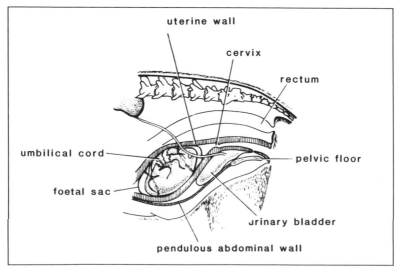

Fig. 6.3 **A puppy near term in the uterus**

(ii) First signs

Your bitch should have stopped panting and become rather more quiet, but you should see big expelling abdominal contractions as she presses down towards her hind end. The reproductive tract is making even deeper contractions inside. Your first tangible sign of imminent birth is the appearance at the vulva of a black fluid-filled bag. This is the amniotic sac (also known as the water-bag), the outer membrane which has surrounded each foetus during gestation and has now served to lubricate its passage out into the world. The water-bag may emerge and then retract a few times, or it may have burst higher in the vagina producing a gush of its fluid contents. Do not be too concerned about the water-bag for it does not contain a puppy, but one should soon be born. The bitch may stand, crouch, or lie down for the actual birth. When the head appears at the vulva, the rest of the puppy should slide out quickly.

If however, there is a lapse in expelling contractions once a puppy has appeared at the vulva, you can help your bitch by applying gentle traction on the puppy. Thoroughly scrubbed and well-lubricated hands or surgical gloves are a necessity, as you do not want to introduce an alien infection into the vaginal tract. Take the puppy, which should still be enclosed in the inner, allantoic membrane, between your first and second fingers, with the back of your hand upwards, and as the bitch strains, pull very gently, *not directly towards you* but *gently downwards* (remember the anatomy and angle of the birth canal – see Figure 6.4). Ease the puppy out of the vulva, applying more lubricating jelly as necessary. You may only have to do this with the first puppy as this one will be enlarging the passage for the others. Episiotomy, a vertical cut in the vulva to let a puppy through when the vulva has remained tight, is seldom used by veterinary surgeons.

If the first puppy to be born is coming hind feet first, this is a little more difficult as the widest part of the puppy is not pioneering the way, and the lie of the puppy's fur does not help. However, about half of all puppies are born hind feet first and, unless they happen to be the first one, this presentation should give no problems. A feet first presentation is *not* a breech birth – that term is reserved for a puppy presenting rump first with hind legs tucked under the body.

Where the head is deflected or one leg is tucked behind the puppy, you may be able, with the aid of lubricating jelly and your forefinger, to ease the body into a straighter line.

Often a slight rotation of the puppy will help enormously. Beware of pulling strongly on an exposed head or limb. A gentle pull, timed to coincide with the bitch's own efforts, is what is needed.

At this stage, when the puppy is so nearly born, it is useless to ask for veterinary assistance as the foetus would be dead before help arrives. Keep calm and see what you can do yourself. You may be able to stimulate the bitch to give an extra strong push by stroking your fingers against the inside of the vulva. This is known as 'feathering' and is much used as a stimulant for whelping bitches in the United States, where this method is said to be as effective as giving injections of oxytocin.

Bitches are often surprised, if not shocked, at the birth of their first puppy, and it is said that the straining which has been needed may be confused in their minds with passing a bowel movement in a 'forbidden' place. When the puppy makes its first cry, traditional maternal behaviour usually takes over. However, probably for the first puppy, and perhaps later ones if the

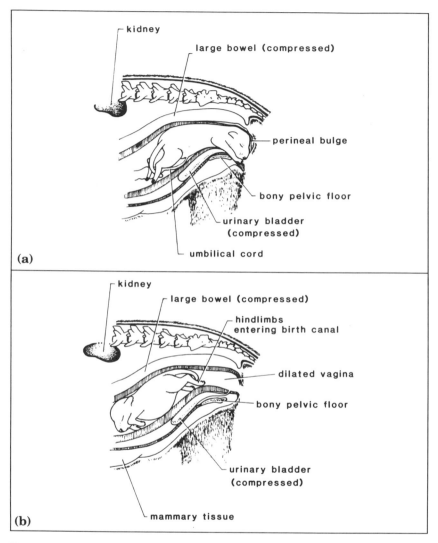

Fig. 6.4 **Normal birth**
(a) anterior presentation
(b) posterior presentation

bitch is tired, the breeder must help open the amniotic sac and get the puppy breathing. Do not be too anxious to take over if the bitch knows what to do.

Sometimes bitches with a very full abdomen cannot reach their hind ends to attend to their new-born although they would like to do so. The breeder can help the bitch fulfil her natural function by bringing the puppy round to the bitch's head, gently pulling on the umbilical cord if necessary. Frequently, the puppy will emerge from the vulva with the umbilical cord and placenta still inside the bitch. Priority, by breeder and bitch, is to get the puppy out of the amniotic sac. The bitch tears the sac with her teeth, and consumes the membranes. She also shreds the umbilical cord with her side teeth, and sets about resuscitation of the puppy. She may seem to be very rough as she turns the puppy over and over in the box, pulling on the umbilical cord, but this is Nature's way of stimulating the puppy's breathing. If the bitch can manage on her own it is better to let her do so, as natural whelping behaviour makes the passage of further puppies easier and facilitates the let-down of milk. It is very important that the bitch should bond with her puppies as soon as possible, recognizing them as her own, as this will help her maternal instinct throughout the lactation period. Bypassing this early bonding stage is one of the drawbacks of birth by Caesarean section.

If the bitch neglects the puppy, the breeder must tear off the membrane and, holding the puppy upside down, drain fluid from the lungs, clean the mouth and nostrils of mucus and deposits with gauze swabs so that as far as possible the airway is clear.

A vigorous rubbing with a warm towel will often start the puppy breathing.

Only when you have done as much as you can for the immediate comfort of the puppy should you ease, with the fingers, the blood within the umbilical cord down towards the puppy, and cut, with scissors which have stood in sterilizing fluid, or tear, with clean fingers, the cord as far away from the puppy as possible. The end may retract within the bitch.

Nothing should be applied to the end of the cord, or to the navel of the puppy. Many people believe that ligaturing the cord can lead to an umbilical hernia. If the puppy is still moribund, hold the head between your first two fingers and the body in the palm of your hand and swing the puppy upside down fairly vigorously beside your body. You may, by this means clear the puppy's airway and stimulate it into giving the first vital gasp as its respiratory system adjusts to breathing on its own. If you do revive a puppy in this way, be sure to mark it so it is recognizable later. Make a note of what you did and how long the puppy took to start breathing – this information may be most valuable to you in connection with any disease, or even temperamental conditions, which the pup shows later in life. Then dry the body so that the puppy is not losing heat – do not do it all yourself but offer the puppy to the bitch to lick.

Stage three
The placenta, or afterbirth, sometimes arrives at the same time as the first puppy. If it does not, it should arrive at the vulva within a short time, or it may come with the next puppy. A great deal of fuss used to be made as to whether all afterbirths had appeared and been counted but less importance is given to this now. It is not unusual for a bitch to pass an afterbirth during urination 24 or more hours after the birth of the final puppy.

In the wild, the afterbirths would represent the bitch's food for several days before she could go hunting again. They are blood-filled and highly nutritious but often they do cause the bitch to produce copious fluid, dark bowel movements at a time when she may be letting her house-training lapse through reluctance to leave her puppies. The fashion therefore began for the breeder to remove as many afterbirths as possible. Now thinking has turned around, and it is believed that consuming at least some of the placentas is necessary to help the uterus contract back to its normal size and to stimulate the milk flow.

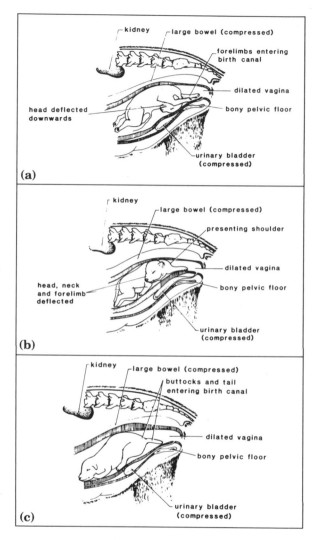

Fig. 6.5 Incorrect presentations
(a) **downward flexion of the head**
(b) **sideways deviation of the head**
(c) **breech presentation**

A bitch which gives birth by Caesarean nearly always has to do without the benefit of eating the placentas, but there is no reason, if you remember at the time, why you should not ask your veterinary surgeon to save and return them to you with the bitch and puppies, so that you can give some to the bitch.

Once a puppy is born, the breeder can be of assistance in cleaning and drying the whelping area. This will be a constant task as each new puppy will drench the whelping bed and often the previous puppies too, but it is still better to leave the pups already born with the dam, already on the teats, because their sucking action is also said to stimulate contractions. Some

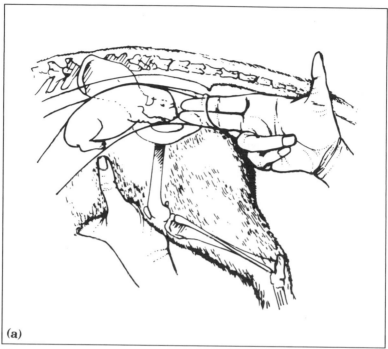

Fig. 6.6 **Puppy delivery**
(a) checking the presentation

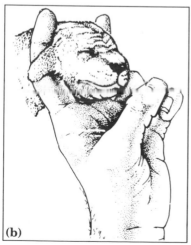

(b) **traction by the head**

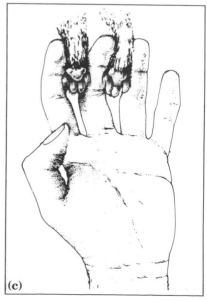

(c) **traction by the hind legs**

authorities advise moving the puppies away to a dry, heated box during subsequent births but this can disturb and distress the bitch and make her restless and it is not advisable. You can give the new puppies some protection by making sure that the bitch's hind end is lying on polyester fur with a thick pad of newpaper underneath to soak up the fluid which will pass through the polyester. Change the paper or add more dry paper, frequently. Mop up as much fluid as you can with absorbent kitchen roll and keep the puppies on the heated portion of the box while others are being born.

(i) Intervals between births

The most skilled part of whelping is deciding how long it is safe to allow between births of puppies before asking veterinary assistance and assessing whether the bitch is in trouble or if she is just having a rest. Intervals during the birth of live, normal puppies can vary so much, but it is generally agreed that about two and a half hours is a reasonable time to allow between puppies. You should have alerted your veterinary surgery when your bitch went into stages one *and* two of whelping and, as the two hour interval approaches, you may want to warn the vet on duty that help may be needed. Only the observer can describe the events that are happening. Is the bitch straining deeply but ineffectively? Is she not straining at all, but contentedly asleep with her puppies? Can you see puppy movements in her abdomen which make it obvious that there are more whelps to come, or has she perhaps finished whelping?

These factors, together with the age and breed of the bitch and her previous whelping record, will decide whether the veterinary surgeon wishes to make a home visit to give treatment or whether the bitch had better be taken to the surgery for more extensive examination and a Caesarean section if the need arises.

In view of the many difficulties of whelping, some novices may wonder if they could have the services of a veterinary surgeon or nurse to stay with them throughout the whelping. The answer is almost certainly 'No' – on grounds of time (whelping can take 36 hours or more) and expense.

It may then seem reasonable to ask if the bitch can whelp at the veterinary surgery. This is possible, but not desirable, in view of the fact that bitches give their best performance in secluded quarters in the security of their own homes with familiar people in attendance.

(ii) Dystocia

In about 40 per cent of whelpings, there is some lengthy hold up which may result in the death of one or more puppies. Delays in whelpings are known in veterinary parlance as dystocia. A bitch obviously full of puppies and displaying the other signs of imminent whelping may be reluctant to start whelping at all. This is primary uterine inertia, said to be hereditary and common in certain families and breeds. In other cases, primary inertia is said to be due to breeding from bitches for the first time when they are over five years old, to lack of muscle tone, to obesity, lack of fitness, or to an over-stretched uterus which is unable to contract because it has already expanded to full capacity to contain a very large litter.

Secondary uterine inertia is the term for the cessation of uterine contractions or the lack of any impulsion to expel foetuses after one or several puppies have been born. The reason may be sheer fatigue of the uterine muscles. In cases of secondary inertia, the veterinary surgeon turns to an injection of oxytocin, a hormone secreted by the pituitary gland. A fast-acting oxytocin injection usually sets up contractions which will cause the puppy to be delivered within 10 minutes unless there is a major obstruction.

Some bitches require an injection for every puppy but this injection must never be given before at least one puppy has been born, as the uterus may rupture in response to the contractions if the cervix has not opened.

If there is no response to oxytocin, your veterinary surgeon will inevitably begin to consider a Caesarean birth.

(iii) Caesarean

If a Caesarean becomes necessary following the birth of some puppies, leave the puppies in a warm, covered box while the bitch is taken to the surgery. They will come to no harm without food for a few hours. Modern anaesthetics mean that the bitch is awake as soon as the operation is over and, although sometimes it can be a little difficult to get her to accept her offspring, and the pups themselves may be a little less active because of the transmission of anaesthetic to them, Caesarean litters generally thrive.

Despite the fact that the bitch has a surgical wound between the line of her teats, or possibly on her flank, she will nearly always feed the pups diligently and the wound will usually heal without problems. The sutures are removed seven to 10 days later. It is, however, a good plan to examine the wound twice a day and to clean and dry the area between the teats if it is getting dirty and hot. Use only the mildest of antiseptics, if any at all. Your veterinary surgeon will advise.

After the whelping

Your veterinary surgeon will want to see the bitch on the day following the whelping, to check that the uterus is empty and contracting in size and that the bitch has no sign of infection.

Most vets will give an injection of oxytocin to ensure that the uterus contracts down properly and that all its contents have been expelled. Some breeders argue against this injection being given, as it can seem that a bitch which has been passively content with her puppies becomes excited and stressed again under the influence of the hormone, but this stage soon passes.

You will want to keep a close watch on your bitch during the entire lactation period for any sign that she is unwell. A greenish discharge from the vulva, known as the lochia, is normal for 24 hours, followed by a brownish-red blood discharge which continues, in diminishing amounts, often for several weeks. The amount and duration of the discharge is relative to the number of puppies produced since it comes from the sites in the uterus where the placentas were attached. A change to a blackish, foul-smelling discharge is a danger signal which requires veterinary help at once, but advice should also be sought if any discharge continues beyond, say four to five weeks after the birth. Don't forget to keep detailed notes of every incident of the bitch's lactation period. It will help you on another occasion and it will help your breed club if they collect information on the behaviour of bitches.

Table 6.2: Whelping summary

Stage one	Panting, distress, bed tearing.
Stage two	Expelling contractions and delivery of the foetus. This stage may be as short as 10 to 30 minutes, or it may take up to an hour in the slow-whelping breeds (see Chapter 12). Longer than this is cause for concern if the bitch is straining.
Stage three	Begins after the delivery of the foetus and ends with the expulsion of the placenta.

Notes
1. Stage one takes place only once.
2. Bitches which are going to have more than one puppy will alternate between stages two and three. There is no need to worry if a bitch rests for up to four hours between successive stage two's. However a lag of more than one hour with straining is a cause for concern.

Table 6.3: Whelping tips for breeders

- Stay with your bitch throughout stages one, two and three, observing from a distance if all seems to be going well. Do not invite an audience to watch the whelping – the bitch may hold up proceedings if you do.
- Keep all other animals away, even from outside the door.
- Let your bitch do as much as she can herself.
- Warn your veterinary surgery that whelping has started and keep in touch.
- Let the vet know when the bitch has finished whelping if you have not required any help. Your veterinary surgeon need not then be on alert to render assistance to your bitch.
- Try to arrange for a house call so that the veterinary surgeon can check that all is well with the bitch and the puppies once whelping is over.
- Allow about two hours as normal between deliveries of puppies.
- Keep the whelping bed dry and the room warm.
- Offer the bitch glucose/water drinks frequently, but no food.

Up-to-date whelping lore

Those breeders who have been whelping litters for a long time will have seen many radical changes take place in whelping, rearing and selling customs and in the concept of what is best for the bitch.

The breeding environment has changed too; there are now far less big kennels with special blocks of compartments for whelping bitches. The majority of the bitches which are bred from live in the house and are accustomed to a high degree of comfort.

It is useful, when you consult a book about dog breeding, to look at the date it was first published, and to reflect on how other elements in the world have changed since that time. Books written in, or before, the 1950s and 1960s, do not reflect the degree of information available today.

Table 6.4: Modern whelping lore

- 63 days pregnancy from mating day to whelping day is not inviolable – think 57 to 72 days!
- Open tray whelping boxes are not congenial for bitches. Create a cave-like situation with a removable covered top. Abandon permanent whelping boxes for disposable cardboard cartons.
- Infra-red lamps suspended above the box are not the best means of heating whelping areas. It is best to provide heat underneath the puppies to create a warm moist environment.
- Polyester fur rugs for whelping and puppy rearing are the greatest revolution for whelping this century.
- Encysted toxocara larvae in the bitch can be removed by modern worming preparations given during pregnancy.
- It is quite safe to start worming puppies at two-and-a-half weeks and to continue treatment fortnightly up to 12 weeks.
- Umbilical hernias are *not* caused by the bitch pulling on the cord, but are due to incomplete closure of the umbilical ring, and are probably hereditary.
- Nothing should be applied to the umbilical cord or the navel of puppies. No dressings or ligatures are required and to bind on coins or other artefacts serves no useful purpose.
- There is no such thing as 'acid milk'. Think in terms of cleanliness of the whelping box in cases of puppy milk rash.
- Goats' milk is not suitable for early feeding of puppies; it is too low in fat and protein and is only marginally richer than cows' milk.
- The delivery of a dead puppy does not necessarily mean that the bitch will need a Caesar. The majority of dead puppies come at the end of the whelping process.
- Pregnancy can last from fifty seven to seventy two days. Eleven per cent of bitches whelp before the fifty ninth day and in five per cent of bitches pregnancy lasts for sixty seven days or longer – the average duration range is sixty to sixty six days.
- Primary uterine inertia may be associated with small litters and the consequent under-production by the pups of the hormone which triggers whelping. In a few cases the condition may be associated with low calcium and/or glucose levels in the blood.
- An elective Caesarean may deprive the puppies and the anaesthetic risk cannot be completely ignored.
- It is generally not wise to subject a bitch to more than two Caesarean births since adhesions can make access to the uterus difficult and dangerous. Furthermore, if Caesareans are required regularly the suitability of the bitch as breeding stock should be seriously questioned.
- It is probably wise not to decide too hastily to have a Caesarean birth for the last puppy or two in a litter as they are likely to be dead. It may be more sensible for the vet to try to remove them by some other means first.

Emergency 'what ifs', in relation to whelping

What if my whelping bitch is in trouble and I drive her to a veterinary surgery late at night but cannot get an answer?

There is a considerable amount of misunderstanding about the way the 24 hour veterinary service is operated.

While every veterinary practice must have someone available to attend to emergencies day and night every day of the year, it is obviously unpractical for this expensive service to be available at every veterinary surgery. Therefore veterinary surgeons in large practices often operate a duty rota at nights and weekends. Smaller practices will probably share their cover with other practices in the area. There are actually very few veterinary premises which are open for business and are actively working all night, and those that do exist are in the major cities.

However, the practice which is providing cover for the area on any particular night should open up for you, unless of course the veterinary surgeon on duty prefers to make a house call.

For out-of-hours emergencies you have to accept that you may not see your usual vet and you may have to drive to surgery premises you have not been to before. The key to finding out who is on duty and where to go must always be via the telephone.

Always telephone your own surgery first and then ring any other number you are referred to before rushing off anywhere. Even if you happen to know your vet lives on the surgery premises, off-duty time and a full night's sleep is necessary and must be respected, and you cannot expect to get an answer to your knock if cover has been efficiently arranged elsewhere. Keep some change and a phone-card ready in the car in case you want to telephone again along the way, and keep a map of the local area handy too.

What if my whelping bitch needs veterinary help at night?

This is something you should have talked over with your vet well in advance of the crisis happening. Although you cannot predict the actual whelping day or night, your veterinary surgeon will be happy to tell you what the practice arrangements will be for the weekends or weekday when you may need help urgently. You will then at least be forewarned if your own vet is not on duty.

What if I cannot get in touch with the veterinary practice I usually use when my bitch needs help?

Once again make the telephone work for you. Look up Veterinary Surgeons in the Yellow Pages and telephone the surgeries. If all else fails, police stations have this information and in a real emergency, if telephone lines are down, they may be willing to contact a vet for you.

What if my vet doesn't make house calls?

This is again a matter to be sorted out well in advance of whelping day. There are many whelping situations where it is beneficial for the bitch to go to the surgery; primary uterine inertia is one where the car ride may actually start off the contractions. If the bitch is going to need a Caesarean, then she will have to go to the surgery anyway.

But there are times when the breeder feels strongly that a house call is necessary. Many people feel they do not want to take the bitch to the surgery for her post-whelping check-up. Talk to your vet and see what can be done. It may be that if there are daytime traffic and parking problems, your vet will consider coming out in the evening to check the bitch.

It is as well to be aware that house calls take the vet a lot of time, that bitches may be more difficult to handle on their own territory and in less than ideal conditions, and that the cost of house calls is understandably high. However, if you have a good professional relationship with your vet, an arrangement that satisfies you both can be achieved.

What if my bitch has a puppy in the car?

This is not at all unlikely, especially if the bitch has been given an oxytocin injection. Throughout the time when whelping is imminent your car should be as organized as a maternity ambulance. According to the size of your bitch, convert the back of the car into a flat area on which she can lie, and have your pad of newspapers and a sheet of polyester fur there. Carry some sterilized scissors, gauze swabs, towels and absorbent kitchen roll in a plastic box. Keep two hot-water bottles ready to fill before you put the bitch in the car, and a puppy box or warmly-lined carton too.

What if my bitch's insurance cover does not extend to whelping costs?

Breeders with several animals and some experience of whelping can take out insurance which will cover treatment for bitches during pregnancy and a Caesarean birth (except for Bulldogs and Boston Terriers), as well as any necessary post-whelping treatment for the bitch, including the cost of necessary house calls.

What if I am finding all the necessities for whelping expensive to buy? Can I hire or borrow?

The answer must be a very firm No! However clean a whelping box or the polyester fur may look, there is always the possibility that these and other articles may carry invisible 'bugs' to which your own bitch and puppies are not immune. The same situation would apply if you lent your equipment elsewhere, because every dog household has its own resident low-level infections. It is particularly important to avoid bringing in outside infections at a time when your bitch and the puppies are so vulnerable.

The polyester fur blankets must be bought but they will be invaluable to you as dog bedding, car seat covers etc. for many years to come – polyester fur never dies, it just gets greyer!

Bottle feeding equipment is not very expensive and must be ready to hand if you need it. Surgical scissors, a stubby-ended thermometer, and a small electric heating pad will also be useful throughout your dog's life.

The whelping box costs nothing, and the sides of the playpen will come into use in the garden or can be sold for that purpose locally later on.

If such costs really do represent a problem, you really should not be thinking about breeding from your bitch. You could well find yourself in the position of having no puppies and a very large veterinary bill.

CHAPTER 7
CARE OF YOUR NEWLY-WHELPED BITCH AND PUPPIES

Care of the
   newly-whelped bitch

Care of the puppies

Docking and dew-claw
   removal

Inherited defects

Bottle feeding

Weaning

Care of the bitch
   post-whelping

Selling puppies

Care of the newly-whelped bitch

Newly-whelped bitches sometimes sacrifice their house-training to a compulsion to remain with their puppies. You may find it difficult to get your bitch to go outside for the first three days after whelping. If you have somewhere you can walk the bitch on the lead without encountering other dogs, a walk on the lead for about 15 minutes a day is ideal.

When she has finished whelping, the bitch will appreciate an easily-digested meal. There is no need to give milk as this can promote diarrhoea in some adult bitches.

Make life easy for your bitch; she has a big job to do on her own. Feed her in her bed, so that she is not worried about leaving her puppies, and offer frequent drinks of water too, as she is unlikely to get out of bed even when she needs a drink. It is essential that she takes sufficient fluid to produce the amount of milk the puppies will need.

If there is a really big litter, you may want to get up once in the night to check that all is well with the puppies and also to feed the bitch.

The bitch will stimulate her puppies to pass urine and faeces by licking them, and she will consume all their faeces until they are about 20 days old. If your bitch is reluctant to do this, smearing the puppies with sunflower oil, or honey, may attract her to licking them. It may be that the bitch has mouth ulcers or that her tongue has become sore through cleaning up the whelping fluids. If you find that this is the case, your veterinary surgeon will be able to help.

Take the opportunity when you can to groom the bitch and to keep her clean.

Increase feeding as described in Chapter 4, and encourage the bitch to take periods of exercise, but respect her need to be secluded with her puppies and do not allow other animals or people to invade her privacy.

Care of the puppies

The first 36 hours after the birth are the most critical of the puppies' lives. There must be important adaptations at birth to the major body systems, especially the heart, lungs and liver. In the normal pup, the lungs should contain a foamy substance known as surfactant. If this is not present, the lungs will collapse at each breath the puppy takes and it will soon die. A human baby with this condition would be put on a ventilator. In puppies, this may be part of the fading puppy syndrome (see page 151). The blood supply which has short-circuited the liver while the pup was in the uterus now has to alter its route and there are also changes which must take place in the circulation of the blood within the heart. If any of these modifications do not happen, the puppy may be cold, flabby and weak, and may only survive a short time.

Puppies are born in a very immature state. Their body temperature is low compared with that of adult dogs and they can only keep up their body heat by lying against something warm, either the mammary glands of the bitch or a heated pad.

Other new-born puppy statistics are shown in Tables 7.1 and 7.2.

Puppies are born with an immature brain and nervous system, and with eyes and ears tightly closed. An enormous amount of development must take place within the next few weeks.

New-born puppies are never still, they twitch and jerk and stretch their

Table 7.1: Vital statistics of the new-born puppy

Body temperature	0 to 14 days 15 to 28 days 35 days	94– 99°F 97–100°F 101.5°F (adult temperature)
Respiration rate	at birth 7 to 35 days over 35 days	average 12 breaths per minute 20 to 30 breaths per minute 15 to 30 breaths per minute (adult rate)
Pulse	at birth 7 to 35 days at 12 weeks	up to 130 beats per minute up to 200 beats a minute approaching adult rate of 70 to 100 beats per minute
Birth weight	should double in 8 days	
Fluid requirement	2 to 3 oz per pound body weight per day	
Fluid excretion	about twice as much as an adult dog New-born puppies are 80 per cent water, a bigger ratio for their weight than adults which are 60 to 70 per cent water	
Calorie requirement	60 to 70 K cal per day per pound of body weight	

Table 7.2: Puppy development

Milestones	Average age
PHYSICAL DEVELOPMENT	
Eyes open	7 to 10 days
Ear canals open	14 days
Primary teeth through	14 to 21 days
First adult round worms (*Toxocara canis*) passed	14 days
Body twitching in sleep	0 to 28 days
DEVELOPMENT OF PUPPY SKILLS	
Can see	10 to 15 days
Barking	18 days
Early play movements	18 to 20 days
Stand upright	21 days
Urinate and defecate without stimulation by bitch	21 days
Balance for passing urine and bowel movement	21 to 26 days
Eat from dish	24 to 27 days
Play with other pups	25 to 28 days
Walk and run	28 days
Sight as good as adult	28 days
Hearing acute	35 days
Play with toys	35 days
Play constructively with litter mates	40 days
Learning mouth and paw skills and body control	40 to 48 days
Voluntary control of urination and defecation	begins at 10 to 12 weeks – perfected at 4 to 6 months

limbs constantly. This reflex action, called activated sleep, serves to develop and exercise the nerve and muscle system. A pup which lies completely still is likely to be in trouble, so is a pup which is constantly crying. If polyester fur is used as the lining of the box pups can move around on it safely and comfortably and without the frustration of trying to get a grip on newspaper. Wood shavings, straw and similar materials should never be used in puppy boxes as the material may be toxic from sprays used upon them.

One instinct present in all normal pups at birth is the urge to gravitate towards a teat and to hang on to suck. The breeder should be ready to help, by expressing a little milk from the teat or by putting a weaker pup on to the more productive teats near the bitch's hind quarters. Sometimes in the larger breeds, the bitch's teats will be too large for the puppies' mouths. The pup must take a lot of the teat into the mouth before it can draw milk. In particular, bitches which have had previous litters may have gross teats. In this case, it is important that the bitch should be hand-milked into a cup and the milk then given to the pups by bottle or syringe. As the pups grow and get more vigorous they will be able to draw milk for themselves.

You will notice that pups which are sucking make paddling movements with their paws on the bitch's mammary glands. It is important to keep the pups' nails cut short, taking off any curved part of the nail twice weekly, otherwise the bitch may be scratched badly, even enough for her to be reluctant to feed the puppies.

Feeding the puppies

It is important that the puppies are fed by the bitch as soon as possible after the birth so that they get maximum benefit from the colostrum, the first milk. Although colostrum may be present in the teats for several days, puppies can only utilize it properly for a limited amount of time, perhaps for as little as 12 to 36 hours after whelping. Colostrum contains antibodies to all the diseases which the bitch has encountered in her life and also those she has been vaccinated against. It is beneficial for the puppies to have this passive protection until they themselves can be vaccinated. Puppies which are known never to have sucked from the bitch should have very early vaccine protection about which you should consult your veterinary surgeon.

It is not wise to turn to feeding an artificial formula if it can possibly be avoided, so resist the impulse to top up the puppies with a bottle feed. Unless the bitch is ill, or shows very poor maternal behaviour, normal puppies will get enough milk from the dam for at least two weeks, and probably longer.

Weak or orphaned puppies may be bottle fed (see page 113) but it is best to avoid this if at all possible as part-bottle and part-bitch feeding can confuse the pup's digestive system and lead to problems.

Puppies should gain weight steadily, although loss of an ounce or two or no gain for a day or so may be ignored. Puppies which are thriving well should double their birthweight in a week after birth. Weighing daily will help the breeder pinpoint some event which either took the bitch away from the puppies, or caused her to produce less milk. Do not forget to note any such incident in your records.

The handling the puppies receive at weighing time is important for their future socialization even if they protest loudly at being put on the scales. As the pups grow larger, it may be possible to borrow baby scales so that the pup feels more secure in the weighing pan, or improvisation can be made by tying a small cardboard box on the scales and adding on weights to compensate.

Aim for an evenly-sized litter at seven weeks old, just a few ounces in difference between males and females. Puppies which are smaller at birth often catch up rapidly when weaned. If there is a wide divergence in weight between the pups it can be due to poor management on the part of the breeder, i.e. the larger puppies are being allowed to bully the others and so get more than their share. There is also the possibility that a very small puppy has some congenital condition which will prevent it from thriving.

You will find some customers enquire for 'the runt of the litter'. Responsible breeders don't have runts, or any other type of sub-standard puppy.

Healthy new-born pups are quiet, sleepy, warm to touch, round, firm and plump. They make a contented, low murmuring noise interspersed with an occasional sharp cry if one gets squashed or pushed off a teat.

Abnormal pups are limp to pick up, have a damp, wrinkled, cold skin, purplish bellies and feet, and may utter a persistent, plaintive, seagull-type cry, or may be silent and chilled. The bitch will often instinctively ignore pups which are not normal, possibly they smell and sound wrong to her and they do not react to licking as a normal pup would.

It is rare for an entire litter to survive. Breeders must expect a proportion of the pups which reach maturity in the uterus to be born dead. Of those born alive it is probable that as many as 25 to 30 per cent will die during the first week due to becoming chilled, through lactation problems in the bitch, being dropped or squashed, having a heavy worm burden or poor maternal behaviour by the bitch. See Fading Puppy Complex, page 151. If a pup lives to two weeks, it stands a good chance of surviving until the next hurdle –

weaning time – when inherited defects tend to show as the puppy begins to stand and play, and to digest solid food.

Distinguishing puppies

It is extremely important that you are able to distinguish your puppies individually from the moment of birth – this is not easy when there are several puppies of the same colour.

There are alternative ways of marking pups.

- Make a light neck collar of several plaited strands of knitting wool.
- Mark each pup with a different colour blob from a felt-tipped pen. The colour chosen will be the pup's temporary name – (orange, blue, green etc.); a favourite marking site is the top of the tail. A white pen can be used for dark-coloured puppies. The marking will have to be renewed as it fades or when the bitch licks it off.
- Cut out discrete patches of hair on thighs or flanks and make a note of the shape cut out.
- Obtain from your vet coloured paper collars used for operation cases. These are self-adhesive, like a hospital bracelet.

Docking and dew-claw removal

British legislation states that lay people can no longer legally dock puppies of any age or breed. Veterinary surgeons are now the only people who can legally carry out this procedure, although they have been advised by their governing body, the Royal College of Veterinary Surgeons, that to do so for purely cosmetic reasons can be perceived as an act of disgraceful professional conduct and so render them likely to disciplinary proceedings.

As a result, many veterinary surgeons have decided against docking puppies. The Kennel Club has stated that docking is optional in those breeds where docking was customary, so a longtailed dog can be shown alongside docked specimens. Taildocking is no longer permitted in Scandinavia, but it is still normal practice in the United States and Canada.

If your bitch is a working gun dog and it is likely that the puppies will go to shooting homes, some veterinary surgeons may be prepared to dock the tails to prevent injury in the future.

Most breeds still have their dew-claws removed, as these can grow long and curved and can also be painfully torn. Dew-claws are normally found on front legs but occasionally on hind legs too. In just a few breeds the Kennel Club standard requires the dew-claws to be left on – Briards have two pairs which must be retained – so check with your breed club or stud owner on what is customary for your breed.

Any docking and dew-clawing must still be done on days 3 or 4 after the birth. Do not leave it later as the tails grow very thick quite quickly and the central nervous system, by which the puppy will feel pain, is also developing rapidly.

If a vet does agree to dock either by cutting with scissors or by using an elastic tourniquet and is to come to your home to dock the tails, warn them if there is a large litter and that the job may take some time, as you will want to create a situation which will cause the least possible distress to the bitch. Let the docking take place in a room as far away from the bitch as possible. Warm the room well in advance and prepare a warmed box with a hot water bottle for the puppies, which should be taken from the bitch one or two at a time so that she does not feel deprived of all her litter.

Inherited defects

On day one of its life, a puppy should be checked for obvious congenital defects. Inspect all four limbs, feet and toes; the anus (puppies can survive a surprising number of days with an imperforate anus); and check for harelip and/or cleft palate.

It is also important to check the umbilicus daily for any sign of infection, and to weigh the puppies daily to check for a steady but small weight gain.

A further crisis point comes around the time at which puppies are sold. Some defects may only become apparent when the puppy is separated from the litter, and the stress of changing homes may reveal defects which were not obvious before.

During the first four weeks of life puppies should be examined daily for the following conditions, some of which may become evident as the pups become more active.

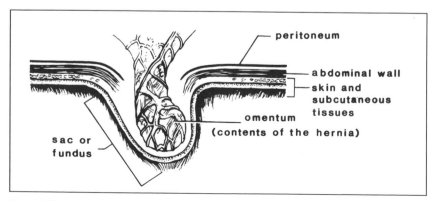

Fig. 7.1 **The structure of a hernia**

Umbilical hernia

A hernia is a protrusion of a part of the body organs through an abnormal opening in the surrounding tissues.

In the case of an umbilical hernia, a pad of fat or part of an abdominal organ protrudes through an incompletely-closed umbilical ring. The tendency for the umbilical ring not to close properly is familial and hereditary in some breeds. The explanation, given by some people, that umbilical hernias are caused by the bitch or breeder pulling too enthusiastically on the umbilical cord is now largely discredited.

A small umbilical hernia is likely to disappear as the puppy gets older. However, if a bitch puppy has a large hernia, or one which can be pushed back into the abdomen by a finger, then a veterinary surgeon should be consulted about a relatively simple operation to repair the hernia, as if it is left it may cause trouble when she is bred from.

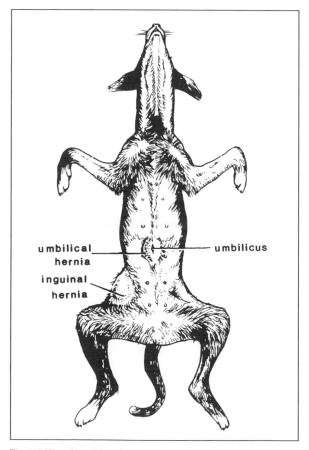

Fig. 7.2 **The site of inguinal and umbilical hernias**

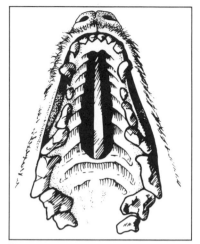

Fig. 7.3 **A cleft palate**

Inguinal hernia

This term is used to describe the protrusion of an abdominal organ or part of the abdominal contents through the inguinal canal in the groin. This is the canal through which the testes descend in the male puppy. These hernias are not uncommon in bitches. Very often they contain one or both uterine horns which would certainly cause problems if the bitch became pregnant. It is as well to have large inguinal hernias corrected surgically.

Cleft palate

This condition is the result of both halves of the hard palate in the roof of the mouth failing to fuse together. This is seen most commonly in the

Fig. 7.4 **A harelip**

short-nosed breeds, such as Pekes and Pugs, but may be found in many breeds. All puppies should be carefully examined for this condition at, or soon after, birth. If you have missed identifying this condition, you may see milk coming down the nose when the puppy tries to suck, as the mouth cannot form a vacuum to enable it to draw milk. All puppies with any degree of this condition should be culled immediately. It makes no sense to attempt to feed a puppy which has a partial cleft because it will never be a healthy specimen of its breed.

Harelip

This inherited condition is not seen so often as it used to be. It is sometimes seen together with a cleft palate. It is the result of a failure of the upper lip to join properly in the midline. Although it can be corrected surgically it is probably more sensible to cull such puppies at birth as they may well also have some other inherited fault which is not so obvious.

Under- or overshot jaw

In a normal canine mouth the upper front teeth (the incisors) just overlap the bottom teeth in what is known as a scissor bite. If the overlap is abnormally large the dog is said to be overshot, but if the lower teeth overlap, i.e. lie in front of, the upper teeth the dog is said to be undershot. Some breeds, for instance the Boxer, are required to have an undershot mouth but many breeds, particularly gun dogs, require a level bite. Where the bite is incorrect, it is not only a breed fault but it leads to undue wear on the teeth and even the possibility of teeth in one jaw cutting into the gum of the other. It is not usually possible to identify this condition until the second

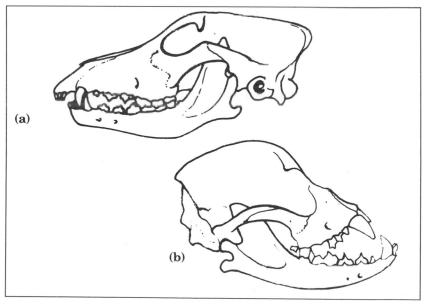

Fig. 7.5 **Jaw structure**
(a) **overshot**
(b) **undershot**

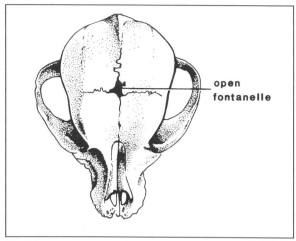

Fig. 7.6 **An open fontanelle**

teeth are through, at about four months. If the condition is exaggerated it may be possible for the veterinary surgeon to correct the fault, but he will require an undertaking that the bitch will not be bred from as this is a strongly hereditary fault. Naturally correct mouths are regarded as very important for the show ring.

Open fontanelle

The bony plates which make up the skull are normally fused together in the middle of the forehead. In some small breeds with very domed foreheads, e.g. Chihuahuas, this fusion may not occur, leaving a gap or fontanelle. Such puppies are very susceptible to brain damage and are constant liability and worry as a pet. A badly-affected puppy is best painlessly destroyed to save it from the greater pain of accidental injury.

Anasarca or waterlogged puppies

Puppies are sometimes born with a generalized accumulation of water in their tissues. They are often called 'walrus' puppies from their resemblance to this animal. It is not known why the condition occurs but it is almost certainly fatal, so it is kindest to have an affected pup destroyed at once.

Screw-tail/Kinked tail

A screw-tail is shorter than normal and resembles a corkscrew. It is probably sensible to cull a puppy with this defect as this may be external evidence of further deformity of the spine. In Bulldogs a screw tail is normal.

Kinked-tails can be felt, even if not noticed at birth. They usually give no problems except for spoiling the dog's chances at show, but it is as well to seek veterinary advice as an amputation may be required.

Dermoid Cyst

This is a cystic tumour enclosing skin tissue or any skin-like substance. Such cysts can occur in any part of the body and present singly as 'lumps' or discharging sinuses. However, in the Rhodesian Ridgeback, dermoid cysts, usually in the centre of the back, are a breed problem. Consult your veterinary surgeon for advice on this condition.

Hydrocephalus

Simply interpreted, this means water on the brain. The condition is brought about by an accumulation of cerebrospinal fluid in the ventricles of the brain and will be noticed in growing puppies by an obvious enlargement of the head, so much so that sometimes the pups cannot lift their heads at all. Affected puppies may also show a variety of nervous signs. These puppies should be painlessly destroyed by a veterinary surgeon as soon as the condition is confirmed.

Swimmers

These are puppies born with a broad, flattened chest, which seem unable to get up on to their feet when their litter mates can. A swimmer keeps its forelegs at right angles to its flanks, and the hind legs are usually extended behind the pup, or they may also be at right angles to the body. Typically, an affected puppy moves around the whelping box in a swimming motion. The condition is thought to be due to weakness of the muscles or a deformity of the bones. Mild cases can be treated by harnessing, or hobbling, the front legs with tape into the correct walking position and deliberately exercising the puppy. In view of the vast over-population of dogs it is doubtful if attempting a cure is sensible as there may be associated difficulty in breathing together with heart problems.

Other problems which may occur during rearing

Breathing problems

Some puppies do not seem to breathe as easily as their siblings – you may hear wheezing and rattling in the chest when you hold them close to your face. It may be that this pup's lungs did not expand effectively at birth or fluid may have got down into the lungs. Ask for veterinary advice as a simple treatment, maybe a brief spell in an oxygen cage, can help enormously.

Juvenile pyoderma (milk rash, nappy rash)

Many puppies develop tiny spots which eventually contain pus, often on the lower abdomen, the groin, hind-quarters and back. When the spots are in the coat, as opposed to a hairless area, the hair will drop off giving the puppy a moth-eaten look. The pups continue to grow and eat normally and seem unaffected. The rash was once attributed to 'acid milk', but that theory has now been discarded. It is probably due to the bitch not cleaning the puppies sufficiently.

Pyoderma seems less prevalent now that newspaper is no longer used as the surface on which puppies lie. Polyester fur, which does not support bacterial growth, is the easiest bedding to keep clean and to change once or twice daily. Bathing the spots with antiseptic lotion helps, as does extra attention to cleanliness in the nest; however the spots have to go through their natural course of enlarging, bursting, drying-up and scab formation. They usually leave no permanent marks. In extreme cases, veterinary help and possibly the administration of antibiotics may be required.

Conjunctivitis

Even before the pups eyelids open you may notice a slight pus-laden discharge from the corner of the eye probably caused by an infection under the eye-lid.

It may be necessary to open the eye to let the pus drain. Ask for veterinary advice directly this condition is noticed or there may be permanent damage to the eye.

Hypoglycaemia

This condition of low blood sugar sometimes affects puppies of the toy breeds at times of maximum stress, especially when changing homes, when meals are missed or even from becoming exhausted from too vigorous play.

The signs may be weakness and depression, whole body muscle tremors and, later, convulsions. The puppy could even die. Give honey and water by mouth at once, and report to the veterinary surgeon who may want to give an intravenous drip. Warn the new owners not to let their puppy become chilled, and to serve meals at regular times and allow plenty of sleep.

Puppy head gland disease (puppy strangles)

This is a serious staphylococcal infection which may affect one or more puppies in the litter from three to 12 weeks of age. Sometimes the bitch will have similar cases in subsequent litters. It starts with a few spots or swollen areas, usually on the head, but progresses very rapidly to swelling of the lymph glands in the neck and grossly enlarged ears, eyes, nose etc, or sometimes the swelling can cover nearly the whole body. The swellings usually turn into abscesses and burst to release their burden of pus. 'The pup was one big abscess', is a comment made by breeders who have experienced this condition.

The puppy affected in this way is a pitiful sight and often gives off an unpleasant smell.

The basic cause of puppy head gland disease is now thought to be a failure in the pup's immune system or a hypersensitivity to bacteria.

Puppies remain surprisingly cheerful; they will eat and grow, but it is fairly evident that they do experience some pain. The affected pups will have to be removed from the litter and will require a great deal of nursing and cleaning. A lot of veterinary assistance will be needed, with possibly expensive laboratory tests to find the antibiotic which will kill the bacteria most effectively. It may also be necessary to give corticosteroids to reduce the inflammation. If you suspect that one of your puppies is affected with this condition seek veterinary help without delay. The earlier treatment is started the more effective it is likely to be.

The hair is likely to be permanently lost from the sites of the abscesses. It is possible to nurse puppies through this disease although the time and expense committed may be out of all proportion to the success achieved and it may be many months before they can be sold as pets. It is not known whether these pups will have an impaired immune system or special sensitivity to bacteria all their lives. With this in view, it is important to discuss with the veterinary surgeon whether it is sensible to attempt a cure. A bitch puppy which has recovered from puppy head gland disease should not be bred from and deep consideration should be given to breeding from the dam again.

Selling imperfect puppies

Some breeders feel it is an indication of a caring attitude to expend a great deal of time and effort in rehabilitating a young puppy with a serious illness or deformity but it is as well to take an introspective look at the motives for doing so.

A puppy which has had a poor start in life is of no use as breeding stock, and it is not sensible for a breeder to keep passengers. Is it right to sell such a puppy as a pet, even at a reduced price? It can be unwise to do so unless both the breeder and the purchaser sign a statement to say why the puppy was sold cheaply, just in case legal proceedings arise in the future. Does your customer realize the implications of buying a less-than-perfect puppy, in terms of possible veterinary expense and shorter life span? Is there any real future in this overcrowded world for pups of less than perfect quality? Would not the breeders' time be better spent on a more intensive socialization programme for the normal pups? All these questions are worthy of serious consideration before embarking upon rehabilitation for a swimmer, or nursing a puppy head gland case, etc.

Attention should be given to the wisdom of breeding again from bitches which have produced puppies with these problems and also from the apparently healthy siblings in a litter where one or more of the puppies was affected, since brothers and sisters may be carriers of the condition. Puppies which have had any congenital deformities repaired must never be bred from. It is likely that the veterinary surgeon will require an undertaking to this effect before even considering surgery.

It is also a matter for debate whether dogs and bitches which have had repair operations should be exhibited. Their presence and possible wins in the show ring may mislead others about the true genetic worth of the line.

Bottle feeding puppies

Supplementary feeding of pups at any stage before weaning is best avoided, but if the bitch dies, has eclampsia or for any reason loses her milk supply, there may be no alternative. It is best to have the equipment available even if it is not used, as it is not alway easy to obtain at an hour's notice – this may be your time schedule if the bitch's milk fails.

Puppies may be fed by means of a tube passed down the oesophagus into the stomach where a calculated amount of milk formula can be deposited via a syringe. Most breeders do not favour this method, preferring to use a feeding bottle in an attempt to satisfy the puppies natural sucking reflex. Medicine droppers seem easy to use but they convey too much air into the puppy. The best bottles to use are the Belcroy premature baby feeder for large breeds and a Catac miniature bottle for small pups. Your veterinary surgeon can obtain these for you. Both come equipped with teats which should be boiled before use. You will also need a small bottle brush. Do not be tempted to enlarge the holes in the teats to make sucking easier – the puppy should have to work at pulling the milk, as it would from its dam. The right speed for the milk flow is shown by holding the bottle upside down, when a few drops (but not a stream) should drip out.

The teats supplied with human baby bottles are too hard for puppies and too large, except in the case of the big breeds.

The bottles must be washed and sterilized after use and kept submerged in sterilizing fluid between feeds. Rinse thoroughly before using again. The formula should be fed at blood-heat, which will mean standing the jug containing the milk in a saucepan of hot water if you have many puppies to feed.

Human baby formula milks, even made up to double strength, are unsuitable for puppies as the protein level is still too low. Cows' milk and goats' milk is a long way from being as rich as bitches' milk, which is very high in protein and fat. Your veterinary surgeon may have replacement bitch milks to offer, but in an emergency a very satisfactory puppy feed can be made by using four parts of canned evaporated milk to one part of boiled water. This is a very rich mixture, giving 1264 K cal per kg, whereas bitch milk is about 1200 K cal per kg. If you use a milk which is not as rich in fat and protein as bitches' milk, then you will have to give more feeds in 24 hours in order to nourish the puppies. On a rich milk supplement you need feed only every four hours around the clock for the first few days. If the pups are doing well, then make it six feeds in 24 hours. By the time the pups are 10 days old you can afford to take a longer rest, missing out on one of the night feeds. Feeding every two hours, day and night, is unnecessary unless a weak formula is being used.

It is important to hold the puppy correctly while bottle feeding. Hold the bottle and the puppy's head in your right hand and support its body with your left, leaving the front legs free to paddle, as they would against the bitch, and also the hindlegs free to kick (see Figure 7.7).

If the bitch is not able to take any interest in the puppies at all, the breeder must take over the role of stimulating the puppies to pass urine and defecate. Very recent work shows that the bitch performs this service before

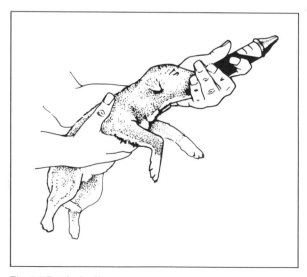

Fig. 7.7 **Bottle feeding a puppy**

she feeds the puppies and not after. Rub the puppy's abdomen with a pad of warm, damp cotton wool and do not give up until you get results. Mark down on a chart what has been passed, as this can be a valuable indicator that the puppy is doing well.

Constipation can be an ailment in bottle fed puppies. Inserting the well-lubricated tip of a stubby thermometer gently into the anus can be a help, so can injecting a tiny amount of olive oil via a medicine dropper into the anus as well as massaging the abdomen.

Bottle fed puppies must be kept clean, as milk etc. which dries on the coat can result in matts which have to be cut out. Also, dry the skin of the abdomen carefully so that it does not become sore.

One of the problems with bottle feeding a whole litter is that they tend to suck at each other and in doing so they can become very sore. Try giving warm, boiled water (bottled still water is best at this stage) in case the pups are thirsty, but most likely the sucking behaviour is instinctive and cannot be curtailed. You can also try separating them in a compartmented box, but by doing this you are depriving them of the huddling behaviour which is one of the essentials of being part of a litter.

Puppies which are not with the dam must be kept very warm and they should have a slightly damp atmosphere too – a piece of damp towelling in the box will generate humidity. The puppies should lie on some source of heat (e.g. heated pad, well-wrapped hot-water bottle etc.) and also the room they are in must be very warm, day and night. The temperature should not drop at all, especially after dark, but the environment should be constantly monitored in case the sun is shining on them for part of the day and they become too hot. If you find one of the puppies chilled warm it up very slowly and do not attempt to feed it until it is warm again. The best warmer is being held or carried close to a human body – put the puppy in your pocket or inside your jumper and let it take your body heat. On no account warm a puppy up quickly. Your consolation for all this work is that bottle fed puppies wean very early; you could begin feeding meat at just over two weeks. Except for their coat texture, it is possible to bring bottle fed pups along so that they are just as satisfactory as pups on the bitch. It never seems possible to get the sleekness which the bitch's tongue can achieve but since puppy coat is lost within the next few months, this is not a long-term disadvantage.

Table 7.3: Tips on bottle feeding puppies

- Do not bottle feed if you can possibly avoid it.
- It is preferable not to alternate bottle and bitch feeding. It is probably better to take some pups right off the bitch if necessary.
- Have the equipment ready in case you need it.
- Use a high protein/high fat formula.
- Keep all equipment sterilized.
- Attend to elimination prior to feeding.
- Keep the puppies clean.

Weaning

In the wild, a litter would get its first semi-solid food by the dam regurgitating some of her own kill. Some domesticated bitches will still regurgitate their own food for their pups, but since we do not want our bitches to lose condition by not getting their proper nourishment, it is a good idea to keep the bitch away from the pups for about an hour after she has been fed once they are three to four weeks old.

The puppies' first teeth will be through by now, and they will be quite ready to taste scrapped meat or a small amount of canned puppy food placed in a little ball in their mouth (see Chapter 4). It is also around this time that the litter should move location, out of the seclusion which has been necessary for the lactating bitch into a place where they can see and be seen.

The puppies should be provided with a covered area – a large cardboard carton will do – in which they will sleep. They must also have an attached run in which they will play and defecate. Puppies must be kept in an enclosure, otherwise they may be accidentally injured and they are equally likely to cause an accident themselves. Panels sold to make up compost bins are useful for the run as they are made to hook together and extra panels can be added to the run as the puppies grow. The run can stand on a sheet of hardboard to protect the floor.

The puppies' bed should be lined with polyester fur, but the run must be carpeted thickly with newspaper which should be constantly changed as it becomes soiled. The puppies will also need sponging over several times a day as their coats become soiled with food.

The puppies will still need warmth, especially overnight when the temperature of the house normally drops. They may still need shading from bright daylight.

The bitch will cease to clean up after her puppies once they are eating solid food, and she may also cease to lick their coats. She should, however, be allowed access to them whenever she wants, although she may make her visits very brief, just jumping in and out of their pen within minutes. If the bitch is left in the same room with the puppies overnight, she must have a bed apart from the litter which the puppies cannot reach.

It is a cruelty to shut a bitch in with a litter when her milk is diminishing. You will notice however that the bitch still has a role to play with her puppies – she will break up puppy fights and she will console any pup which is hurt. She is also very quick to admonish a puppy which takes liberties with her, by pulling on her ears or tail. Take heed of the warning growl and quick snap which is the bitch's way of enforcing her discipline; this may well be imitated by dog owners when correcting puppy behaviour.

The breeder now has a full time task in beginning the education of the puppies – teaching them to be handled, to stand on a table to be groomed, to be familiar with the noise of hair driers, to go out in the car, and even for each puppy to be alone for a short time. Remembering the time when you bought your bitch, you will endeavour to copy and enlarge upon the education your own puppy was given to make those early days in the new home easier for the people who will come to you to buy.

Give your puppies the opportunities to acquire physical skills, by supplying them with play material which should be constantly changed. Everything put in the playpen should be carefully checked for safety. Cardboard cartons with holes to climb in and out of, toys tied to a line strung

Fig. 7.8 **Puppy playpen**

above the playpen, a plastic bucket to roll around, a carrot or apple to chew, all provide mental and physical exercise.

Invite people to see the pups, especially the type of person your own family lacks – perhaps children or old people, men if you have a predominantly female household etc. We do not always realize how very different the voices, the gestures, even the body shape of different categories of people must be to dogs, but during this learning period they should be exposed to all types of people. Children should be encouraged to handle the pups only when sitting on the floor, and they must always be well-supervised. You will, of course, be conscious of the need to avoid infection being brought in to unvaccinated puppies at a stage when their maternally derived antibody may be waning. Sensible precautions will include insisting that shoes are left outside the room, having overalls to offer to cover top clothing (especially trousers which may carry infection through casual encounters with dogs in the street), and passing around disinfectant-soaked cloths to wipe over hands.

If the litter consists of six or more puppies it can be very useful to have a second playpen, for use while you clean the first one. You will soon find that keeping the run clean is a never-ending task which is not made easier by the puppies wanting to play while you try to roll up newspaper. The soiled paper will need to be burnt, or put into sacks to be taken to a refuse dump.

When you clean the soiled floor of the box use hot water and detergent first, then use disinfectant solution and leave for 30 minutes. Finally rinse with hot water and allow to dry. Beware of using household disinfectants which may not kill the viruses and bacteria you need to destroy. Your veterinary surgery can probably let you have some suitable disinfectant. Beware of room sprays which are often irritant, and in summer do not hang fly repellent strips which contain organophosphorus chemicals in the same room as the puppies.

Care of your bitch after whelping

Although most breeders are anxious to wean their puppies early as a safeguard against the bitch losing her milk later, the bitch should be permitted to visit her puppies whenever she wants to, but she must not be forced to stay with them for any length of time. You will find that nearly all bitches terminate their lactation gradually at a time when the pups no longer need food from this source, and there is seldom any need to take any steps to dry up the bitch's milk.

The bitch will gradually resume her normal place in the household. Check her weight, and if she has 'milked off her back', that is converted most of her food intake into milk for the puppies, she will need building up again. This may mean giving a vitamin and mineral supplement under veterinary guidance and feeding rather more than her maintenance diet until she reaches target weight again. If the bitch is being fed a prepared pet food vitamin supplementation should not be needed, as such foods are complete and balanced. Conversely, the bitch which comes off a litter overweight will need a reducing diet.

Most bitches will benefit from a thorough bath and trim when they are away from their puppies, with all dead coat stripped out and tattered fringes removed to promote the growth of new hair as soon as possible. Sometimes bitches will acquire a crusted nose while rearing puppies through constant licking; soften the crusts with applications of lipsalve or vaseline.

Lack of exercise may have resulted in the overgrowth of toe nails, so have them clipped or take the bitch for walks on a shingle beach.

Help your bitch to get her figure back by giving plenty of exercise. Swimming is an excellent way to restore the mammary glands to normal size but many bitches will never be as neat in that region as they were before the litter.

It is extremely unwise to think of breeding from your bitch at the next season unless there are overwhelmingly urgent reasons for doing so, or unless she had a very small litter this time. The next season is likely to be delayed for a few weeks beyond her normal cycle.

If you are considering having your bitch spayed before her next season, talk the matter over with your veterinary surgeon. Spaying should wait until the bitch is back to prime condition but should be done before the next season is imminent. Plan the timing carefully.

Make a fuss of your bitch. Tell her what a good job she has done in producing and raising the puppies. This is particularly necessary if you are keeping one of the litter, as when all the attention is directed to an attractive puppy, it is not unknown for the dam to endure a type of post-natal depression when she feels she is no longer the centre of your world.

Make a deliberate effort to revert to the things you used to do together before she was pregnant – the games she played, the little tricks she had, the obedience routines you put her through. Allow her some privileges the puppy does not have and make sure visitors talk to her as well as the pup, so as to restore her pride in being a very important member of your family.

Selling puppies

Timing

Start showing the puppies to buyers from four weeks old so that the pups can go to new homes at the optimum time for adjustment, around seven weeks old. Waiting until eight weeks takes them into the sensitive period when major changes and upsets are not advisable. Puppies as young as seven weeks bond with their new owners very well and take changes more easily than an older puppy.

If your customers are proposing to feed their pup on a particular kind of food because they are, say, hoteliers, butchers, or vegetarians, do your best to wean the puppy on to that food, so that the new owners do not have to make a change.

Advertising

Join one of the Puppy Finding Associations which circularize buyers with lists of puppies available immediately.

Advertise locally within a 50-mile radius.

Let the stud dog owner know how many puppies are for sale.

Advise your breed club secretary that you have puppies – a lot of enquiries go to breed clubs.

Tell the staff at your veterinary surgery that the puppies they so kindly helped with are now ready for new homes.

Beware of making advertising claims which are excessive or unsupported. Puppies by a champion dog should not be advertised as 'champion puppies'.

Paperwork

Get the paperwork ready well in advance. Register the litter with your National Kennel Club when they are about two weeks old. In the UK many breeders insure puppies for the first few weeks after they leave for their new homes. This is not common practice in the USA. Make out and have duplicated a feeding chart, with advice on how to increase the amount of food given as the puppy grows. Write your own sheet of puppy care advice and the special information which refers to your breed, especially on grooming. Make a note of the tools needed and where to buy them.

Write out a pedigree for each puppy – new buyers prize them so much. Pedigree forms cannot be bought at local stationers, so send away for them from addresses to be found in the canine press well-ahead of needing them. It can be useful to put the colours of dogs under their names. Don't forget to underline the champions in red, but don't honour any near champions or open show winners in this way. Copy the pedigree carefully. Errors in names and transpositions of lines go down the generations and make a nonsense of the pedigree system. Be absolutely accurate on the date of birth; don't for any reason adjust it, as making the puppy older or younger than it really is could confuse vaccination timing and may even result in the death of the puppy from virus disease months later.

If you are selling a puppy with any kind of defect, ask your veterinary surgeon exactly what you should say to your customer about it. People go to law much more eagerly nowadays so it is as well to get all details clear and in writing. If the puppy has a defect which can be repaired later, you may feel obliged to bear all or half of the cost, or you may want the operation done by your vet. Get it in writing and keep a copy so that no misunderstanding arises.

The sales package

Pleasant additions to your sales package may include the following.
- A photograph of sire and dam, and one of the whole litter.
- Details of membership of breed clubs and local canine societies, and the dates of shows or rallies where more of the breed may be seen.
- A book on the breed and a book on puppy rearing. *The Doglopaedia* says it all!
- A small piece of used polyester fur which will seem familiar to the puppy.
- A photocopied price list for folding crates, bean bags, polyester fur and other dog accessories which may be unfamiliar to the new buyer.
- A Puppy Pack available from many dog food companies which contains a number of leaflets giving much useful information.

Interviewing customers

This can be a tiring business since you have to find out so much about the prospective purchasers and the way they are likely to treat the puppy, without seeming to overstep the bounds of civility. Although breeders are perfectly correct in being very particular about the homes to which their puppies go, we have to remember that this is probably the only purchase your clients ever made at which they had to justify their suitability to own the object they are proposing to buy.

Some puppy clients resent the cross-questioning they are put through. Point out that they are possibly being saved from considerable expenditure of money, and probably heartbreak and family strife.

You may want to ask your customers some of the following questions which will help you to build up a picture of, not only the welcome your puppy will receive, but also the long-term tolerance that a growing dog can expect.
1. Do your clients live in a house, or a flat?
2. Do they have a separated (i.e. not communal) fenced garden?
3. Why did the other permanent members of the household not come to see the puppies? Is some family member reluctant to take part in this exciting purchase, or is the puppy to be a surprise?
4. Does everyone in the family want a puppy?
5. Have they had a dog before? Have they had a dog of this breed before?
6. Will there be someone at home for the greater part of each day?
7. Have they thought about provision for the dog when they are on holiday or away on business trips?

8. Do they really appreciate the running costs of dogs in your breed? Estimate the annual expenditure on food, vaccination, insurance premium, accessories, trimming, boarding – can they be sure of taking this expense on board?
9. Have they an elderly parent living with them or who frequently visits? (This is especially applicable when selling very small fragile breeds or medium to large boisterous ones.)
10. What are their hobbies and are they compatible with dog ownership?
11. Is any member of the family very house- or garden-proud?
12. What do they see as the life-style and environment for their puppy (e.g. do they visualize it living in a kennel or the boiler room)?
13. Will the puppy be left with 'staff' for a lot of the time? Nanny, the gardener, or other employees may resent having to look after the puppy and may not treat it well.
14. Have they considered the danger a covered swimming pool in the garden can be to a puppy? What are they going to do about theirs?

More subtle probings are needed to also find out the following:
● Status and permanence of life partner. Break-up of households are the reason for 50 per cent of rejected dogs and a puppy is often bought as a last-ditch consolation present.
● Do they hope to have children soon? Many young animals are cast out when a first or second baby comes along.

Don't be taken in by:
● 'We are in an apartment but hope to move soon to a house with a big garden'. It is best to wait until they have moved.
● 'I'll take the dog to work with me'. It is unlikely that the environment will suit a young puppy.
● 'I'm only out for four hours in the morning'. Four hours employment can easily mean six hours away from home with travelling, shopping etc.
● 'Will you house-train him for us?' This betrays a lot about the attitude of the purchasers and is, in any case, an impossible task as the pup must learn house-training in its new environment.

Deposits
Take a deposit of 20 per cent of the purchase price when your client decides to buy, the balance to be payable when the puppy is collected. If no more is heard of the buyer after the date of collection has passed, despite attempts to contact them, you are entitled to re-sell the puppy and keep the deposit. In the UK the law is flexible on the length of time you are obliged to keep uncollected animals, but two or three weeks seem acceptable if the prospective owners cannot be traced.

Veterinary checks and the possible return of puppies
Advise your customers to collect their puppies early in the day, so that they can, if they wish, take the pup immediately to a veterinary surgeon for a check-up. Make it clear to your clients that you will take the puppy back and cure any defect if the vet finds one, or that alternatively you will refund their money in full, but put a time limit in days on this offer. You cannot be expected to take a puppy back on these terms if it has been away from your kennel for weeks.

If the puppy has to be returned for any reason, probably largely because it does not fit in with the buyer's life-style, make it clear that you will take the puppy back and re-sell it for your clients, but that you will deduct your expenses for re-advertising and the keep of the puppy. Some breeders try to insist that any puppy or dog bought from them must not be re-sold or parted with unless the breeder gives permission. This condition is unenforceable. Once bought, the puppy is the buyer's possession, and although the breeder will always want to hear news of the dog or will willingly give advice, they have no rights over the dog unless it was sold on breeding terms or some similar agreement which must be composed and signed by both parties. However, morally the breeders are responsible for life for the animals they breed, and so, many years later you may be obliged to take into your home a dog which you last saw as an eight week old puppy.

Many breed rescue schemes exist but they should not be used until the owners and the breeder have made exhaustive attempts to re-home the dog themselves by advertising privately. If breed rescue is used, consideration should be given to providing some money for the expenses incurred in transporting and selecting a second home. Despite the very best intentions towards the care of the dog, we should not make it too easy for owners to divest themselves of their obligations to their pets.

SECTION THREE: ANATOMY, PHYSIOLOGY AND MEDICAL PROBLEMS

Anatomy and physiology

Medical problems specific to bitches

CHAPTER 8

ANATOMY AND PHYSIOLOGY

PART I

THE STRUCTURE OF THE REPRODUCTIVE ORGANS

Ovaries

Oviducts

Uterus

Vagina

Vestibule

Vulva

Mammary glands

Introduction

An understanding of how bitches are 'made' and how they 'work' is essential if they are to be kept properly and the full benefits offered by bitch ownership realized. Furthermore, owners who know the names of the various parts and organs, and their functions, can more easily describe any signs and symptoms shown by their bitch to a veterinary surgeon or breeder when seeking advice. They can also better understand why a specific treatment or course of action has been advised.

It is therefore sensible for all owners, especially those who have not owned a bitch before, to read this chapter right through as one would do with a manual for a new car. Thereafter, it should be necessary only to 'brush-up' on specific points. The information has been provided in such a way that details can be quickly referred to when required.

This part of Chapter 8 concentrates on the anatomy, or structure, of the female genital tract and the related organs. In Part II, the role of the hormones, the chemical messengers which are responsible for bringing about the oestrous cycle in all female mammals including bitches, is described.

A full appreciation of how the hormones involved interact one with another is the key to understanding why bitches come on heat, why they suffer so often from false pregnancy, mammary tumours and the life-threatening disease of the uterus called pyometra. Such knowledge is equally helpful whether an owner wishes to produce a litter of puppies or avoid pregnancy.

Many owners have kept and bred from bitches in the past without knowing about these matters but there is no doubt that time spent studying the essentials of both anatomy and physiology will make bitch ownership more rewarding, possibly prevent suffering and may lead to more successful breeding.

The anatomy of the reproductive tract

The reproductive organs of the bitch include the ovaries, the uterine tubes (oviducts), uterus, vagina, the vestibule and, the external opening, the vulva. These organs are situated in the abdominal cavity as illustrated in Figure 8.1. Their relative size and shape is indicated in Figure 8.4.

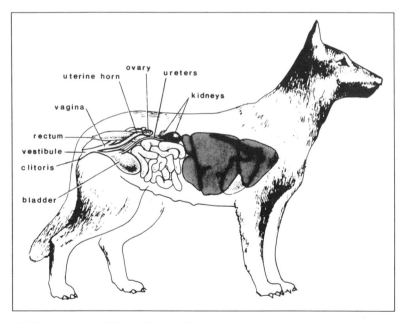

Fig. 8.1 **The female genital tract in situ, illustrating its relationship with other structures**

Metric measurements have been used in this book. One Inch = 2.4cms.

The ovaries

In common with other female mammals, bitches have two ovaries. These organs are situated just behind the kidneys near the abdominal wall to which they are anchored by strong, short, fan-shaped ligaments. The ovaries are on average about 2 cm in length and they are oval in shape. Each ovary is concealed in a fat-filled pouch, or 'bursa', which has a slit-like opening on the underside.

Each ovary is made up of an outer layer or rim called the cortex and an inner layer called the medulla, which contains supportive tissue, nerves, and blood vessels. The eggs, or follicles, are produced from cells in the cortex. Newly-born bitch puppies have thousands of eggs in their ovaries but most of these never reach maturity and indeed many are lost even before the bitch has her first heat. An examination of the cortex of mature bitches at different stages of the oestrous cycle reveals egg-producing cells, developing and degenerating follicles together with recently formed corpora lutea and the remains of corpora lutea resulting from earlier ovulations.

Besides producing eggs, the ovaries manufacture the female sex hormones, oestrogen and progesterone. These are responsible for bringing about the secondary female sex characteristics such as a more refined body shape and the development of the mammary glands (see also The Hormonal System, page 138).

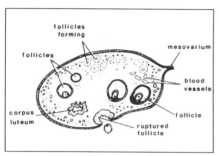

Fig. 8.2 **The ovaries**

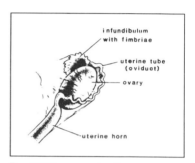

Fig. 8.3 **The ovary** *in situ* showing the uterine tubes

The uterine tubes or oviducts

These are thin tubes which average about 5 to 8 cm in length. They lie mainly in the ovarian bursa, mentioned previously, and their fringed and funnel-shaped open ends, designed to catch mature eggs as they are shed, are situated close to the surface of the ovaries. This means that there is little chance of eggs being released accidentally free into the abdomen. The inner surface of the uterine tubes is covered with finger-like processes (cilia) which sweep rhythmically carrying fluid and any eggs that have been caught towards the end of the oviduct which is attached to the uterus. The opening into the uterus is very small.

The uterus or womb

The uterus of the bitch is a hollow, tubular, muscular organ with a very short body and extremely long, narrow horns which are quite uniform in diameter. In a bitch the size of a Cocker Spaniel which has never been pregnant, the body of the uterus is about 2 to 3 cm long and the horns measure 12 to 15 cm in length. The uterine horns diverge from the uterine body towards each kidney making the uterus as a whole appear Y-shaped. The body of the uterus joins with the vagina posteriorly through a narrow canal, called the cervix, which protrudes downwards into the vagina. The cervix is normally closed but opens during oestrus, to allow the passage of spermatozoa from the male. The cervix must open again at the end of

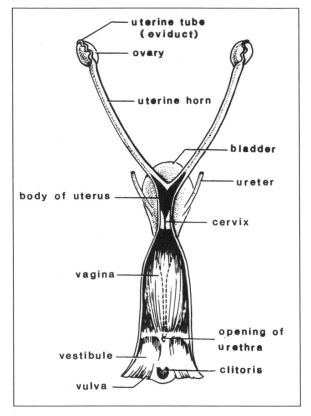

Fig. 8.4 **The genital organs of the bitch**

pregnancy to allow the puppies to be born. The peculiar structure, narrowness and position of the cervix in the bitch makes it very difficult, if not impossible, to see it from the vagina or pass instruments through it into the uterus.

Between heats the uterine horns are no thicker than a piece of string, but when the bitch is in season they increase in size to become rather thicker than a pencil. The pregnant uterus has a tremendous capacity for expansion and has a diameter of 5 to 10 cm according to the breed and may contain, in the case of the large breeds, as many as 12 or 14 puppies.

The walls of the uterus consist of four layers as shown in Figure 8.3. The two muscle layers are, of course, very much involved at the time of birth and, acting in concert, they propel the puppy towards the vagina. The lining of the uterus, the endometrium, contains the uterine glands, connective tissue and a rich blood supply. The endometrium changes character dramatically during the oestrous cycle, if the bitch becomes pregnant or develops pyometra.

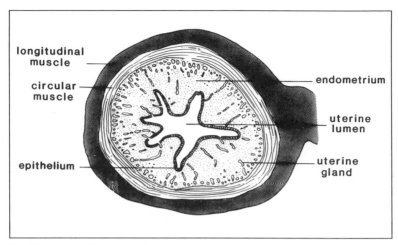

Fig. 8.5 **Cross-section through the uterus**

The vagina

In bitches the vagina is a very long, hollow, muscular organ which is capable of great dilation. It lies wholly within the pelvis. In an average-sized bitch the vagina is 12 to 14 cm in length, making it impossible in all but the very smallest of bitches for the cervix, which enters at its anterior end, to be reached for examination purposes, by a finger inserted through the vulva. The vagina is lined by epithelial cells that are shed throughout the oestrous cycle. The character of these cells changes at different phases of the cycle. This feature may be utilized when vaginal smears are used, for example to determine when a bitch should be mated or whether ovulation has occurred (see Table 8.3). Posteriorly the vagina is separated from the vestibule by a constricting muscular ring which should not be confused with the cervix. Very occasionally a band of fibrous tissue which can interfere with mating or the free passage of puppies may occur across the ring.

The vestibule

The word 'vestibule' is used to describe that section of the female genital tract which links the vagina to the vulva and is probably most sensibly regarded as being part of the vulva. The urethra, the tube leading from the urinary bladder, opens through an elongated protrusion into the floor of the vestibule just behind where it joins the vagina. The clitoris, which contains mostly fat and some erectile tissue, also lies under the floor of the vestibule.

The vulva

The vulva forms the external opening of the genital tract of the bitch. The lips of the vulva form a vertical slit and, where they meet ventrally, come to a point which projects downwards and backwards from the body. The vulval lips are soft and pliable and become much enlarged when the bitch is on heat.

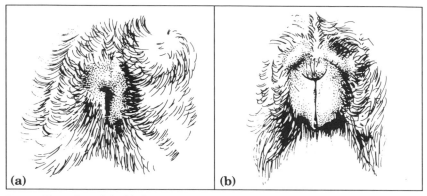

Fig. 8.6 **The vulva of the bitch**
(a) in anoestrus

(b) in pro-oestrus, i.e. when on heat

The mammary glands

The mammary glands are in fact skin glands that have become modified to produce milk. There are usually 10, arranged in pairs on either side of the

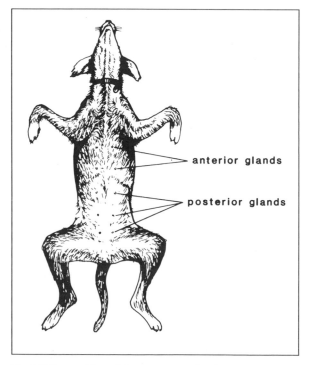

Fig. 8.7 **The position of the mammary glands**

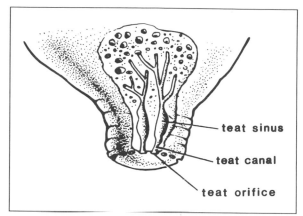

Fig. 8.8 **The structure of a mammary gland and teat**

bitch's body, extending from the chest to the groin. To have one or more missing glands is not unusual. The teats or nipples are normally short and have, most commonly, six to 12 small openings rather like the rose on a watering-can. Both the teats and the glands become much enlarged when the bitch is suckling a litter of puppies.

Table 8.1: Notes relating to the anatomy of the bitch's genital tract

- The ovaries are hidden in a fat-filled bursa or pouch.
- Developing follicles, mature follicles and corpora lutea can usually be seen as projections on the surface of exposed ovaries in mature bitches.
- The uterus of the bitch has a short body and two long, narrow horns – it is thus Y-shaped.
- The lining of the uterus, the endometrium, changes character very dramatically at different stages of the oestrous cycle, during pregnancy and if the bitch develops pyometra.
- The vagina of the bitch is very long making it impossible, in all but very small bitches, to reach the cervix with a finger inserted through the vulva. It is therefore seldom possible to know if the cervix is open to allow pups to be born.
- It is important not to confuse the constricting muscular ring, which separates the vagina and the vestibule, with the cervix.
- Missing mammary glands are not uncommon.
- In contrast to a cow's teat, which has one large duct, bitches' teats have several openings.
- During coitus, spermatozoa ejaculated from the male penis are deposited around the cervix. They pass through into the uterus and up the uterine tubes where the eggs are fertilized.
- Spaying (ovariohysterectomy) involves the complete removal of the uterus and the ovaries of the bitch. This is carried out under general anaesthesia and is a major operation.
- Very occasionally the lining of the vagina will protrude through the vulva after whelping. This is called a vaginal prolapse and requires veterinary attention (see also Chapter 9).
- Vaginal hyperplasia is the term used to describe a swelling and protuberance of the lining of the vagina that sometimes occurs during heat, particularly in Boxers and Bulldogs (see also Chapter 9).

CHAPTER 8

ANATOMY AND PHYSIOLOGY

PART II

THE OESTROUS CYCLE AND THE PHYSIOLOGY OF REPRODUCTION

The oestrous cycle

Vaginal smears

The hormonal system

Physiology of
the oestrous cycle

The oestrous cycle

The signs and frequency of heat in bitches

In scientific terms bitches are described as monoestrus since they have only one oestrus during each breeding season. This unique situation is in marked contrast to polyoestrus animals, such as rats, mice, cows and women, which cycle at regular intervals of two to four weeks throughout the year, giving many opportunities for mating and conception.

The objectives of the oestrous cycle are to produce eggs, to stimulate the bitch to accept the male, and prepare the reproductive tract to nurture fertilized eggs and the foetal puppies as they develop in the uterus.

The bitch's cycle can be conveniently divided into four phases as shown in Figure 8.9 and described separately in Table 8.2.

It should be noted, however, that the stages are not separate entities – they do merge into each other.

It is traditional for owners of bitches to refer to the summation of pro-oestrus and oestrus as 'heat'. A bitch is often described at this time as being 'on heat' or 'in season'. There is no specific lay terminology for the other two phases of the cycle.

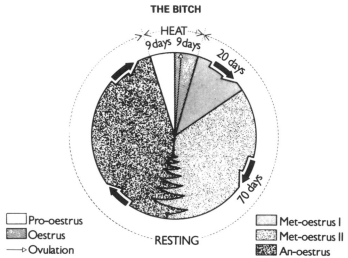

Fig. 8.9 **The phases of the oestrous cycle in bitches**

Table 8.2: The stages of the oestrous cycle

Stage of Cycle	Duration	Comments
Pro-oestrus	Average 9 days (range 2 to 27 days)	This stage is the beginning of heat. The vulva is swollen and there is a blood-stained discharge. Although the bitch is attractive to dogs she will not allow them to mate her.
Oestrus	Average 9 days (range 3 to 21 days)	This stage is defined as the period when the bitch will accept the male. The vulva is much enlarged and turgid. The discharge is straw-coloured rather than blood-stained. Ovulation occurs spontaneously usually about 2 days after the start of oestrus.
Met-oestrus	Average 90 days	This stage occurs in the unmated bitch and hormone levels equivalent to those seen in pregnancy are present. During this stage the bitch may show signs of false pregnancy.
Anoestrus	Variable – but on average 75 days	This is the period of sexual inactivity between cycles. The duration of anoestrus largely determines how frequently the bitch will come in season.

The average age for the onset of puberty is six to seven months but it may occur as early as four months or as late as 22 months. *If a bitch of two years old has never been in season veterinary advice should be sought.*

Owners should note, in connection with the figures given in Table 8.2, that:

● Considerable individual variation in the duration of the phases can occur.

- The signs by which pro-oestrus and oestrus are recognized vary from animal to animal, making it difficult to assess accurately the duration of these phases.
- The duration of met-oestrus cannot be readily determined by simple observation, as the beginning and end are not characterized by specific outward signs.

All these factors, true and apparent, are of great importance when considering when to mate a bitch or the administration of agents to control the oestrous cycle. This difficulty can, however, be largely overcome by consulting your veterinary surgeon who may utilise one of the diagnostic procedures available to identify, more precisely, the current stage of the cycle.

For a full discussion of the techniques, noted below, see Appendix 1.

Table 8.3: Detection of the stages of the oestrous cycle

Techniques	Stage of oestrus detectable	Changes detected
Vaginal cytology	Pro-oestrus, oestrus and met-oestrus	Cell population in a vaginal smear
Vaginoscopy	Oestrus/ovulation	Wrinkling of vaginal lining
Measurement of progesterone levels in the blood	Oestrus/ovulation	Increase in serum progesterone

Table 8.4: Notes relating to the oestrous cycle in bitches

- Some bitches may show signs of abdominal discomfort for some days before heat commences.
- Many bitches will start territory marking just before and during pro-oestrus, by passing small amounts of urine at frequent intervals around the garden or when they are taken for walks.
- Since ovulation results from a surge of luteinizing hormone eggs are usually released by all the ripe follicles over a period lasting only about 24 hours.
- Bitches usually cycle throughout their lives – there is no equivalent to the menopause.
- About two-thirds of bitches show signs of false pregnancy usually during late met-oestrus, i.e. one to two months after they have been on heat.
- The life-threatening condition called pyometra occurs most commonly one to two months after a bitch has been in season.
- On average the inter-oestrous period lasts seven months but periods of between five to 10 months are considered normal. The cycle length in German Shepherd Dogs is significantly shorter (four to four-and-a-half months) and African breeds, such as the Basenji, are said to cycle only once a year but this is altering after many years of domestication here. (See also Chapter 12.) More frequent heats, that is at intervals of less than four months, are often associated with infertility.

Table 8.5: The endocrine glands and the hormones they produce

Gland	Situation	Hormone/s produced	Action
Thyroid	The gland lies alongside the trachea at the end nearest the mouth	Thyroid hormone	Controls the activity of the body tissues. Deficiency (hypothyroidism) results in poor growth in young animals. Older animals, lacking in the hormone, become sluggish, over-weight, and have poor hair growth. Excess amounts of the hormone cause hyperactivity.
Parathyroid	The two parathyroids are small glands situated alongside the thyroid	Parathyroid hormone	Controls the calcium stores in the body and is therefore important in the development of the skeleton.
Adrenal	The two adrenal glands are small glands which lie near the kidneys	Adrenaline – produced by the centre of the gland (the medulla)	Prepares the animal for action and is excreted in quantity if the animal is frightened, needs to fight or run away.
		Corticosteroids – produced by the outer layer of the gland (the cortex)	One group of these hormones controls the salt and water content of the body. The other hormones produced by the adrenal cortex enhance the animal's resistance to stress and infection. Excessive production of corticosteroids causes Cushing's syndrome. Addison's disease is caused when too little hormone is produced.
Pancreas	Lies in a loop in the small intestine	Insulin	Controls the amount of glucose in the blood. Animals with sugar diabetes are lacking in the hormone.
Testes	The two testes are situated in the scrotal sac	Testosterone	Responsible for the male characteristics of dogs, particularly aggression.
Ovaries	Situated in the abdomen near the kidneys	Oestrogen	Responsible for the female characteristics of bitches. Stimulates the genital tract and causes bleeding when the bitch is on heat. Also brings about development of the mammary glands.
		Progesterone	Progesterone is responsible for preparing the uterus so that it can support the foetuses. It maintains pregnancy. It causes the mammary glands to develop so that they can eventually produce milk.

Table 8.5: (cont.)

Gland	Situation	Hormone/s produced	Action
Pituitary	Situated at the base of the brain. The gland is divided into two parts, the anterior part which produces the first four hormones listed in the next column and the posterior part which produces the remaining two	Thyrotropic hormone	Controls the action of the thyroid.
		Corticotropic hormone	Controls action of the adrenal cortex.
		Growth hormone	Controls the animal's growth particularly up to puberty.
		Gonadotropins – Follicle stimulating hormone Luteinizing hormone Prolactin	Promotes the ripening of eggs in the ovaries. Causes ovulation. Stimulates the mammary glands so that they are ready to produce milk.
		Anti-diuretic hormone	Acts on the kidney to prevent excessive excretion of water.
		Oxytocin	Makes the pregnant uterus contract as whelping and stimulates the release of milk from the mammary glands.

Footnote: The hormone relaxin should also be mentioned. It is produced by the follicles, the corpora lutea and also the uterus and placenta. It is generally accepted that the major function of relaxin is to allow the bones of the pelvis to separate thereby making an easier passage for the foetus during birth. It may also prime the uterus to the affect of oxytocin, and it has been suggested that relaxin affects the uterine musculature so that developing foetuses become equally spaced throughout both uterine horns regardless of their side of origin.

The physiology of reproduction

The hormonal system

A number of glands called 'endocrine glands', situated in various parts of the body, produce hormones which are spread by the bloodstream throughout the body. They instruct the organ or body system which they control to perform a specific function. Many organs which are under hormonal control receive messages from one hormone which makes them work more actively, and from another which makes them work more slowly or stop. Thus the hormones act rather like the accelerator and brakes on a car – they control very precisely the body's activity.

Besides their effect on specific parts of the body, the hormones also work together in concert, conducted by the hormones produced by the pituitary gland which is situated at the base of the brain. The amount of hormones present in the blood is being continually monitored by the body and adjusted to meet the animal's need at any particular time.

All the hormones involved in maintaining body functions are summarized in Table 8.5. Those that are principally involved with reproduction in bitches have been highlighted.

The physiology of the oestrous cycle

In the bitch, as with other female animals, it seems that there is an inborn cyclic activity in the hypothalamus, a specific area in the brain which is in fundamental control of reproductive function. This part of the brain is, however, also sensitive to both internal and environmental stimuli such as heat and light, particularly the length of daylight. Furthermore, it may be stimulated, through pheromones, by the presence of other bitches and male dogs. The oestrous cycle is controlled by a complex interplay between the hypothalamus and the reproductive tract with the anterior pituitary, an endocrine gland situated at the base of the brain, acting as a central relay. Figure 8.10 summarizes the effects of the three hormones produced by the anterior pituitary (the gonadotrophins), which are controlled by releasing factors secreted from the hypothalamus; and the sex hormones, oestrogen and progesterone produced by the ovaries.

Fig 8.10 **The interaction between the gonadotrophins and the sex hormones**

Hormone	Follicle stimulating hormone (FSH)	Lutenizing hormone (LH)	Luteotrophic factors(s)	
Site of Action	Follicle	Follicle and corpus luteum	Corpus luteum	Mammary glands
Effect	Follicular growth Simulates secretion of oestrogen	Ovulation and formation of corpus luteum Initiates secretion of progesterone	Maintains secretion of progesterone	Stimulates lactation
Action on Anterior Pituitary	Positive and negative feedback	Progesterone has a negative feedback		

The sequence of events in simple terms is as follows. At the end of the period of sexual inactivity, anoestrus, the hypothalamus produces a releasing factor which stimulates the anterior pituitary to produce follicle stimulating hormone (FSH) which controls the development of the ovarian follicles, which in turn secrete the sex hormone oestrogen. At low levels this hormone exerts a positive feedback on the anterior pituitary stimulating more FSH to be released resulting in further follicle growth and increased oestrogen levels. This process continues until the follicles are mature and about to rupture. At this stage the higher levels of oestrogen produced by the ripe follicles have a negative feedback effect inhibiting FSH secretion but at the same time triggering the release of luteinizing hormone (LH) from the anterior pituitary in a pulse, which causes ovulation. The ruptured follicle is rapidly converted into a solid glandular body, the corpus luteum. The development of these corpora lutea is initiated in response to LH and is maintained by the luteotrophic factor(s). The corpora lutea secrete progesterone which has a negative feedback effect at high concentrations, inhibiting the secretion of the gonadotrophin which maintains these secretory bodies. Thus it is the balance of the two sex hormones oestrogen and progesterone that ultimately controls the oestrous cycle through their feedback mechanisms on the anterior pituitary. They also bring about changes in the reproductive tract and mammary glands as illustrated in Table 8.6.

Table 8.6: The effects of the sex hormones on the reproductive tract and mammary glands

Sex hormones	Target organ	Effect
Oestrogen	Endometrium Cervix, Myometrium Vagina Mammary glands	Proliferation of glands Relaxation Proliferation of mucous lining Duct proliferation
Progesterone	Endometrium Mammary glands	Secretory changes in glands Alveolar proliferation

Footnote: Both sex hormones also have a direct affect on the brain causing changes in behaviour and temperament.

The hormonal changes described above, which bring about the oestrous cycle in the bitch, are illustrated in Figures 8.11 and 8.12. These serve to show that the bitch is unusual in three respects.

Firstly, low levels of progesterone are present before ovulation. It seems that the bitch is stimulated to stand for the dog (to allow mating) by rising progesterone levels superimposed on falling oestrogen levels.

Secondly, progesterone levels are maintained for a very prolonged time. This long period of progesterone dominance is possibly fundamental to the development of pyometra in bitches.

Thirdly, the hormone levels in bitches are similar whether or not they have been mated and become pregnant. Although progesterone levels descend very rapidly at the end of pregnancy whereas at the end of met-oestrus they taper off more gradually over a longer period.

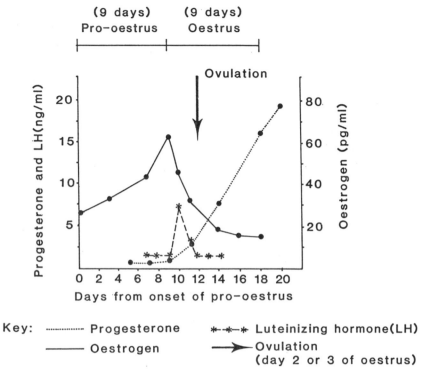

Fig. 8.11 **Oestrogen, progesterone and LH blood levels during pro-oestrus and oestrus**

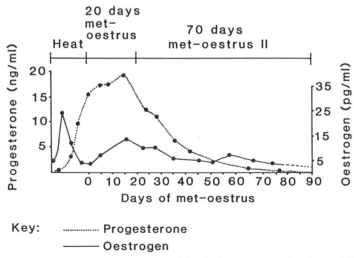

Fig. 8.12 **Oestrogen and progesterone blood levels during met-oestrus in the bitch**

Table 8.7: Notes relating to hormone treatment in bitches

- FSH is sometimes used by veterinary surgeons to bring a bitch into season. However it is not regularly effective even when doses are repeated daily for several days.
- Although ovulation occurs on average 10–12 days after the onset of pro-oestral bleeding, the timing of this event is very variable (5–25 days). The time of ovulation can be pin-pointed by the examination of vaginal smears and also by demonstrating rising progesterone levels in the blood. The identification of the time of ovulation allows the whelping date to be accurately determined since it occurs very consistently 60 days after actual conception time which can be three to five days after the bitch is willing to stand for the dog.
- LH is quite often used to try to synchronize ovulation with mating. It is difficult to judge the effect of such medication because dog spermatozoa are very long-lived, in the female genital tract.
- Four days after ovulation the eggs are in the right stage of development and ready for fertilization. If they are not fertilized within 24–36 hours they die.
- Hormones with physiological actions similar to progesterone (the progestogens) are quite commonly used to control the oestrous cycle (see Chapter 9) and also to treat false pregnancy (see Chapter 9). They work through the negative feed effect on the anterior pituitary.
- Synthetic and natural oestrogens are sometimes used by veterinary surgeons to terminate pregnancy in bitches which have been mismated and also in the treatment of false pregnancy.
- Bitches housed in close proximity tend to synchronize their oestrous cycles, probably as a result of the excretion of pheromones.

CHAPTER 9
MEDICAL PROBLEMS SPECIFIC TO BITCHES

Observing for signs of illness

Signs and symptoms

Diseases and conditions

Disease prevention

Feminine 'what ifs'

Mishaps and problems about the house and outdoors

Introduction

The prompt recognition of illness is important, not only to save pain and suffering, but also because early treatment is likely to be more effective.

The object of this chapter is to help the owner to identify, and to describe accurately, the signs of pain and illness in their pet and to know when to seek veterinary advice. The observant owner will then be able to supply an accurate and detailed account of the bitch's condition should veterinary treatment become necessary. An accurate history of events can be a crucial factor in helping the veterinary surgeon to arrive at a correct diagnosis and is thus a prelude to effective treatment. Your veterinary surgeon may appreciate having the history in writing. Remember to include dates of oestrus, mating or attempted mating.

Signs and symptoms

Most canine illnesses are shown by a combination of signs and symptoms.

Signs of illness are: Objective evidence that something is wrong which is readily *apparent to an observer*, e.g. diarrhoea or coughing.

143

Symptoms of illness are: A change in sensation of bodily function *experienced by the patient*, e.g. the pain caused by trying to put an injured foot to the ground. Although dogs are at a disadvantage in being unable to describe their symptoms they are nevertheless able to indicate in a number of ways what they are experiencing, but it is necessary to learn how to interpret these indications correctly.

It is important for the owner to keep an open mind about the nature of an illness during the early stages.

Not all cases of a particular illness show all the signs and symptoms associated with that illness. Furthermore, many signs are common to a number of different diseases. Jumping to the wrong conclusion too early may prevent help being sought at the right time and delay the start of proper treatment.

The signs associated with specific diseases that affect bitches are listed under the description of the condition. In order to help the owners at the time of need the significance of various signs of illness shown by bitches will be found at the end of this chapter under the heading 'Feminine what ifs'.

Table 9.1: Tips on observing for signs of illness

- The concerned owner will spend time observing the normal habits, reactions and detailed appearance of their bitch when in full health, so that any alterations which may be indicative of the beginnings of illness will be noticed quickly.
- Any small change in behaviour or any unusual physical sign should mean that the bitch is kept under close scrutiny for a few hours, or a few days, until either more positive signs develop or she has returned to normal. A bitch under observation for illness should not be given strenuous exercise nor should she be taken to a training class, a dog show or into any situation which may cause her stress.
- It may not be beneficial to seek veterinary advice in the very early stages of discomfort, as the vet will usually want some positive signs to develop before treatment can be started. The discerning owner will be aware when this stage is reached, and will have a note of the earliest signs to hand.
- Bitches, like many women, may have days when they feel 'off colour' for no obvious reason. If these episodes occur often in your bitch, a note of days, times and circumstances should be made. Veterinary advice should then be sought in order to interpret the information collected in this way.
- Bitches may show signs of depression and illness in response to worry or grief affecting the owner or the household in which she lives. Human alterations in behaviour may be subtle, but the devoted dog recognizes mood changes in her owner. The bitch will return to normal when her owner is feeling happier and on no account should she be given anti-depressive drugs prescribed for human use.
- It is particlarly important to be extra observant on the days when you expect your bitch to be coming on heat and for the two months after she has been in season. Note in particular increased thirst, frequency of urination, vaginal swelling and/or bleeding and more frequent licking, particularly of the genital organs.

Temperament and behaviour changes

Bitches are creatures of habit. Any marked changes not associated with changes in the household may be indicative of illness. However, allowances should be made for jealousy, resentment and pining, as well as undue persecution by a puppy, kitten, child or other dogs.

Temperature taking

The normal temperature of a newborn puppy is 94–97°F. The normal adult body temperature of 101.5°F is not achieved until the pup is about four weeks old. It is not wise or helpful for an inexperienced owner to take a bitch's temperature unless specifically requested to do so by the veterinary surgeon – thermometers can be broken in the rectum all too easily! Furthermore, readings need skilled interpretation, as any form of excitement can cause the temperature to rise by two or three degrees when the dog is in normal health.

Pain

Pain is probably the most significant symptom of illness or injury and it is important to understand the ways that bitches indicate that they are suffering from pain in a particular area or organ. For example abdominal pain is often indicated by continual glancing round at the site of pain, biting and licking at the area or the bitch may be reluctant to leave her bed. The bitch may hold herself in a hunched up position when standing, or she may take up the 'prayer position' (down on forelegs with hindlegs standing). In some cases bitches with abdominal pain will show persistent straining to pass a bowel movement. More general hind end pain will be shown very often by frequent whirling round in the response to 'hind end' discomfort from a burr or matt of fur in the region, or from blades of grass which have not been passed properly with a bowel movement and which are still protruding from the anus. As with anal gland pain, the bitch may also turn round suddenly and frequently to inspect the affected area, often with a cry.

Two general signs of pain that are frequently shown by dogs are:

Vocalization

Dogs do not cry by means of tears, but they will utter a vocal cry at a sudden injury, such as being stepped on, or when an external injury or a painful internal organ is touched. Unprovoked whining or vocalization may indicate internal pain. Some bitches are much more stoical than others and will endure considerable pain without any vocalization.

Aggression

Any radical change in temperament may be a reaction to pain. A sudden tendency to aggression may stop when the pain is alleviated, so give the veterinary surgeon a full history before concluding that a pet has become vicious.

Diseases and conditions

The major diseases and conditions that are specific to the bitch or affect bitches more commonly are listed below in alphabetical order. It should not be forgotten, however, that bitches do also, of course, suffer from other diseases and conditions that affect dogs generally, such as canine distemper, parvovirus infection, vomiting, diarrhoea and so on. Information on all these will also be found in *The Doglopaedia*.

Anatomy, physiology and medical problems

Major diseases and conditions specific to bitches

ABORTION

Definition
Dictionaries define abortion as 'the act of bringing forth young prematurely' or loosely as 'a miscarriage'. In fact it is rare for bitches to give birth prematurely to recognizable puppies from mid-pregnancy onwards. In contrast, however, it is quite common for some successfully conceived puppies in a litter to fail to reach maturity and to be re-absorbed early in their development. There is evidence indeed that whole litters may be re-absorbed in this way. This process occurs before there is significant skeletal development, the foetus and the membranes being first liquefied. In later foetal losses the 'puppies' may become dehydrated to a black mass or 'mummy' which is expelled, often unnoticed, when the viable puppies in the litter are produced 'at term'.

Cause
The cause of abortion in bitches is not yet clearly understood but this condition has been associated with the factors listed below:

Infection –   (a) bacterial – particularly streptococcal infections and possibly *Brucella canis* infection.
  (b) viral – canine herpes virus.
  (c) toxoplasma infection.
  (d) non-specific – any infectious condition which causes a persistent high rise in body temperature in the bitch.

Hormonal imbalance –possibly a continued failure of progesterone production by the corpora lutea.

Inadequate nutrition – some vitamin deficiencies have been associated with puppy loss.

Severe trauma –   such as a road traffic accident or a fight late in pregnancy.

Teratogenic agents –   Some chemical compounds such as those contained in crop sprays and weed-killers ingested accidentally during pregnancy have been incriminated as the cause of foetal death. Most medicines are tested stringently to ensure that they are not teratogenic (i.e. cannot affect foetuses in the uterus) but despite this it is always wisest, wherever possible, to avoid medication during pregnancy.

146

Treatment
It is essential to obtain professional assistance for bitches that are aborting, or where excessive foetal re-absorption is suspected, since successful treatment depends on an accurate diagnosis of the cause.

Prevention
Ideally breeding bitches should be kept separate from other stock.

Bitches intended for breeding should be 'acclimatized' in the kennel before they are mated.

Practise good husbandry paying particular attention to disinfection and nutrition.

Avoid, wherever possible, the administration of medicines during pregnancy.

In commercial kennels consideration should be given to retiring bitches that have problems in respect of abortion or re-absorption since the fault could be an inherited one and furthermore preventive measures are unlikely to be cost-effective.

Comment
Normal exercise is most unlikely to cause abortion in pregnant bitches. There is no need to restrict normal exercise during pregnancy or to be particularly anxious if a pregnant bitch is as energetic as usual. Indeed the bitch should be encouraged to take as much exercise as she wants to, right up to whelping time.

However, training for agility contests and field trials should cease during pregnancy as these activities involve considerable effort on the part of the bitch.

It is also wise to discontinue beauty shows and obedience classes directly the bitch is mated as canine gatherings of this kind may be the source of infections.

ACROMEGALY

Definition
This is a chronic hormonal disorder characterized by an increase of soft tissue and bony structures.

Cause
Typically the condition occurs in adulthood and is caused by the production of higher than normal amounts of growth hormone by the affected animal. The disease occurs principally in intact bitches during metoestrus but it may be associated with the administration of the early progestogens for oestrus control.

Signs
Affected animals snort as they breathe in as a result of increased amounts of soft tissue around the larynx. In advanced cases the skin becomes folded, there is abdominal enlargement, thirst, increased frequency of urination, raised blood sugar levels, and fatigue. In some affected animals the spaces between the teeth become much larger than normal.

Treatment
If this condition is suspected, veterinary assistance should be sought. Cure is

often possible and may simply involve spaying or stopping medication for oestrus control.

AGALACTIA

Definition
Agalactia means, simply, failure to produce milk.

Cause
Possibly hormonal dysfunction, stress, systemic disease or in association with mastitis.

Signs
The absence of milk; restless, hungry and crying puppies.

Treatment
Veterinary assistance is required so that the cause can be identified and appropriate medication given. This may involve the administration of post-pituitary hormone by injection.

Gentle massage of the mammary glands may help to stimulate milk production in some cases.

Prevention
Ensure that nursing bitches are not stressed. In a breeding enterprise it is sensible to keep for breeding only those bitches which are proven good mothers.

CYSTITIS

Definition
Inflammation of the urinary bladder. This condition occurs quite frequently in dogs and, as is the case in other species, it is more common in females.

Cause
Cystitis is most commonly caused by a bacterial infection which ascends from the genital tract. It may also be caused or aggravated however by urinary retention resulting from an obstruction, possibly by bladder stones, or a growth, or trauma to the urinary tract, or even by prolonged confinement of a house trained bitch. Very long car journeys combined with a refusal to urinate on unfamiliar surfaces may lead to cystitis.

Signs
Affected bitches usually make frequent attempts to pass urine. Typically they will squat and strain for some time but succeed in producing only small amounts of blood-stained, often foul-smelling thick fluid. Some bitches may show signs of pain when passing urine or cry out and turn suddenly to lick the vulva immediately after urine has been passed. Do not confuse cystitis with constipation, since the straining motion may look much the same. When bitches strain to pass faeces their back is usually arched but they mostly have hollowed backs when they are passing urine.

Treatment
Veterinary assistance is required since medication involves diagnosis of the cause. It is often necessary to examine a urine sample to identify the

changes in the urine and to isolate any bacteria which may be involved so that the most appropriate antibiotic may be selected. It is essential that cases are treated without delay since once the condition becomes chronic it can become exceedingly difficult to effect a cure.

Prevention
No specific action can be taken to prevent cystitis but it does make sense to ensure that bitches always have ready access to an adequate supply of clean drinking water and that they are given frequent opportunity to pass urine. House-trained animals have been known to hold their urine for more than 24 hours when confined. The area around the vulva should be kept clean, especially in breeds with long coats, when bitches are in season and after whelping.

Comment
It is important to differentiate between the signs of cystitis and the frequent urination shown by bitches when territory marking, just before they come on heat and when they are fully in season. Such frequent squatting and the passing of small amounts of urine is a normal behaviour and requires no treatment.

DIABETES MELLITUS

Cause
Sugar diabetes results from the lack of insulin production by the pancreas or failure of the tissues to respond to the effects of the hormone leading to raised sugar levels in the blood.

Signs
The principal signs of the condition are increased thirst, more frequent urination and a voracious appetite. It mostly occurs in bitches over eight years in age.

The condition is three times more common in bitches than in dogs and its onset often occurs soon after a bitch has been on heat.

Treatment
If the signs described above are seen veterinary help should be sought without delay. Remember to take a urine sample. Such cases can often be successfully treated especially if they have not been allowed to become chronic.

DOG POX

Definition
Blister- or papule-like lesions in the vestibule which may cluster together in groups to form a raised granular area.

Cause
Unknown but probably due to a herpes virus infection.

Signs
Usually none but some bitches may periodically suddenly turn and lick their genitals.

Treatment
Veterinary help is required since cautery and the use of antibiotics may be required.

Prevention
None recommended although since the disease may be spread through coitus it is wise to avoid mating bitches to dogs which have similar lesions on their penis or sheath.

ECLAMPSIA (lactation tetany, milk fever)

Definition
In human medicine, eclampsia is defined as 'a convulsive seizure, without loss of consciousness, occurring during pregnancy or childbirth'. Although the signs are similar in bitches they occur almost invariably *after* whelping so the term eclampsia, although widely used, is technically incorrect.

Cause
The condition is associated with lowered levels of calcium and possibly glucose in the blood but the precise cause is obscure. The condition can occur even when apparently adequate amounts of calcium are being given by mouth.

Signs
Typically eclampsia occurs in bitches of the small breeds that have recently whelped, or up to 21 days post-whelping, and those that are nursing a large litter of vigorous puppies. Very occasionally bitches are affected just before whelping.
    Characteristically affected bitches become anxious, restless and hide from light, they often reject their puppies, behave abnormally, salivate and lack co-ordination. In the absence of treatment, violent contractions of the muscles occur, the bitch becomes extremely excitable and often yelps continually, or may be found collapsed. The body temperature is usually extremely high (often more than 105°F) and the heart rate is greatly increased. If the convulsions are allowed to continue the bitch will eventually become weaker and pass into a flaccid paralysis, become comatose and die.

Treatment
This is a true emergency. Veterinary attention must be sought without delay.
Usually intravenous and subcutaneous injections of calcium and glucose are given and the result of such medication is often quite spectacularly effective. Occasionally the condition will recur and further treatments will be necessary but this is by no means as common as one might expect.

Prevention
There is nothing that can be done specifically to prevent eclampsia although it makes sense to feed bitches an adequate, well-balanced diet throughout pregnancy and during lactation. It is sometimes stated that over-supplementation of the diet with calcium during pregnancy is counter-productive in that it may actually increase the likelihood of the bitch suffering from eclampsia. In small bitches with large litters it can be helpful

to give supplementary feeds to the most vigorous puppies to reduce the demand on the bitch's milk supply. The risk of this remedy is that stress will be put on the puppy's digestive system through alternating between the dam's milk and an artificial supplement which can never accurately reproduce the natural product. However, as the puppies approach two-and-a-half weeks of age, supplementation is much less likely to cause any problems.

FADING PUPPIES (the fading puppy complex, neonatal mortality)

Definition
Puppies which are apparently healthy at birth but which fail to thrive and die before they reach 14 days of age.

Cause
The condition may be associated with the following factors acting alone or in concert.

Infectious agents – (a) bacteria, particularly ß haemolytic streptococci (BHS) and *Escherichia coli (E.coli)* but possibly brucella species and anaerobic organisms.
(b) *Toxoplasma gondii.*
(c) Viruses, particularly canine adenovirus (CAV-1) and canine herpes virus.

Hypothermia – low body temperature.
Bad mothering – cannibalism and crushing.
Dystocia – difficult birth.
Congenital defects – e.g. cleft palate, absence of an anus.
Parasites – particularly *Toxocara canis* infection.
Poor nutrition of the dam – possibly too little protein, vitamin A or K deficiency or inappropriate fat content in the diet.

Signs
Affected puppies are generally vigorous and appear healthy at birth and suck avidly for the first 24 hours. Thereafter they become progressively weaker and make no further attempt to suck. They lose weight, are restless and may vocalize continually. They often have muscle spasms with over-extension of the forelimbs and spine. Occasionally the production of blood-stained faeces and urine precedes death. Not all litter-mates are necessarily affected and fading puppies may or may not be produced in subsequent litters. The signs shown by fading puppies are much the same regardless of the cause, essentially they all look the same. It is important not to dismiss the idea that the condition does not exist because one or more of the signs mentioned here is not seen.

Treatment
The treatment of fading puppies is generally unrewarding. However it does make sense to seek veterinary help in case some medication, such as the administration of an antibiotic and/or fluids, may be of help in affected puppies and possibly in litter-mates to prevent them fading too. The bitch herself may also need some treatment.

Anatomy, physiology and medical problems

In some cases it may be necessary to remove the puppies from the bitch and to feed them artificially, at least temporarily. The provision, under veterinary supervision, of an oxygen enriched atmosphere for affected puppies to breathe can be advantageous in some cases. Puppies suffering from hypothermia should be rewarmed gently; carrying them close to the human body by placing them in the pocket of a loose garment is one useful way of warming puppies gently, or an older or immobilized member of the family can hold a chilled puppy on their lap. Too rapid re-heating can be counter-productive. In breeding kennels the bodies of puppies should not be discarded before seeking veterinary help since a post-mortem examination can be extremely useful in establishing the cause of the problem.

Prevention
If a pet bitch produces a litter of fading puppies it is sensible not to have her mated again. However if there is a particular reason to breed again, the actions listed below, which are generally recommended in the case of kennels where bitches are bred regularly, should be followed.
(a) *Husbandry*
Ensure that all puppies suck within the first hour or so of being born so that they get an adequate amount of colostrum.
Provide a secluded whelping area that is adequately heated and properly ventilated.
In the case of large breeds, use a whelping box that will give protection against possible crushing.
Adopt a sound disinfection policy.
Do not introduce new dogs or bitches into a breeding kennel without a period of isolation.
● Do not introduce bitches that are already pregnant into a breeding kennel.
Instigate a regular worming policy for all stock. Consider using the more recently introduced products that are active against migrating worm larvae.
(b) *Feeding*
Provide the bitch with an adequate quantity of a well-balanced diet. Pay particular attention to diet in the last third of pregnancy and during lactation.
Do not over-supplement the diet with vitamins, especially vitamin A.
Weigh puppies daily and give supplementary artificial feeding to weak puppies, those that are less than 75 per cent of the normal birth weight for the breed, and those that are not gaining weight steadily and are on course to doubling their birth weight in a week.
(c) *Medication*
Where fading litters have been shown to be due to a bacterial infection seek veterinary advice before the bitch is mated again. A course of antibiotics given at mating, to cover the whelping period and possibly during pregnancy may be recommended. It should be realized however that this may prevent the digestive organs of the puppies from working properly and may in fact cause diarrhoea and failure to thrive. Never give antibiotics without precise veterinary advice on dosage and duration of use. Ensure that breeding bitches are properly vaccinated and boosted.
(d) *Culling*
Bitches that have dystocia, are bad mothers, or which produce abnormal

numbers of puppies with congenital defects should not be used for breeding.

(e) *Record keeping*

● Good record keeping is paramount to successful breeding. Ideally an individual record card should be kept for each breeding bitch together with a separate mating/whelping register. See also Chapter 11.

Comment

Kennel owners with a fading puppy problem should be prepared for a lengthy veterinary inspection of their premises and records, and a detailed examination of all their stock. In the majority of cases too there will be a need to examine bacterial swabs taken from the throats of all dogs, from the vulva of bitches and the sheath of any stud dogs. There may also be the necessity to examine blood samples (often a series) from bitches, puppies and dogs on the premises and to carry out post-mortem examinations on puppies that have faded. It will be obvious therefore that such an investigation can be an expensive, time-consuming necessity. Thus the rigorous application of preventive measures is well worthwhile in that considerable expense can be saved and the possible loss of a breeding line prevented.

FALSE PREGNANCY (pseudopregnancy, pseudocyesis)

Definition

This term is used to describe the condition in which bitches show the signs of pregnancy, nursing and lactation, and yet have no puppies, either because they have not been mated or have failed to conceive.

Cause

The cause of the condition is still obscure but it is probably brought about by hormonal changes at the end of met-oestrus which result in the over-production of the luteotrophic factors (prolactin).

Signs

The signs mostly occur late in met-oestrus, i.e. one to two months or so after the bitch last came on heat, and vary in type and severity from one bitch to another. Characteristically, however, most bitches will produce milk and display obvious maternal behaviour. Many of them show nervous signs including panting and breathlessness. A lot of bitches will carry shoes and other toys around the house and collect them in their bed. In severe cases some bitches will actually strain as if they are producing a litter. Once a bitch has had a false pregnancy she will probably do so again after each heat with the signs becoming progressively more severe on each occasion.

Treatment

With regard to treatment, it is worth noting that the condition is really a normal occurrence in that something like 60 per cent of bitches have false pregnancy to some degree. Indeed, in the wild state or in a breeding kennel, false pregnant bitches will be capable of nursing a litter from a bitch that has died, so the condition serves a useful purpose for the species. If the signs are mild it is probably better not to give treatment. The nervous signs will disappear more quickly if the bitch is denied sympathy and if toys and brooding objects are removed. Less milk will be produced if the carbohydrate content of the diet is reduced, if the bitch's water intake is reduced somewhat (she must not of course be denied access to water entirely for long periods) and if the amount of exercise is increased.

If the signs are severe and the actions mentioned above do not lead to an improvement, veterinary assistance should be sought. A course of hormone tablets or a hormone injection may be advised and in some cases it may be considered necessary to bathe the mammary glands with a concentrated solution of Epsom salts in water, or possibly with diluted alcohol, to help the milk to be reabsorbed. Sedatives may be prescribed to control the nervous signs, especially if the bitch is very disturbed and cannot rest.

Prevention
Veterinary surgeons often advise that bitches that have severe false pregnancy be spayed, since bitches that do not come on heat do not have false pregnancy. Spaying must wait until the false pregnancy has ended and the bitch is in full health, as bitches spayed whilst producing milk will go on doing so, often for months! The chemical control of heat, by giving regular hormone injections, helps to reduce the incidence of false pregnancy and may be advocated in some cases (see also page 171). There is no truth whatsoever in the 'old wives' tale' that it is beneficial for bitches that have false pregnancies to be mated and have one litter. Once a bitch has had a false pregnancy it will continue to do so to varying degrees after each and every subsequent heat.

INFERTILITY

Definition
The inability to produce young.

Cause
Infertility may be the result of a number of, often complex, factors acting alone or sometimes together. Usually an exhaustive veterinary investigation, often involving the examination of samples, is necessary before the cause in any particular case can be identified.

Infertility in bitches may be the result of:

(a) *Mating wrongly timed* or under the wrong conditions, e.g. when the owner and or bitch are stressed, or in unsuitable, distracting surroundings.

(b) *Physiological anomalies* leading to abnormal cycles, aberrant signs of heat, failure to ovulate etc.

(c) *Anatomical abnormalities* of the genital tract which may be congenital or acquired.

(d) *Foetal re-absorption.*

(e) *Abortion.*

(f) *Stud dog of low fertility.*

(g) *Infection of the urogenital tract* including cystitis, vaginitis and metritis.

(h) *Unwillingness to accept a particular dog.*

Treatment
Unless some obvious management problem is identified it is probably wise to

seek veterinary help early, since much time can be lost because bitches come on heat on average only twice a year. Diagnosis of the cause is fundamental to successful treatment.

MAMMARY TUMOURS

Definition
Growths within the mammary glands which increase in size at a variable rate.

Cause
Unknown, but may be sex hormone linked.

Signs
A separate, well-defined or diffuse 'lump' in the mammary gland which may show increased growth when the bitch is on heat or more regular growth throughout the cycle.

Mammary tumours are very common in bitches. Indeed surveys have shown that as many as 75 per cent of bitches will develop mammary tumours if they are left entire and allowed to have normal oestrous cycles. Approximately 40 per cent of mammary tumours in bitches are malignant resulting in secondary growth in the lymph glands, in the groin or arm pit, and in the lungs. Where there is spread to the respiratory system affected bitches become easily fatigued, breathless and may have bouts of coughing.

Treatment
Early detection is the key to successful treatment (see Chapter 3). If a 'lump' is detected in a bitch's mammary gland, even if it is only the size of a pea, veterinary help should be sought for it will certainly grow. Surgical removal involves sometimes just the excision of the lump itself or sometimes the removal of several mammary glands (mastectomy) and the local lymph nodes. The results of surgery are variable but total cures can be effected. In some cases post-surgical radiation therapy or medication with anti-cancer drugs is given.

Prevention
The risk of mammary tumour development may be reduced by spaying. Studies have shown that the incidence of mammary tumours in bitches spayed before their first heat is about one in one-hundred; in bitches spayed after their first season and before their second the incidence increases to one in ten. Bitches spayed between their second and third heats have an incidence of about one in four. Thus, in this context, early spaying has much to commend it but the matter should be discussed in depth with a veterinary surgeon since there is a need to consider other factors, such as the possible development of an infantile vulva, lack of guarding ability, incontinence and coat changes. The incidence of these side effects varies between the breeds.

The chemical control of heat can affect the incidence of mammary tumours in bitches, some of the older products may lead to an increased risk whereas the use of the more modern preparations may reduce the chance of tumour development. Again this matter should be discussed with a veterinary surgeon.

MASTITIS

Definition
Inflammation of the mammary glands.

Cause
Mastitis usually results from a bacterial infection and most commonly bacteria called streptococci are involved.

Signs
Painful, hard, hot, swollen mammary glands and the production of abnormal-looking, possibly blood-stained, milk. Usually only one gland is affected. These signs are accompanied by general malaise, fever, inappetence and, occasionally, vomiting. In some cases an abscess may form in the affected gland and this may burst to the outside.

Treatment
Veterinary assistance is required since it will usually be necessary to give a course of antibiotics by injection or by mouth. Bathing the gland with warm water containing an antiseptic or hot fomentations may be advised. In some cases careful milking by hand is advocated. In very severe cases it may be necessary for the veterinary surgeon to resort to lancing or surgical removal of the affected gland.

Prevention
It helps to ensure that all the glands are evenly used by the puppies and where this cannot be achieved, possibly because the litter is small, judicious hand-milking of glands that are very distended should be carried out.

Obviously it pays to keep a newly-whelped bitch's abdomen clean of discharges by regular washing with warm water containing a weak disinfectant such as TCP. After whelping the glands should be inspected at least once daily. If any gland stays hard and swollen despite being sucked properly by the puppies then veterinary help should be summoned without delay.

Comment
In some newly-whelped bitches, particularly those that are producing a lot of milk, some glands, most often the most posterior ones, become congested. The glands are usually hard, feel very warm to the touch and it is often difficult to express milk from the teat. The bitch's body temperature is usually not raised. Bitches affected in this way become listless, will resent such glands being sucked and, if action is not taken, the milk supply may be lost. Owners are usually recommended to bathe the affected glands with warm water and to keep trying to milk the teat gently. It is also often helpful to restrain the bitch and encourage the strongest puppy to suck the gland. If such procedures are adopted the condition will normally be resolved in 36 to 48 hours.

METRITIS (post-partum endometritis)

Definition
An acute inflammation of the lining of the uterus (the endometrium).

Cause

Bacterial infection usually occurring after the birth of a litter of puppies, possibly as a result of an unhygienic whelping, trauma associated with whelping, or the retention of foetal membranes.

Signs

Usually there is a blood-stained, evil-smelling discharge from the vulva, fever, depression, refusal to eat, possibly vomiting and reduced milk production.

Treatment

This condition requires treatment by a veterinary surgeon without delay. Antibiotics and other supportive medicaments are likely to be necessary.

Prevention

It makes sense to arrange for your veterinary surgeon to visit soon after a litter has been born since a hormone injection given at this time will help to ensure that all the afterbirths have come away and that the uterus contracts down properly. If it is considered that a uterine infection may be likely, possibly because the birth has been protracted or manual assistance through the vagina has been required, antibiotics may also be given by the veterinary surgeon prophylactically. Obviously it helps to ensure that whelping takes place in a clean environment and that the rear end of the bitch is not allowed to become caked with blood, other discharges or faeces. If you, as the breeder, have rendered manual assistance to the bitch remember to tell the veterinary surgeon.

Comment

A retained afterbirth by no means automatically leads to metritis although it will aggravate the condition once an infection gains entry to the uterus.

MISALLIANCE

Treatment

If your bitch is mated unintentionally and you do not wish to have a litter of puppies, visit your veterinary surgeon at once, certainly within 48 hours. He will discuss with you the advisability of giving an injection to avert pregnancy.

The effect of the injection will be to reverse the dominating hormones of the bitch's oestrous cycle, so that she will begin her heat all over again. Even more vigilant control will be needed, as the bitch may be even more willing to be mated on a second occasion.

More positive control methods must be employed by the owner at future heats as it is dangerous to the bitch's health to rely on averting the pregnancy after mismating.

In such cases it is possible that your veterinary surgeon may decide, when you first contact him, that it is better to take no action at the time and that he should examine your bitch in three weeks to establish whether she is in fact pregnant. If she is you can at that stage opt to let the pregnancy proceed or to have the uterus, with its developing foetuses, and ovaries removed surgically a week or so later (i.e. the bitch will be spayed). This latter action will of course ensure that such a problem will not arise again! It also avoids the administration of hormones that can cause adverse side-effects such as the development of pyometra.

NYMPHOMANIA

Definition
In bitches the term nymphomania is used to describe not only those animals which have increased libido (sexual activity) but also those that come on heat more frequently than normal and which are almost perpetually pestered by dogs, those that roam persistently and show an increased interest in dogs, and those in which pro-oestrus is abnormally prolonged.

Cause
The cause of the abnormal behaviour described above is not clear but it is generally assumed that it is associated with enlarged or persistent follicles in the ovaries that are producing increased amounts of the female sex hormone oestrogen.

Signs
Increased libido and attractiveness to dogs.
Prolonged pro-oestrus   – bitches may bleed for six weeks or more.
Short oestrous cycle   – bitches come on heat much more frequently than normal.
Roaming.

Treatment
Hormone injections may be used by veterinary surgeons to alleviate the signs in bitches that are required for breeding or to allow easier surgical intervention, but they are by no means regularly effective. Thus spaying is usually the treatment of choice in most cases. Breeders should consider the advisability of breeding from such bitches since the condition could be perpetuated, as it may well be an inherited trait.

Prevention
Nymphomania can be prevented by controlling heat by spaying or by chemical methods. Your veterinary surgeon will advise which is the most appropriate in any particular case.

Comment
Bitches will mount each other when on heat, simulating the role of the male. This is a normal behaviour which is probably better not forceably restricted in breeding bitches unless the bitches are becoming irritable with each other. Sexual behaviour of this kind usually takes place well before the bitch will stand for a male, so beware of moving the mating day forward just on the grounds that the bitch is mounting her companions.

PYOMETRA

Definition
This is probably the most important disease of the bitch's reproductive tract in that it is very common and is potentially life-threatening. As the name suggests, typically the uterus becomes filled with an accumulation of large amounts of fluid which may or may not contain bacteria.

Cause

The cause of pyometra is not entirely clear but natural causes are probably associated with a progressive hormonal imbalance and probably result from the sensitivity of the canine uterus to progesterone. The condition can be induced by the injudicious use of the older progestogens to control oestrus, or the administration of oestrogens in cases of misalliance.

Signs

Typically the condition occurs four to six weeks after a bitch has been in season and is seen primarily in older bitches (over five years old) which have not been used for breeding. The condition can occur, however, in younger bitches and cases have even been recorded in bitches after their first heat. Occasionally signs may be shown only a week or so after a bitch has been on heat. It thus makes sense for owners to observe their bitch very closely during the two month period after she has been on heat.

The toxaemia (blood poisoning), which results from the fluid in the uterus being absorbed into the blood stream, gives rise to the characteristic signs of the condition, **particularly excess thirst**, frequent urination, abdominal distension, vomiting, inappetence, shock and death.

Male dogs may be confused by the odour of a bitch with this condition and may follow her about or attempt to mate her. This may be the earliest sign the owners will have that their bitch is developing the condition.

Two main types of the condition occur, open and closed. In open cases there is a thick, red-brown, evil-smelling discharge from the vulva. In closed cases there is no discharge and the animal is much more acutely ill.

Treatment

If you suspect that your bitch is suffering from this condition, *it is most important to seek veterinary advice without delay*, since an emergency operation involving surgical removal of the uterus and ovaries may be needed to save the animal.

In some open cases it may be possible for the veterinary surgeon to treat the condition medically, by giving drugs which cause the uterus to contract or by flushing the fluid away using catheters. However, even if such methods are successful at the time the condition is very likely to recur after the next heat.

Prevention

The obvious way to prevent the condition is to have bitches spayed (ovariohysterectomy), but if the bitch is required for breeding or showing, and in some other circumstances, such a course of action may not be feasible. The chemical control of oestrus with some modern progestogens can reduce the risk of pyometra by tenfold, or possibly even a hundredfold. (Chemical control of oestrus is discussed later in this chapter.) It is wise to seek veterinary advice on this matter.

TUMOURS

Signs

Apart from mammary tumours which occur frequently and can be serious (see page 155) bitches may develop tumours in any of the organs which make up the genital tract. The signs associated with such tumours will be variable depending on the tissue affected. For example, vaginal tumours may be associated with a persistent discharge, and ovarian tumours may produce abnormal amounts of sex hormones which can lead to nymphomania, irregular cycles, persistent bleeding, coat changes and hair loss. It is always sensible to seek veterinary help if a bitch has a chronic vaginal discharge, changes in hair character or areas of hair loss, which are usually bilaterally symetrical if hormones are involved.

Comment

The condition called transmissible venereal tumour is not generally encountered in the British Isles but it may very rarely be seen in bitches around seaports and occasionally in animals leaving quarantine kennels. The tumour may take months to develop after infection. The signs are a vaginal discharge, which is usually blood-stained, and frequent licking of the genitals. Diagnosis involves endoscopy and possibly exploratory surgery. The tumour may often be successfully removed surgically and subsequent spread is rare.

UNEXPECTED PREGNANCY

Treatment

If your bitch is found to be pregnant unexpectedly, consult your veterinary surgeon without delay. He will advise you whether it is possible to spay the bitch, by removing both uterus and foetuses, if you decide that you do not want to keep the puppies.

If this is not a practical proposition, or if the bitch is wanted for breeding in future, the only option is to allow the pregnancy to proceed, and whelping to take place naturally, but resolving to cull the litter down to a maximum of two puppies which should be left to assuage the bitch's maternal instinct and to utilize the milk supply.

It may be difficult to persuade your veterinary surgeon to cull the litter, as his training has been orientated to preserving life. However, if the litter cannot be reared conveniently, and there is no assured market for the puppies, it is kinder to have them destroyed soon after birth, rather than allow them to swell the very large numbers of unwanted dogs already waiting for a home. You may have to insist firmly but gently that you want this done.

Comment

Rearing a large litter properly is an expensive exercise, and there can be no hope of recouping the cost of a litter of cross-breds and mongrels.

VAGINAL HYPERPLASIA (vaginal prolapse)

Definition

An excessive proliferation of the vaginal lining which may protrude through the vulva.

Cause

Hormonal stimulation from repeated oestrous cycles.

Signs
The condition occurs in association with heat in mature bitches and is most common in Boxers and Bulldogs. Typically a red, swollen mass, which may be as big as an egg, appears suddenly protruding through the vulva. Affected bitches spend much time licking the lump but otherwise it does not seem to cause too much concern or discomfort.

Treatment
The mass may subside without treatment as heat comes to an end but surgical removal, which is usually not too difficult, may be necessary, especially if the swollen tissue becomes traumatized. Antibiotics may need to be given to prevent the swelling from becoming infected so it is wise to seek veterinary assistance.

Prevention
In most cases veterinary surgeons will advise that bitches in which the condition has occurred are spayed to prevent recurrence.

Comment
Vaginal hypoplasia, the opposite of the condition described above, may occur in bitches that are spayed before their first oestrus. In such cases the vulva does not enlarge to its normal size and becomes sunken in the surrounding skin. The folds around the 'infantile' vulva may become infected leading to frequent licking and further inflammation so that a vicious circle is set up. A surgical operation and possibly hormonal medication may be needed to correct the condition.

VAGINAL POLYPS

Definition
The development of polyps, smooth growths, which often have stalks, on the mucous lining of the vagina.

Cause
An overgrowth of tissue, possibly resulting from continued hormonal stimulation.

Signs
A smooth mass of tissue usually 1 to 2 cm in diameter which appears suddenly, protruding through the vulva often when a bitch is coming to the end of being on heat. The swelling may be traumatized through over-zealous licking.

Treatment
Seek veterinary help; surgical removal is usually simply accomplished.

Prevention
No specific action can be taken but the condition does not occur in spayed bitches.

VAGINITIS

Definition
Inflammation of the vagina.

Cause
Usually associated with a bacterial infection.

Signs
A vaginal discharge (which is usually thick and creamy), inflammation of the lining of the vagina, frequent licking of the vulva and possibly inflammation of the surrounding skin. The colour of the discharge depends on the particular bacteria involved and the stage of the oestrous cycle when the infection occurs.

Treatment
Seek veterinary advice since it may be necessary to give a course of antibiotics, often selected following the bacteriological examination of a swab from the vagina, coupled with a vaginal douche.

Prevention
No precautions are recommended in individually owned bitches. In breeding kennels it pays to ensure that all cases are treated promptly and vigorously to reduce the weight of infection and thus the likelihood of the condition spreading.

Comment
A mild form of the condition may be seen in prepubertal bitches particularly of the larger breeds. In such cases there is usually a clear or slightly opaque discharge which often resolves without the need for medication. However if the discharge is persistent and/or the bitch licks her vulva excessively, it is wise to seek veterinary help.

Vaginitis may be associated with infertility but that is not necessarily the case.

Where many bitches in a kennel are affected treatment, usually a protracted course of antibiotics, should be given to all the animals as failure to do so is likely to lead to breeding problems and possibly fading puppies.

Bacteria can virtually always be isolated from vaginal swabs taken from bitches as the genital tract is seldom sterile. The organisms isolated are mostly harmless commensals. The results obtained from bacteriological examination of vaginal swabs need expert interpretation.

There is little point in swabbing bitches before mating to see if they are clear of infection. Elimination of bacteria from the bitch's vagina is virtually impossible and furthermore although bacteria are exchanged between dog and bitch at coitus there is no permanent affect on the normal bacterial population of the genital tract in either sex.

WORMS

A great variety of internal parasites (endoparasites) affect dogs but three types of worm (helminths) are particularly common in all breeds of dog in the British Isles:
(a) *Toxocara canis* – a roundworm

(b) *Toxascaris leonina* – another type of roundworm
(c) *Dipylidium caninum* – a tapeworm
Since bitches play a special role in the life cycle of *Toxocara canis* details relating to this parasite are given below. Information relating to the other worms can be found in *The Doglopaedia*.

Toxocara canis

Description
A round, white worm 3 to 6 in long and pointed at both ends which infects, most frequently, pregnant nursing bitches and young puppies. Adult worms are passed by puppies with or without accompanying faeces. Often several worms are passed at one time coiled up like a spring or in a loose hank.

Life cycle
The release of hormones during pregnancy activates roundworm larvae which may be lying dormant in the tissues of the bitch. Some will migrate to the uterus, mammary glands, and into the developing puppies, while others will continue their life cycle in the intestine of the bitch.

Larvae already within the puppy at birth develop into adult worms by the time the puppy is two weeks old.

The puppy will also receive more toxocara larvae via the bitch's milk, from being licked by the bitch and from her coat where traces of faeces may remain. Additionally, the bitch will take into her body eggs, larvae and adult worms when she cleans up the faeces of her puppies. Within the puppy, ingested toxocara eggs hatch into larvae which burrow through the gut wall and migrate via the liver to the lungs, where they undergo further development. As they pass through they may cause respiratory problems. Some of these larvae are distributed by the blood to other tissues where they remain dormant. Other maturing larvae are coughed up, swallowed, and pass down into the digestive system where they mature into adult worms, which lay thousands of eggs within the intestine. These eggs, with or without adult worms, pass out in the faeces, to lie on plants, grass or soil, sometimes for many months, until ingested by another susceptible dog, when they start the toxocara life cycle all over again.

Signs
It may be taken that all young puppies and nursing bitches have a roundworm burden, whether you see any live adult worms or not. A very heavy worm burden in puppies will cause breathing problems, coughing and possibly pneumonia, while the larvae are migrating through the lungs. Abdominal pain, diarrhoea, retarded growth, a pot-bellied, poor appearance, and harsh coat will be seen when the stomach and intestines are full of worms, which may eventually form a complete blockage of the digestive system. Badly affected puppies whine and adopt a characteristic straddle-legged position.

Action
In puppies especially, a heavy toxocara burden can be very debilitating, even life threatening, and because of the added risk that puppies are most likely to be handled by children, it is very important indeed that they are wormed early. Medication should be given at two-and-a-half to three weeks

of age, and at two week intervals until three months of age, again at six months old, and then twice yearly for the rest of their lives. If you have just purchased a puppy find out whether it has been wormed and if so with what. Discuss with your veterinary surgeon the need for further dosing.

If you have a litter of puppies, weigh the bitch and each of her puppies, and obtain from the veterinary surgeon an effective wormer (vermifuge) at the right strength for each animal. Worming lactating bitches, as well as the puppies is particularly important.

When you have carried out a worming for any infestation, or if you see worms in the faeces, be sure to pick up and dispose of the faeces properly. Worm infected faeces should not be put on to a compost heap, nor should they be dug into the garden, as many worm eggs can survive for years in soil. Burning, or putting into the WC, is the best disposal method. In kennels the number of eggs can be reduced by vigorous scrubbing with large quantities of hot water and detergent and, if practical, the use of a flame gun – the eggs are resistant to most common disinfectants.

Comment
Recent research has produced a vermifuge which is said to act on the encysted larvae in the bitch's tissues during late pregnancy and soon after whelping. This remedy is only available through veterinary surgeons, but if you mean to breed your bitch it is well worth making enquiries about this new development.

Wormers purchased over the counter are not likely to be so effective and the old-fashioned remedies may cause purging and abdominal discomfort.

With many modern wormers, you are unlikely to see any live worms passed, as they are digested within the animal and pass out unnoticed in the faeces. **Do not discontinue worming because you see no worms passed**.

Risk to humans
The sticky eggs of *Toxocara canis*, too small to be visible to the eye, may be picked up from soil, grass or from an animal's coat or bedding, and may be subsequently swallowed – children run the greatest risk. Eggs that have been eaten in this way can hatch into larvae in the human gut but will not develop into adult worms. Instead, the larvae, which are very small, will travel around the body and become embedded in the body tissues, usually causing no problems at all. Very rarely, however, these migrating larvae may settle, by chance, in a particularly sensitive tissue such as the retina. In some cases where this has happened there has been impairment of vision. Sensible precautions will reduce any such risks to infinitesimal odds.

Precautions
● Insist that any puppy you buy has been wormed at least twice, with an effective wormer, before it is eight weeks old.
● Continue with a worming programme as described earlier.
● Dispose of puppy faeces and post-worming faeces properly.
● Do not allow small children to handle very young puppies and nursing bitches, and do not allow dogs to lick children's faces or to share biscuits or ice-creams.
● Do not allow dogs to eat off crockery used by humans.
● Insist that children wash their hands and faces after handling a puppy.
● Keep long-haired pups well-groomed especially around the hindquarters.

Note
Freshly passed dog faeces are not a hazard in this respect, as the eggs of *Toxocara canis* need some time to mature outside the host before they are infective, so that while stepping in a pile of faeces is unpleasant, it is not dangerous. *Toxocara canis* cannot cause threadworm infection in children since that condition is due to another species of worm.

Disease prevention

There is no doubt that when it comes to illness, prevention is far better than cure. By taking sensible precautions you can save your bitch suffering and save yourself expense and inconvenience.

Emergency operations and treatment cost more and invariably they are needed at an inconvenient time – typically over Christmas or just before you are about to depart on holiday. Thus, wherever possible, the wise owner will think ahead and take precautions.

Essentially, it is sensible to think in terms of:
- vaccination;
- health checks – carried out by yourself and professionally;
- preventing obesity;
- controlling heat.

It makes sense too, to consider taking out insurance to help pay those unexpected bills. Most veterinary surgeons will be able to give you some details on the schemes that are available and help you decide which policy will be most appropriate for your needs. For example, one company accepts payments of annual premiums by quarterly instalments, thus making it easier for the new owner to start on insurance cover immediately.

You should note that all the insurance companies exclude preventative vaccinations and elective spaying and most have an upper age limit beyond which they no longer accept dogs for enrolment, but it is important to choose a company which will insure your dog for life if it is enrolled when young. It is often the early years, and again old age, which prove to be the most expensive in terms of veterinary fees.

One company will also insure your bitch for veterinary fees which may occur during pregnancy and whelping, so it is worthwhile reviewing all the policies on offer. Ask your veterinary surgeon which company he finds the most satisfactory to deal with.

Third party insurance cover is a social necessity in case your dog injures another person, possibly quite innocently by tripping them, or in case it kills livestock. It is more satisfactory to have this insurance with a company specializing in animal insurance.

The major infectious diseases affecting dogs

1. Canine distemper
A life-threatening disease caused by a virus infection and usually complicated by secondary bacterial invasion. The initial signs of the disease are a cough accompanied by high temperature, lethargy, lack of appetite, reddened eyes, runny nose, noisy breathing and, possibly diarrhoea and vomiting. Subsequently, usually after some weeks, nervous signs – a

Anatomy, physiology and medical problems

nervous twitch (chorea), fits or paralysis – may develop often accompanied by thickening of the pads and the nose (hyperkeratosis). The latter signs earned this stage the name 'hardpad', once thought to be a separate disease but now known to be a sequel to distemper.

Dogs that develop nervous signs are most unlikely to make a full recovery.

Canine distemper used to be rife nation-wide before effective vaccines were introduced more than 25 years ago. Now the disease is mostly confined to unvaccinated populations in large cities. Thus dogs in more rural surroundings do not receive a natural boost to their immunity by exposure to infected animals and therefore booster vaccinations are most important.

2. Infectious canine hepatitis (also known as Rubarth's disease or canine viral hepatitis)

This highly contagious disease is caused by a canine adenovirus (CAV-1). It has no connection with hepatitis in man. Puppies in their first year of life are most commonly affected but all ages of dog are susceptible. The major early signs are generalized illness and lack of appetite, with pale conjunctivae and gums, greatly raised temperature, vomiting, diarrhoea, abdominal pain. Yellowing of the whites of the eyes (jaundice) may occur. Some 20 per cent of dogs which are recovering from hepatitis show a blue clouding over the whole of the cornea of one or both eyes (blue eye). In most cases this clouding will disappear within a few days without additional treatment but, if it persists, veterinary advice should be sought. A similar clouding of the eye may be seen in some puppies after vaccination against infectious canine hepatitis when live CAV-1 vaccines are used.

This infection has been linked with puppy mortality in breeding kennels.

3. Leptospirosis

This is a disease caused by a group of bacteria called Leptospires. Dogs can be infected by two of these, *Leptospira icterohaemorrhagiae* and *Leptospira canicola*.

Leptospira icterohaemorrhagiae
Incubation Period
Five to 15 days.
Transmission
This bacteria is carried by rats, and is transmitted to dogs which kill rats or play with dead vermin. Dogs may also be infected by rat urine on the ground, in ponds or water bowls, or on fallen fruit etc., which may be eaten by dogs. The disease is particularly prevalent amongst dogs on farms, at ports and in mining areas. The disease is characterized by high temperature, severe thirst, increased frequency of urination, abdominal pain, depression, possible ulceration of the mouth, coated tongue, diarrhoea containing blood, jaundice and persistent vomiting.

Leptospires excreted in the urine of the dog during this illness, and possibly for months after apparent recovery, can infect other dogs and also humans, where the illness is known as Weils disease. Particular attention should be paid to hygiene when attending to a sick dog, and especially when clearing up urine.

Leptospira canicola (also known as lamp post disease and Stuttgart disease)
The signs shown by infected bitches are similar to those described under

Leptospira icterohaemorrhagiae except that jaundice is much less frequently seen and less marked. Mild cases with few signs occur quite frequently. This infection can cause damage to the kidneys which may become critical later in life.

Most of the dogs which recover will excrete bacteria in their urine for up to a year. It must be a matter for consideration whether such dogs should be kept on the same premises as young puppies.

It should be remembered that these infections can be passed on to man. Great care must be taken when nursing affected dogs.

4. Canine parvovirus infection (CPV)
Two forms of canine parvovirus infection are recognized.

Canine parvovirus myocarditis
Where the dam of a litter has not been vaccinated and has not been infected by the disease, she will have no protection to pass on to her puppies. Canine parvovirus, which always seeks out the cells of the body which are multiplying most rapidly, will concentrate in the heart muscle of newly born puppies which are exposed to the virus. The heart muscle is weakened or completely destroyed. The effect is not usually seen until the puppies become active, at four to 10 weeks, when seemingly healthy pups will suddenly collapse and die after playing or feeding. The whole litter is usually affected, although some individuals may survive longer than others, none of them should be sold as sound puppies. This form of CPV is now becoming rare, as most breeding bitches will have some antibody to the infection either through previous exposure to the disease or through vaccination.

Intestinal form of canine parvovirus infection
This is the most common form of CPV. It affects dogs from four weeks of age into old age, but it is most severe in their first year when the disease can be quickly fatal. The signs seen in this form of the disease are depression, severe protracted vomiting, abdominal pain, refusal of food and water, and very profuse diarrhoea, often with considerable blood content. CPV infection is usually rapid in resolution, and if the dog is going to survive it will be noticeably better within four to five days from the start of the illness. When puppies are badly affected by CPV, growth may be stunted and the puppy may be bald for up to a year. The digestive system of affected puppies may always be delicate and they may never make completely satisfactory pets.

It is very difficult to eradicate CPV from a home or a kennel. Sodium hypochlorite (domestic bleach) and formalin are the only common disinfectants active against CPV. However some modern commercial products are effective in this respect and offer other advantages such as prolonged activity and efficacy in the presence of organic material. Your veterinary surgeon will advise. Where a single puppy has died of CPV on domestic premises, it is wise to wait at least six months before introducing another puppy.

5. Kennel Cough (infectious canine tracheobronchitis)
This condition is caused by a complex package of viruses and bacteria which may vary in content at each outbreak, so making it possible for susceptible dogs to have kennel cough more than once during the season (usually May to November), or to have kennel cough every year.

While this disease is mainly transmitted from dog to dog where a number of animals are gathered under one roof, e.g. at a dog show or in boarding kennels, it is possible for the singly-owned pet dog to suffer from kennel cough too. Dogs become infected by breathing in infected airborne particles. The infective agents are carried in the air in a manner similar to the way human colds or influenza are spread. The peak time for infection is the summer, when dogs which do not normally mix with others are gathered in boarding kennels.

The most important, and often only, sign is a protracted harsh cough which sounds as though the dog has a bone stuck in its throat. Some affected dogs may have a discharge from their eyes and nose, and tonsillitis. Affected adult dogs usually remain relatively cheerful, their body temperature is normal and they continue to eat as usual. In puppies however the disease may be complicated by a secondary pneumonia which can cause death.

While this disease is trying and can be long lasting, it is seldom life threatening except possibly in the case of very young puppies.

Problems arise because dogs may be infectious to others before they show signs and after they have apparently recovered. Chronic carrier dogs may also exist.

Vaccination

Fortunately it is possible these days to protect dogs against all the diseases described above by prophylactic vaccination. In the case of canine distemper a modified live virus vaccine is used. Live and killed CAV-1 vaccines have been produced for many years to stimulate immunity to infectious canine hepatitis, but more recently live vaccines based on a related virus CAV-2 have become available. These latter vaccines have the advantage of stimulating good protection generally and in the respiratory tract, with a much reduced incidence of side effects; there is no risk that dogs will develop blue eye post vaccination.

The leptospiral vaccines that are available contain killed bacteria and two doses are required to stimulate immunity. The first parvovirus vaccines to be made available were, in fact, cat vaccines but these were rapidly replaced by vaccines containing killed virus obtained from dogs. More recently vaccines containing live modified dog virus have become available and the latest vaccines in the latter category are claimed to have the ability to stimulate protection even in young puppies that have received passive protection from their mothers through the first milk (colostrum). Their availability has simplified considerably the vaccination of puppies and many fewer doses are required than was the case previously.

All the vaccines mentioned above are given by injection under the skin and they are often combined together to reduce the number of injections that are required.

The vaccine designed to give protection against the bacterium *Bordetella bronchiseptica* – the major cause of kennel cough – contains live organisms and it is given as drops into the dog's nose. Administration by this route stimulates dogs to produce protective antibodies locally in the respiratory tract just where they are required and so provides a prompt immunity. Some of the combined distemper, hepatitis and leptospiral vaccines also contain live canine parainfluenza virus which may be a cause of kennel cough.

As will be appreciated from the information given above, vaccination of dogs is not a simple matter. Not only is there a need to choose a specific vaccine to suit a particular case but also veterinary surgeons have to decide the best times to vaccinate, bearing in mind the dog's background, the risk of infection and local circumstances. There is certainly much more to vaccination than just giving a 'jab'.

New owners are advised to contact a veterinary surgeon by telephone as soon as they get their puppy – if not before – to seek advice in respect of vaccination. It is likely that he will advise that the puppy is vaccinated initially at six to eight weeks of age and then again when she is 12 weeks old. No doubt too he will advise that booster doses are given annually to maintain immunity to the life threatening diseases. Vaccination against kennel cough will mostly be advised before boarding, usually once a year, but in the case of bitches that are likely to be exposed continually to the risk of infection, e.g. in animals taken regularly to shows, vaccination at six monthly intervals may be advised.

Finally, the details given above apply equally to dogs and bitches. In the case of breeding bitches however there may be a need to 'time' vaccination so that maximum amounts of antibody are passed by the bitches to their puppies at birth to give them early passive protection. Vaccination may sometimes be advocated during pregnancy. Your veterinary surgeon is the best person to advise in respect of this matter and it is wise to consult him before your bitch is mated so that the need for vaccination can be considered and optimal timings worked out.

Health checks

Vaccination is a very obvious way to help ensure that your bitch stays fit and well, but you can do more! You should check her regularly yourself for signs of illness and take her regularly to the veterinary surgery for a routine health check – often that can be done at the same time as booster vaccinations.

In *The Doglopaedia* there is a table which indicates what checks should be

Table 9.2: Health checks

Daily	Eyes	Look for the presence of excessive discharge or pus in the conjunctival sac. Check that the cornea is clear and not cloudy that the dog can see clearly. The sight can be checked readily by throwing a titbit for the dog to catch.
	Faeces	Note consistency, colour. Check frequency. Look for undigested food, foreign bodies (plastic bags, cardboard etc.).
Weekly	Ears	Check that there is no discharge or odour coming from the ear canal. Examine ear flaps for presence of wounds or swelling.
	Paws	Examine for wounds, cracks, cysts between the toes and nail-bed infections.
Monthly	Skin/Coat	Look for areas of thickened skin and baldness, particularly on elbows and hocks. Check for evidence of excessive scratching and the presence of abrasions. Test the skin's mobility. Look for worm segments around the anus. Check the whole body for new warts, lumps under the skin, etc. It is a good idea to chart these on a sketch of the dog's outline so that you can monitor their rate of growth.
	Claws	Check nail beds for signs of inflammation. Examine claws for length and presence of splits. Don't forget the dew-claws.
	Teeth	Check the teeth and mouth for dental decay, accumulation of tartar and inflammation of the gums.

made and when. In short we advocate that the regime in Table 9.2 is adopted.

If any significant abnormalities are noted veterinary attention should be sought since in the majority of conditions early treatment is likely to be more effective and less costly.

In the case of bitches, the following additional checks should be made:

Table 9.3: Additional health checks for bitches

Daily	Urination	Note the frequency of urination and if possible the colour of urine passed. More frequent 'squatting' may indicate that your bitch is about to come on heat or that there is an impending infection of the urogenital tract.
	Thirst	Try to gain some idea of how much water is being drunk by your bitch. Excessive thirst may indicate impending pyometra, diabetes or a urinary tract infection.
	Behaviour	Take note of any abnormal behaviour that might indicate that your bitch is about to come on heat, have false pregnancy or indicate the onset of some illness.
Weekly	Vulva	Look for wounds, signs of excessive licking or a discharge. Pay particular attention at the time the bitch is on heat and for the following three months.
	Mammary Glands	Look for the presence of milk by gently squeezing the teats. Feel all the mammary glands for the presence of tumours and record their size. It is particularly important to carry out this examination when the bitch is on heat and weekly in the subsequent three months.

Finally remember to take your bitch for her annual booster vaccination and ask for a health check to be carried out at the same time by your veterinary surgeon. If you spot the need for an insecticidal shampoo, a worming dose or the like, then get them from a reputable source, preferably the veterinary surgeon – cheaper products can prove more expensive in the long run.

Preventing obesity

If you want to have a fit, active bitch that you can breed from and which will give you real pleasure, don't let her get fat. It pays to monitor your bitch's weight and girth regularly and if you find that she is becoming obese it pays to do something about it because fat dogs are prone to: joint disease; heart disease; breathing difficulties; liver disease; skin disease; infectious diseases; diabetes; and digestive disorders.

Furthermore, they are likely to die prematurely.

In theory, controlling obesity is easy – all that you have to do is reduce the calorie intake by 10 to 20 per cent and gradually increase the amount of exercise the bitch is given. However, such a procedure is difficult to implement as most owners have no real measure of how much their bitch eats and the calorific value of the many and varied items that are fed. Furthermore, such a procedure, by its very simplicity, offers little in the way of incentive. Feeding home-made slimming diets is also mostly doomed to failure because of the anthropomorphic tendencies of most owners, the need for messy cooking arrangements, which is aggravated by the requirement to feed dogs that are slimming more frequently, and the fact that such diets can lead to vitamin deficiencies. Far better to feed one of the ready formulated low-calorie diets that are available in cans or as dry food. If such diets are fed precisely as directed and with perseverance, having set goals, a steady weight reduction will result in great benefit to the bitch. Animals that have become lethargic and less playful will be restored to a new vigour giving increased pleasure to their owners. These products can be obtained from your veterinary surgeon. (See also Chapter 4.)

Controlling heat

In the 1950s it was common for veterinary surgeons to spay bitches on request for the convenience of owners. The operation, an ovariohys-terectomy (removal of the ovaries and uterus), was essentially carried out to limit the nuisance of heat – the unsightly vulva swelling, blood spotting and persistent pestering by roaming males. Such a major operation is regarded by many as being a mutilation and the morality of following such a course of action is questionable. However, the situation is changing since it is now recognized that ovariohysterectomy offers a health advantage to bitches in that it will prevent pyometra and false pregnancy and will, particularly if it is carried out at an early age, reduce the incidence of mammary tumours. Furthermore, modern chemical methods of heat control have been developed which mean that such benefits can be obtained without having to resort to surgery, where that is considered unsafe or to carry an unacceptable risk of side-effects such as incontinence, hair loss, obesity and so on.

Such methods can be used also, in contrast to spaying, where bitches are already on heat when presented or where owners may wish to breed from their bitches some time in the future.

The benefits of heat control, by spaying, can be summarized as follows:
- To provide a health advantage – properly done, it is good preventative medicine.
- To help prevent unwanted puppies. Such animals often provide much ammunition for the anti-dog lobby.
- To make bitches more consistently companionable.
- To make bitch owning easier.

But how does chemical control compare? How is it done and what method is recommended?

In order to answer those questions it is necessary to explain briefly the development of progestogens, the synthetic hormones which were developed originally for use in the human contraceptive 'pill'.

Progesterone, the female sex hormone responsible for maintaining pregnancy, was first isolated in the mid-1930s. In 1937 it was discovered that this naturally occurring hormone inhibited the release of eggs in rabbits.

This finding naturally excited the interest of the pharmaceutical companies since it was realized that it could pave the way to effective contraception in women. The first hurdle to overcome was the fact that progesterone is only short-acting and was effective only when given by injection. Work concentrated therefore, on finding new related drugs that could be given by mouth. In the event several thousands of compounds were developed which could be taken orally and which were more potent than progesterone itself. The great majority, however, fell by the wayside because of toxicity and other side-effects, or because they were too expensive to produce. These substances, which act like progesterone in the body, are called progestogens.

Experiments in various animal species showed that the progestogens have a variety of effects; for example, they prevent the development of eggs in the ovaries and their release, they interfere with the movement of eggs and sperm through the female sex organs, and affect the timing of all those events which need to be very closely synchronized if an animal is to become pregnant. Not surprisingly, therefore, they are extremely effective contraceptives.

Apart from these desired effects the compounds also stimulate the lining of the womb in bitches and it has been shown that large amounts given for a long time can cause severe changes such as pyometra.

In respect of the actions noted above, it is important to stress that not all progestogens produce all the effects mentioned to the same degree. In scientific terms it is said that 'the biological activity of progestogens is related to their structure'. Thus a fundamental point to appreciate is that although the drugs may be related in general terms, they do not all have identical effects. That variability is particularly true in respect of side-effects on the womb.

Researchers interested in the application of progestogens in bitches investigated three possible methods of use:

1. *Suppression of heat* – the administration of the compound at the beginning of pro-oestrus to shorten the duration of heat and to prevent pregnancy if mating does occur.
2. *Temporary suppression of heat* – medication just before an anticipated heat, to delay the heat until a more convenient time.
3. *Permanent postponement of heat* – continued dosing at regular intervals after suppression or temporary postponement of heat to keep the bitch in a permanent state of anoestrus.

The first compounds to be used strongly stimulated the lining of the womb, and precisely controlled methods of administration had to be devised to make them reasonably safe. It was necessary, for example, to control very carefully the amount given, to avoid dosing at certain stages of the oestrous cycle, and to limit the duration of medication. The original injectable preparation used in bitches is a good example – its use in the United Kingdom being restricted by strong contra-indications and warnings. In fact, the product was withdrawn from use in the United States many years ago and is not permitted for use in that country to this day.

Similarly, the oral product developed in the United Kingdom cannot be used for permanent postponement of heat because prolonged dosing can cause pyometra. It can, however be used for temporary postponement and suppression of heat, but in the latter situation dosing must be carefully timed if the problems of rebound or early oestrus, subsequent to dosing, are to be avoided. The advent of a more recently discovered progestogen has changed that situation dramatically since it is very effective in blocking the development of eggs and ovulation but has much less effect on the womb. In practical terms this means that it can be given without impediment by injection at any stage in the oestrous cycle and can be used for long-term permanent postponement of heat, by giving injections at three and four monthly intervals to begin with and then every five months, as well as for the suppression of heat.

Spaying offers some significant advantages to bitches principally in terms of improved health. How do the modern products produced for the chemical control of heat compare? First, spaying, properly done will remove any risk of pyometra or false pregnancy. Chemical control with the latest products will reduce the incidence of these conditions by at least tenfold and possibly one-hundredfold. Seventy-five per cent of unspayed bitches will develop mammary tumours, this incidence is reduced to just under 10 per cent in bitches spayed between their first and second heats. Unfortunately the older progestogens had a tendency to increase the risk of mammary tumours developing possibly because they induced growth hormone. The more recently developed compounds do not appear to have such a side-effect and clinical trials have shown a numerical reduction in the incidence of mammary tumours in animals given regular injections for the permanent postponement of heat.

Thus it will be seen that the most modern products can also offer a significant health advantage without many risks. Spaying offers more in respect of health advantages but does, of course, carry some risks because it is a major abdominal operation requiring full anaesthesia. Furthermore, side-effects like urinary incontinence, especially in large breeds such as Old English Sheepdogs, obesity, infantile vulva and excessive hair growth or hair loss (especially in the short-coated breeds) are quite commonly seen following the operation. It is necessary, therefore, for bitch owners to weigh in the balance with the aid of their veterinary surgeon, which is the best option for their particular pet. Sometimes, for example, in small Terrier breeds or Poodles, where there is no intention of breeding in the future, the balance will swing in favour of spaying. But in the case of large breeds, with short hair or which are already obese, hormonal control may be the better option. In situations between these extremes, the balance may be one way or the other.

Finally, it should be stressed that hormonal control of oestrus does not replace spaying, it is simply another option to consider where there is a reason to hesitate to spay a particular animal.

What to do in relation to heat control

Whether you intend to breed from your bitch or not, discuss with your veterinary surgeon how you can obtain the advantages offered by heat control. It makes sense to talk to him about this matter at the time your dog is given her primary vaccination course.

Spaying is a once-only operation which is generally safe and very effective, but it may not be a sensible procedure in some animals and, of course, it is not applicable in bitches intended for future breeding. The operation needs to be planned in advance since it is not usually done when bitches are already on heat. The initial cost is relatively high but looked at in the long term it is the least expensive and most convenient way to obtain all the health advantages offered by heat control.

Chemical Control

Suppression of heat

If your bitch comes on heat unexpectedly at an inconvenient time consult your veterinary surgeon without delay. He may give a simple injection or dispense a course of tablets for you to give daily for about a week or so. In either case the period of bleeding and attractiveness to dogs will be shortened from three weeks to four to five days and if your bitch is mated after that time she should not become pregnant. Spaying is not an alternative in this situation. Suppression of heat does not, unfortunately, offer the health advantages that can be obtained with other methods of heat control.

Temporary postponement of heat

If you think it is likely that your bitch will come on heat at an inconvenient time, e.g. when you are about to go on holiday or before a particularly important show or series of shows, ask your veterinary surgeon about the possibility of postponing heat temporarily by chemical means. Again he may advise a course of tablets to be taken daily or give a simple injection depending on how long you need to delay the onset of heat. Ideally in this situation you should consult your veterinary surgeon, preferably one month, but at least 14 days, in advance.

In breeding kennels temporary postponement can sometimes be used with advantage to achieve litter spacing, your vet will advise. Temporary postponement of heat does not offer the health advantages that can be obtained with other methods.

Permanent postponement of heat

Regular hormone injections given usually at five to six monthly intervals, may be used to prevent bitches coming on heat permanently. This is a valid alternative to spaying where veterinary surgeons hesitate to spay and does keep open the option of breeding in the future. If dosing is stopped bitches usually come on heat six months (range three to nine months) after the last dose is given. Permanent postponement with modern products offers the health advantages of heat control but not to the same extent as spaying. In the long term chemical control is more expensive than spaying and, of course, it is necessary to remember to take your bitch for injections at the appointed time, so it is less convenient. If you wish to consider this option ideally it is best to let your bitch have her first season naturally and contact your veterinary surgeon about three months later to discuss what action should be taken.

Feminine 'What ifs'

Introduction

The first part of this section seeks to answer questions which worry bitch owners when signs are seen which may indicate illness. Each topic begins with the words 'What if my bitch......?' and it is hoped that the details given will help owners decide whether:

● The sign is normal and no action is required.
● Some simple 'treatment' is needed.
● First aid action is indicated.
● Veterinary help should be obtained and, if so, how urgently.

Use Figure 9.1 or the list on page 176 to identify the relevant number.

In the second part we provide some solutions to common problems and mishaps which occur in the household and generally in respect of bitch ownership. The information given will, hopefully, help owners decide what action to take in the short and long term to overcome and prevent the difficulty.

Note

Ideally readers should refer to the 'Feminine what ifs' in conjunction with Chapter 4, Part I and Chapter 7 in *The Doglopaedia*.

'What if my bitch . . .?'

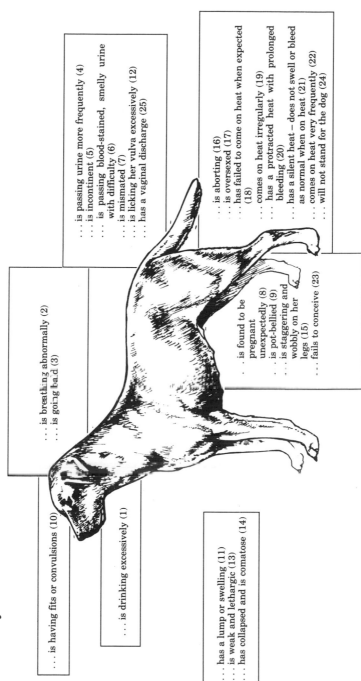

. . . is having fits or convulsions (10)

. . . is drinking excessively (1)

. . . is breathing abnormally (2)
. . . is going bald (3)

. . . is passing urine more frequently (4)
. . . is incontinent (5)
. . . is passing blood-stained, smelly urine with difficulty (6)
. . . is mismated (7)
. . . is licking her vulva excessively (12)
. . . has a vaginal discharge (25)

. . . is aborting (16)
. . . is oversexed (17)
. . . has failed to come on heat when expected (18)
. . . comes on heat irregularly (19)
. . . has a protracted heat with prolonged bleeding (20)
. . . has a silent heat – does not swell or bleed as normal when on heat (21)
. . . comes on heat very frequently (22)
. . . will not stand for the dog (24)

. . . is found to be pregnant unexpectedly (8)
. . . is pot-bellied (9)
. . . is staggering and wobbly on her legs (15)
. . . fails to conceive (23)

. . . has a lump or swelling (11)
. . . is weak and lethargic (13)
. . . has collapsed and is comatose (14)

Figure 9.1. Feminine 'what ifs'. Use the figure to identify the relevant 'what if number. The 'what ifs' are also listed numerically on page 178.

Diseases and conditions – 'what if my bitch ....?'

1 is drinking excessively
2 is breathing abnormally
3 is going bald
4 is passing urine more frequently
5 is incontinent
6 is passing blood-stained, smelly urine with difficulty
7 is mismated
8 is found to be pregnant unexpectedly
9 is pot-bellied
10 is having fits or convulsions
11 has a lump or swelling
12 is licking her vulva excessively
13 is weak and lethargic
14 has collapsed and is comatose
15 is staggering and wobbly on her legs
16 is aborting
17 is over-sexed
18 has failed to come on heat when expected
19 comes on heat irregularly
20 has a protracted heat with prolonged bleeding
21 has a silent heat – does not swell or bleed as normal when on heat
22 comes on heat very frequently
23 fails to conceive
24 will not stand for the dog
25 has a vaginal discharge

Table 9.4: "What ifs" in relation to diseases and conditions

No.	What if my bitch....	Possible causes specific to bitches	Action/Comment
1	is drinking excessively (Normal water consumption is 40–50 ml/kg)	Pyometra, diabetes mellitus – usually related to a recent heat in middle-aged bitches.	This is a serious sign in bitches and unless it is obviously associated with hot weather, excessive exercise, or the demands of lactation, *veterinary help should be sought without delay*. It may be useful to take a urine sample with you when consulting your vet.
2	is breathing abnormally	First stage of labour. Eclampsia. Possibly mammary tumours that have spread to the lungs.	Veterinary assistance will be required so that the cause can be identified and the appropriate medication given. The urgency will depend on the severity, the acuteness of the signs and the well-being of the bitch in other respects.
3	is going bald	In association with spaying. Ovarian tumours. The baldness is usually bilaterally symmetrical where it is associated with abnormal hormone levels or balance.	Because successful treatment depends on correct diagnosis, which in turn may be supported by the examination of samples, veterinary consultation is sensible but is not urgently required.
4	is passing urine more frequently	Cystitis, pyometra, diabetes mellitus, acromegaly, vaginitis. Territory marking in association with heat.	Unless obviously associated with territory marking, veterinary attention should be sought within 24 hours so that the cause may be diagnosed and proper treatment instigated. Take a urine sample.

Table 9.4: (cont.)

5	is incontinent	In relation to spaying, particularly before puberty (and in large breeds), over submissiveness, cystitis.	Seek veterinary help. Unless the urine contains blood there is time to try to establish whether the incontinence is linked to some specific factor or event.
6	is passing blood-stained, smelly urine with difficulty	Cystitis, vaginitis, vaginal tumours, possibly metritis and pyometra.	Obtain veterinary treatment without delay, unless it is certain that the problem is simply associated with heat or recent whelping. Take a urine sample to the surgery.
7	is mis-mated		If you wish to prevent the risk of pregnancy consult your veterinary surgeon without delay and certainly within 48 hours. (See also page 157.)
8	is found to be pregnant unexpectedly		Consult your veterinary surgeon as soon as is convenient, since it may be possible to spay the bitch if pregnancy is not too far progressed and you are anxious not to have a litter of puppies. (See also page 160.)
9	is pot-bellied	Pregnancy, false pregnancy, cystitis with urinary retention, pyometra.	As there are numerous causes veterinary attention should be sought. If the abdominal enlargement is gross and has appeared suddenly, or if the bitch is also vomiting or collapsed, seek help urgently.
10	is having fits or convulsions	Eclampsia.	This is a true emergency, *call the vet day or night*, be sure to tell him if your bitch is suckling a litter.
11	has a lump or swelling	Mammary tumour, mastitis, mammary congestion, vaginal hyperplasia, vaginal polyps.	Except in the case of suspected mastitis or vaginal prolapse that has become traumatized, veterinary help is not required urgently. However it is better to ask for assistance earlier rather than later.
12	is licking her vulva excessively	In association with heat, cystitis, vaginal hyperplasia, vaginal polyps and vaginitis; possibly pyometra, metritis, and dog pox.	Since the causes are legion diagnosis by a veterinary surgeon is required. The urgency of the situation will be determined by the bitch's general appearance and/or the presence of other more worrying signs such as persistent vomiting.
13	is weak and lethargic	Imminent eclampsia, pregnancy, diabetes mellitus.	In such cases it is always wise to seek veterinary attention. This need only be done immediately if the presence of other signs dictates otherwise it might be more helpful to wait for a few days so that the vet will have more information on which to base a diagnosis.

Table 9.4: (cont.)

14	has collapsed or is comatose	Eclampsia, pyometra, in association with diabetes mellitus.	Call a veterinary surgeon urgently.
15	is staggering or wobbly on her legs	Eclampsia, possibly pyometra or diabetes mellitus.	Call a veterinary surgeon without delay.
16	is aborting	See page 146	Call a veterinary surgeon urgently – be prepared to answer queries in respect of when the bitch was mated etc.
17	is over-sexed	A hormonal imbalance.	Veterinary help will be required but first ensure that the circumstances are properly understood so that a good history can be provided.
18	has failed to come on heat when expected	A hormonal problem, particularly thyroid deficiency. General illness, undernourishment. Occasionally old age.	Veterinary help will be needed if the bitch is required for breeding. Often it is necessary to give hormone medication. Introducing the bitch to others that have come on heat may help. Be patient over the winter months. This is not in itself a serious sign or a cause for worry in pet bitches.
19	comes on heat irregularly	Possibly a thyroid deficiency, general illness or undiscovered adrenal gland problems.	This is not necessarily a problem in pet bitches but will need correction in bitches used for breeding.
20	has a protracted heat with prolonged bleeding	Excessively high or prolonged oestrogen levels, possibly associated with follicular cysts, ovarian tumours or treatment for misalliance.	Veterinary help should be sought since the condition may predispose the bitch to other more serious problems and it causes considerable inconvenience and disturbance in the neighbourhood.
21	has a silent heat, i.e. shows most signs of being in season but there is no blood-stained discharge	Possibly lower oestrogen levels than normal.	In pet bitches the condition is only a problem in that they may be mismated and become pregnant. In breeding bitches there will be a need in most cases to have vaginal smears examined so that the correct time to mate the bitch can be determined.
22	comes on heat very frequently	The reason for some bitches cycling every three to four months is not clearly understood.	It makes sense to obtain veterinary help because if the condition is not corrected other problems such as pyometra, metritis, etc., may result. Furthermore it is generally inconvenient in pet bitches and it is difficult to mate such bitches successfully. Hormone medication with the agents used to control heat or spaying may be required.

Table 9.4: (cont.)

23	fails to conceive (infertility)	Anatomical causes, bacterial infection, hormonal imbalance, psychological behavioural problems and mating at incorrect time.	A full veterinary investigation is required so that the cause can be pin-pointed and appropriate medication given.
24	will not stand for the dog	Hormonal imbalance, behavioural problem, incorrect timing of mating.	It may be possible to work out the most likely cause in discussion with an experienced breeder. Veterinary attention will be required in the case of hormonal imbalance.
25	has a vaginal discharge	Open pyometra, metritis, cystitis, vaginal tumour, vaginitis.	Seek veterinary attention without delay especially if the bitch is also vomiting, is obviously 'off colour' and has recently been on heat, since an emergency pyometra operation may be needed. Cases of suspected metritis in newly-whelped bitches also need prompt medication.

Mishaps and problems about the house and outdoors

Homes with dogs can never be as immaculate as those which do not include the pleasure and companionship of pets. *The Doglopaedia*, has a chapter devoted to giving hints on how to cope with those accidents and mishaps associated with dogs which do inevitably occur in and around the home. Those which apply to bitches are reproduced below. Hopefully they will help bitch owners decide what action to take, in the short- and long-term, to overcome and prevent those difficulties which relate more specifically to bitches.

What if my bitch is in season and there are male dogs in the house?

Nearly all male dogs recognize the odour of a bitch in season, as indeed nature intended them to do.

It is undoubtedly cruel to keep a male dog in the same house as an in season bitch; the two would almost certainly evade your attempts to keep them apart, as during the middle-third of her season the bitch is as eager to meet the dog as he is to find her.

Immediate action
Proprietary pills and lotions are generally ineffective in masking bitch odour. Either bitch or, preferably, dog must be boarded elsewhere.

Subsequent action
Consult a veterinary surgeon about the prevention of heat on a temporary or permanent basis. Spaying or chemical methods are available. Castration of the male may be effective but he may still show some mating behaviour.

179

What if my bitch makes blood-stains on the carpet and furniture when she is on heat?

The amount of blood-stained discharge when in season varies from bitch to bitch. Some bitches will lick themselves much more frequently when in season and so cause little problem, other bitches are not so meticulous.

Immediate action
- Use salted cold water to soak the stain out of fabrics.
- Wash in biological washing powder.
- Clean floor and carpets in similar manner.

A number of commercially-formulated stain-removers specific for individual stains, including blood and urine, can be obtained from hardware stores. These have generally been found to be very effective.

Prevention
- Confine the bitch to easily-washed areas while she is in season.
- Cover furniture with old sheets or similar cotton material.
- Consider fitting the bitch with sanitary pads and knickers, which can either be bought at pet shops or improvized
- If the bitch is not to be bred from, consider eliminating all the nuisance of seasons. See pages 31 and 174.

What if my bitch makes bleached circles on the lawn where she urinates?

Immediate action
The grass can be prevented from yellowing by pouring on two to three gallons of water immediately the urine has been passed.

Prevention
With patience the bitch can be trained to use a concrete, gravel or soil area. Prevention is not possible if the bitch is allowed to use the lawn.

What if my bitch is stolen?

There is an increasing risk that pedigree puppies and adult bitches will be stolen from cars, and even from their gardens, or when tied-up outside shops. Check with the police, the local veterinary surgeries, and rescue kennels that your bitch has not been taken in from the street. Check again every other day.

If you are sure that your bitch has been stolen, the best tactic is to have a leaflet printed showing her photograph and giving her description. Circulate it as widely as possible and display it in shops that offer that facility. Also contact the canine press, so that breeders may be on the alert for a new bitch coming into the area under possibly suspicious circumstances.

Offer a reward; however it is illegal to state that 'no questions will be asked if the animal is returned', as this is conniving with the thieves.

Do not give up hope of seeing your bitch again, as she may be turned loose to make her way home several days or even weeks after the theft.

SECTION FOUR:
USEFUL INFORMATION AND DATA

Further useful information

Your bitch's records

Breeding data

CHAPTER 10
FURTHER USEFUL INFORMATION

First aid

Emergencies

Dog care and first aid kits

Dogs and the law

Useful addresses and telephone numbers

Vital signs

Household measures

Further reading

First aid

There will inevitably be times when your bitch will need some first aid before being taken to a veterinary surgeon for treatment. Details of what can be done in such situations are given in a concise form in *The Doglopaedia*. Readers are advised to keep a copy of that book handy so that it can be referred to at times of need. If you are in doubt about what to do telephone the veterinary surgery, and ask the nurse or receptionist for advice if you are unable to speak to the veterinary surgeon at the time.

Emergencies

In general the main objectives in applying first aid in emergency situations involving injured dogs are:

1. *To restrain the bitch* so that she does not run away and possibly sustain further injury. Loop a restraining lead over the dog's head but allow her to adopt whatever position she obviously finds comfortable.
2. *To ensure that the bitch has a free airway and can breathe freely*. This may necessitate pulling the tongue forward and folding it under the side of the lower jaw if the dog is unconscious. Keep her neck straight.
3. *To control bleeding*. This can usually be achieved by the use of pressure bandages but in the case of bright-red, spurting blood it may be necessary

to apply a tourniquet at a suitable point between the heart and the wound. Ensure that a tourniquet is not left on for more than 15 to 20 minutes without releasing it at least temporarily.

4. *To comfort and reassure a dog* by talking in a normal voice. But remember that a dog which is frightened or in pain may react by biting even a well-loved owner.

5. Finally, it is helpful to *keep the dog lightly covered and warm* during transport to the veterinary surgery.

The main conditions specific to bitches which require emergency treatment by a veterinary surgeon day or night are:
- Eclampsia (fits) – see page 150.
- Dystocia (difficult birth) – see page 94.
- Very acute mastitis – see page 156.
- Traumatized vaginal prolapse – see page 161.
- Abortion – see page 146.

The wise owner will seek veterinary help without delay if their bitch is:
- Drinking excessively. This may be due to pyometra, diabetes mellitus, or indicate problems in the urinary tract.
- Has a large swollen mass protruding from the vulva – see vaginal hyperplasia, page 160.
- Has difficulty urinating. This sign may be associated with cystitis, vaginitis or a vaginal tumour.
- Has enlarged and inflamed mammary glands – see mastitis, page 156.
- Is mismated. See page 157.

Finding a veterinary surgeon in an emergency
Try: Police, Post Office, Yellow Pages, or a local breeder, kennel or pet owner.

Always plan to take the dog to a veterinary surgery. A vet is restricted in what he can do to help a dog in the road or at a private house. Telephone first to be sure of locating a vet on duty.

It is as well to be aware that if you are helping an unknown, unowned animal, you may be required to pay some or all of the cost.

If an animal has been killed in an accident, call the police rather than a veterinary surgeon. It is a mis-use of veterinary time for them to be asked to act as undertakers.

Dog care and first aid kit

The following list of equipment, kept in a box labelled 'Dog First Aid Kit', will be invaluable both for you and for anyone who may be taking care of the dog for you.

Your veterinary surgery can provide you with most of these items and will also advise you in respect of a suitable disinfectant to keep handy.

The prudent owner will also carry a few first aid items in the car, in order to be able to help his own dog or another which may be in distress.

When a dog travels in the car, always carry a bottle of water and a drinking bowl. In summer, a towel to soak in cold water to act as a whole body cooler and a flask of ice can be invaluable. Dogs can become dangerously overheated, even while travelling in a car in hot weather. A strong blanket on which an injured dog can be carried is a necessity.

DOG FIRST AID KIT

Tweezers, curved and straight scissors, nail clippers.
Strips of soft strong tape for emergency muzzle.
Conforming bandage which sticks to itself as layers are put on.
Antiseptic – TCP is ideal.
Cotton wool.
Antacid emulsion for indigestion and flatulence.
Liquid paraffin for constipation.
Meat tenderizer – soothes both wasp and bee stings.
Small nuggets of washing soda. (This acts as an emetic but should only be used on veterinary advice.)
Tube of antiseptic cream.
Roll of 2 in or 3 in wide adhesive plaster.
2 in and 4 in open weave cotton bandage.
2 in crepe bandage.
Small sterile container for urine sample.
Small jar or plastic pot for faeces sample.
Small empty bottle for giving liquid medicine.
Anti-flea spray, as advised by veterinary surgeon.
Environmental flea spray.
Shampoo specifically made for dogs.
Glucose powder.
Ear drops ⎱ as advised by your
Eye drops ⎰ veterinary surgeon.
Antihistamine tablets – as advised by veterinary surgeon for use after insect stings.
A small note-book – in which to record the dog's weight and details of previous illness and treatments given. Most importantly the book should contain a note of the veterinary surgeon's telephone number together with two alternative numbers for emergency use and the telephone number of a taxi company. (See also Chapter 11.)

A FIRST AID KIT FOR THE CAR

Strong, washable nylon braid slip collar and lead.
Length of soft tape for an emergency muzzle.
Curved scissors, tweezers.
Small bottle of diluted antiseptic.
Large pad of cotton wool.
2 in crepe bandage, 2 in open weave cotton bandage.
3 in elastoplast.
Leg from a pair of tights to put over the bitch's head if her ears are bleeding.
Bottle of meat tenderizer to put on stings.
Roll of kitchen paper for blotting, cleaning, etc.

Note
A pregnant bitch must NEVER be left in a parked car, even if the day seems cool and the windows are open. Dogs do not lose heat as efficiently as humans and they have greater need for oxygen at all times. (See also 'Dogs and the law', below.)

Dogs and the law in Britain

There are a number of laws which apply to dog-ownership. They are intended to protect dogs from cruelty and misuse, to protect livestock and wild animals from dogs, and to protect people from annoyance by badly-kept dogs.

In addition, many local authorities make their own bye-laws concerning fouling of footpaths, roads and parks where dogs must be kept on leads, beaches where dogs are not allowed during the summer months, and public buildings into which dogs may not be taken. Some local authorities are considering imposing a condition that dog owners *must* pick up and dispose of the faeces passed in public places by their dogs.

Food shops and restaurants are encouraged by the Food Hygiene Regulations 1970 to ban dogs from their premises.

Large land-owners such as the Forestry Commission also create bye-laws prohibiting the chasing of deer, game birds, etc., by dogs on their land.

Licenses and laws that apply particularly to bitch owners

Three activities require licences from the local authority, and involve inspection of the premises concerned. The licence cost is determined by the local authority – annual amounts of up to £60 have been recorded.

The Breeding of Dogs Act 1973

Owners of more than two bitches from which puppies are bred for sale require this licence from the local authority where they live. The premises where breeding is carried on, even if a private house, will receive an annual inspection by an Environmental Health Officer and/or veterinary surgeon. The cost of the licence is determined by the local authority concerned.

Selling dogs

Dogs and puppies may not be sold in the street or any public place, or to a child under 12 years old, or in conjunction with a rag or old clothes dealing business.

Buying dogs and puppies

In general the law decides that it is up to the buyer to be careful what he buys and livestock are bought 'as seen' without any warranty. However, if the buyer states that the puppy is wanted for a particular purpose, e.g. for showing or breeding, and in due course the dog does not fulfil that purpose, the buyer may have a claim under the Sale of Goods Act 1979. If a pedigree is given with a puppy, it must be correct. It may be regarded as an offence of obtaining money by false pretences to give an incorrect pedigree.

The Cruelty to Animals Act 1911

It is an offence to leave a dog in an enclosed car in hot weather. Penalties may be a fine of up to £2000 and/or six months imprisonment.

It is an offence to abandon a dog

Abandoning may be applied to leaving a dog in your home or kennel without regular attention and provision of food and water at appropriate intervals. One successful prosecution involved leaving some puppies from 4 p.m. on one day until 10 a.m. on the next without supervision or replenishment of water bowls.

Diagnosing and treating illness

It is an offence for anyone to diagnose and treat illness in a dog *which is not his own,* unless they are a qualified veterinary surgeon or working under the direct supervision of a veterinary surgeon. All operations, with the exception of the most minor procedures, must be performed while the dog is under an anaesthetic to prevent pain being felt. The only exception is first aid to save life or relieve pain.

Docking tails

Since July 1, 1993, no one other than a qualified veterinary surgeon may dock a puppy's tail *at any age, before the eyes are open or after.* Any person found to have done so risks prosecution for cruelty and a heavy fine.

Dogs and the law in North America

The complexity of the modern world exerts a very strong influence on dogs, their owners and the general interaction of dogs and society. This is fully demonstrated by the numerous laws in effect throughout America which relate to the keeping and control of dogs. Certain laws protect dogs from people and people from dogs. There are laws on the books to provide legal remedies for the destruction by dogs of public and private property and laws to mandate acceptable standards of dog-keeping in a community. Because of the great size and diversity of the North American continent and the tremendous number of large and small communities, laws will vary based on the character and needs of the particular city or town. It would be impractical to cite specifics in this book, but certain generalities must be included in this discussion.

Wherever dogs are kept, owners should take care that they are not allowed to roam unsupervised. Dogs at large are in serious danger of death, injury or theft and may also foul or destroy lawns, gardens or outdoor furniture. Unsupervised dogs can kill or injure pets or livestock and may attack people. In cases where small children or frail elderly are set upon by one or more wandering dogs, the outcome can be disastrous.

Dogs running at large may be seized by authorities and, under certain circumstances, humanely destroyed. A farmer discovering a dog worrying livestock may legally shoot the dog to death without any legal penalty. The owner of an unsupervised dog would probably be held liable for loss and damage to property.

Responsible dog owners obey the law by providing secure exercise areas on their own property for their dogs and keeping them on leash in public places. When responsible dog owners do take their pets out in public, they are prepared to clean up and properly dispose of any of their dogs' faeces. Many American communities have enacted laws obliging owners to do so. To the great credit of dog owners, most willingly comply with these local measures; those who do not give the majority a bad name. If your locality has clean-up and/or leash laws, be an exemplary citizen and comply fully at all times. Dog owners can also run foul of the law if their dogs are allowed to create an annoyance by incessant barking. This can especially be a problem in densely populated areas such as large apartment buildings. In this connection, if you rent your living quarters, check your lease to be sure you can keep a dog at all. Many landlords have a no pets clause in their leases and you can find yourself dispossessed if you acquire a dog over the landlord's objections. If you are planning to get a dog, find out in advance what all your civic responsibilities as a dog owner will be and be prepared to meet them. Otherwise, don't become a dog owner.

Generally, dogs are not allowed in food markets, restaurants and office buildings. Dogs are also not allowed on some forms of public transportation at all; with others they are allowed if confined to a carrier. These rules of public access do not apply to guide dogs for the blind, hearing dogs, service dogs for the disabled and certified therapy dogs.

Most communities require that dog be licensed, but the manner in which licenses are issued will vary. It is best to inquire of the town or the local animal control officer for specific details. Communities will also vary regarding the number of dogs which can legally be maintained on one's property. A kennel license is usually required for anyone wishing to breed dogs as a hobby and the owner is wise to cover him or herself by taking one out.

Any business dealing with dogs is subject to the normal laws of the community in this regard. Pet shops, boarding kennels, grooming parlors and the like must all comply with any regulations governing zoning, cleanliness, humane treatment and all the other many factors which will be involved here.

In recent years some municipalities have enacted a 'puppy lemon' law for the protection of buyers. Under this law, a newly-purchased puppy deemed unsaleable for any reason upon veterinary examination, may be returned to the seller for a full refund or the seller is liable for the puppy's veterinary expenses up to the full purchase price of the puppy. In this connection, buyers as well as sellers have a duty to know their rights as well as their obligations.

Many communities are also enacting dangerous dog laws. Unfortunately, there are too many misguided persons in this world who keep aggressive dogs for all the wrong reasons, not the least of which is pit fighting for wagering. Even in our technologically enlightened age, we have still not fully purged ourselves of the lust for blood sports.

The whole subject of dogs and the law is very complex as you can see. Readers in North America are recommended to acquire a copy of The Complete Guide to Dog Law (New York, Howell Book House, 1994) by Deidre E. Gannon, Esq. for a more complete view.

Vital Signs

Body temperature °F	**100.9-101.7**
Body temperature °C	**38.9-39.7**
Pulse rate	**70-80 beats/minute**
Respiration rate	**15-30 breaths/minute**

Approximate household measures

1 large teaspoonful	=	1/6 fl.oz	=	5ml
1 tablespoonful	=	1/2 fl.oz	=	15ml
1 wineglassful	=	2 fl.oz	=	60ml
1 cupful	=	7 fl.oz	=	200ml
1 pint bottle	=	20 fl.oz	=	568ml

CHAPTER 11
YOUR BITCH'S RECORDS

Illness and medication

Heats and breeding

Whelping

Weight

Introduction

As mentioned in Chapter 9, record keeping is particularly important in relation to the prevention of disease. But that's not all for, armed with good records, you will be able to provide your veterinary surgeon with a much fuller and more accurate history should your bitch need attention. That will make his job of diagnosis more easily accomplished and may well save you time and money and help prevent your bitch suffering unnecessarily.

Additionally your breed club may in the future be researching the incidence of some illness or condition and you will be able to make a valuable contribution from your records.

Keeping records is, of course, a very personal thing and thus we can only give guidance. However we do advise that you purchase a notebook and prepare it along the lines noted below for each bitch you own. If you own three or more bitches it may well be more practical to set up a card index system along similar lines or this information could be put on a home computer.

The front page of the book, or the first card, should be used to record the basic facts such as date of birth etc., relating to the bitch or bitches you own, realizing that in an emergency situation people unfamiliar with the bitch may have to refer to it. Some suggested headings are given on page 190.

The remainder of the book should be divided into four parts to accommodate the types of record indicated alongside the chapter heading above.

Suggested layouts for your bitch's record book
Page 1

RECORD BOOK

Bitch's name: ....

Registered name: .... Breed: ....

Date of Birth: .... Official colour/description: ....
....

Special identifying marks: ....

Photograph:

```
┌──────────────────────────────┐
│                              │
│                              │
│                              │
│                              │
│                              │
│                              │
└──────────────────────────────┘
```

Owner's name: ....

Address: ....

Telephone number: ....

Veterinary surgeon's telephone number: ....

Insurance details: ....
....
....

Taxi telephone number: ....

Record 1

| ....'s Record of illness and medication* | | | |
Date	Signs shown	Medication given and/or surgical procedure undertaken	Comments

*(To include medication given for treatment and prevention of disease, i.e. vaccination, chemical control of heat, etc. Ask your vet to write down for you the name and purpose of injections or tablets he prescribes.)

Record 2

..........'s Record of Heats and Breeding

Heat Number ......

Date started .... Signs seen ....

Date ended ....

Duration of bleeding .... days

Duration of attractiveness to dogs .... days

Date mated .... Stud dog used ....

Date whelped ....

Number of puppies born .... (male .... female ....)

Reared .... (male .... female ....)

Date false pregnancy noted .... Signs ....

Date false pregnancy ended ....

Comments:

Record 3

........'s Whelping Record

Litter number: .... By Stud Dog: ....
Time first stage started: .... Signs: ....
Time second stage started: .... Signs: ....

Puppy no.	Time born	Resuscitation*	Sex	Weight	Description	Congenital Defects**

Bitch behaviour during whelping: ....
Medication given to bitch and times: ....
Date of post-whelping veterinary check: ....
Medication given: ....
Date dew-claws removed: .... Reaction: ....

Summary: No. male pups born: .... No. reared: ....
No. female pups born: .... No. reared: ....
Puppy deaths age: .... Possible reason: ....
Post mortem results: ....
....

*Note whether resuscitation required and if so record what was done.
**Describe defect noted and age when observed.

Record 4

........'s Weight Record			
DURING GROWTH		**IN ADULTHOOD**	
Age	**Weight**	**Age**	**Weight**
Week 1 2 3 4 5 6 7 8 9 10 11 12 Month 4 5 6 7 8 9 10 11 12		Year 1 + 6 mth 2 2 + 6 mth 3 3 + 6 mth 4 4 + 6 mth 5 (etc)	

CHAPTER 12
BREEDING DATA

Average sizes of litters

Average number of surviving puppies

Expected weight at birth

Expected weight in adulthood

Pregnancy and whelping points

Appearance of puppies

Congenital abnormalities

Introduction

Table 12.1 is designed to bring together a wealth of information useful to both novice and expert breeders.

By the use of the table the following questions can be answered:

- What is an average sized litter for my breed?
- What is the average number of those puppies which survive and are registered'?
- What should the puppies weigh at birth?
- What does an adult bitch weigh? (This will allow the correct amount of food and medication to be given.)
- Are there any special points to note about pregnancy and whelping in your breed?
- Will the puppies look like little adults, or are there texture and colour changes to take place in the coat?
- What congenital abnormalities frequently appear in the breed?

In view of the tendency for buyers to sue breeders, it is important that breeders are aware of the likely faults in that breed.

Definitions

Achondroplasia
A disease characterized by inadequate formation of cartilage at the ends of long bones resulting in a form of dwarfism and abnormal angulation of the joints.

Atrial and ventricular septal defects (hole-in-the-heart)
These are holes in the septum or division between the right and left sides of the heart and these lead to circulatory problems of varying degree and usually an overload on one of the chambers of the heart.

Cerebellar hypoplasia
This term is used to describe the condition where the cerebellum fails to develop fully. Affected puppies walk with a staggering unco-ordinated gait and show muscle tremors when they stand up.

Cryptorchidism
In some male animals one or both testicles fail to descend into the scrotum during puppyhood and are permanently retained in the abdomen. A dog with only one descended testicle is known as a unilateral cryptorchid (often incorrectly referred to as a monorchid since there is usually a second testicle in the abdomen), and where neither is descended as a cryptorchid. See page 67.

Diabetes Mellitus
Sugar diabetes – see page 149 for a full description of the condition.

Hermaphrodite
An animal that has the characteristics of both sexes. This defect may not be noted until much later in life.

Megaoesophagus (oesophageal chalasia, oesophageal achalasia)
Failure of the normal contractions of the oesophagus which cause food to pass to the stomach, leading to oesophageal dilation. This defect is congenital and hereditary in certain breeds but may also be acquired. The condition leads to passive regurgitation of undigested food mixed with saliva.

Microphthalmos
A condition in which the eyes appear very much smaller than normal. Such eyes may be functional and normal anatomically, or they may be simply non-functional cysts. Microphthalmos is often accompanied by other congenital abnormalities of the eye, e.g. an opaque lens.

Patella luxation
Dislocation of the kneecap.

Pyloric stenosis
Thickening of the pyloric sphincter, which is situated at the exit of the stomach and the commencement of the small intestine. The condition may be congenital or acquired and leads to regular vomiting unrelated to eating.

Spina bifida
A developmental abnormality of the bony canal surrounding the spinal cord.

Stenotic nares
Failure of the nostrils to open properly – a narrowing of the nostrils.

Urine dribbling
Incontinence often associated with anatomical abnormalities of the urinary tract, e.g. the ureters entering posterior to the bladder sphincter.

Breeding Table:

> **Note:** The difference between average number of puppies born, and the number registered at the Kennel Club is taken to represent the number of puppies which die before 21 days old or which are in some way substandard.

Table 12.1: Breeding table

BREED	THE BITCH				THE PUPPIES			
	Weight in lb	Oestrus behaviour	Whelping and breeding characteristics	Number born	English Kennel Club registration figures	Weight at birth	Coat colour change	Congenital faults often visible soon after birth and up to selling time.
Affenpinscher	7	First oestrus 8 to 14 months	Some Caesareans	2 to 4	2 to 3	3 to 5 oz	None	Cleft palate, waterlogged puppies, patella luxation
Afghan Hound	50	First oestrus up to 2 years	Likes complete privacy for whelping	7	6 to 7	up to 18 oz	Spotting should disappear by 12 weeks	May be allergic to cows' milk
Airedale Terrier	47½	First oestrus at 15 months		8 to 12	6 to 7	12 to 15 oz	Black at birth	Umbilical hernia
Akita	95	False heats common	Slow whelper. Tails curl over back at 6 weeks	6 to 10		16 to 24 oz	Major changes during first year	Umbilical hernia, cerebellar hypoplasia
Alaskan Malamute	75	Early first oestrus		7 to 12	4 to 5	12 to 22 oz	Colour lightens	Hereditary dwarfism
American Cocker Spaniel – see Cocker Spaniel (American)								
Anatolian Shepherd Dog	135	May have only one oestrus per year	Easy whelpers	Up to 8	6	30 to 36 oz	None	
Australian Cattle Dog	35	Normal		5 to 6		12 to 16 oz	Born white. The blue or red speckling appears at 2 weeks	Deafness, wall eyes

198

Table 12.1: Breeding table (cont.)

BREED	THE BITCH			THE PUPPIES				
	Weight in lb	Oestrus behaviour	Whelping and breeding characteristics	Number born	Kennel Club registration figures	Weight at birth	Coat colour change	Congenital faults often visible soon after birth and up to selling time.
Australian Terrier	10½	Normal	Easy whelpers	4 to 5	3 to 4	5 to 7 oz	None	Crytorchidism
Basenji	21	Often only one season per year in autumn	Easy whelpers, good mothers	5 to 6	3 to 4	6 to 8 oz	Dark brown lightens to red, pink noses fill in with black	Inguinal hernia, umbilical hernia, cleft palate
Basset Hound	42½	Normal	Not easy to mate. Slow whelpers	8 to 10	6 to 7	8 to 16 oz	Red and lemon markings deepen	Inguinal hernia, eye conditions
Beagle	20	Normal		6 to 7	4 to 5	8 to 16 oz	Black and white at birth, tan markings show at 3 weeks. Lemon Pieds and Tan Pieds – white at birth	Short or crooked tail, cleft palate, umbilical hernia
Bearded Collie	45	8 to 12 month aneostrus common		7 to 10	5 to 6	10 to 12 oz	Coat greys as puppy grows to maturity	Mismarks, smooth and woolly coats, cleft palate
Bedlington Terrier	20	Long anoestrus common	Dam may injure long tail of pup	4 to 6	3 to 4	6 to 8 oz	Colour lightens	Swimmers, liver function problems
Belgian Tervueren	70	Normal at 10–12 weeks	Short pregnancy	6 to 8		12 to 14 oz	Colour lightens	Pancreatic problems, epilepsy
Bernese Mountain Dog	65	Regular	Caesars common	8 to 10		16 to 24 oz	Colour lightens	Osteochondritis, umbilical hernia, blue eyes

199

Table 12.1: Breeding table (cont.)

| BREED | THE BITCH | | | THE PUPPIES | | | |
	Weight in lb	Oestrus behaviour	Whelping and breeding characteristics	Number born	Kennel Club registration figures	Weight at birth	Coat colour change	Congenital faults often visible soon after birth and up to selling time.
Bichon Frise	18	Irregular cycle-silent heats common	Very sensitive to pain, Caesars not uncommon	4 to 5	4	3½ to 4 oz	None	Patella luxation, attention to teeth necessary
Bloodhound	90		Reabsorption common, slow whelpers, Caesareans	8 to 14	6 to 7	16 to 18 oz	None	Eye conditions
Border Collie	42		Easy whelpers	5 to 8	5 to 6	16 oz	None	Deafness, flea allergy, cryptorchidism
Border Terrier	12½	Silent heats	May resent owner's help at whelping	4 to 7	4 to 5	8 to 12 oz	Coat colour lightens	Kinked tails, heart murmurs
Borzoi	75	Puberty not until 24 months		7 to 8	4 to 5	12 to 16 oz	None	
Boston Terrier	17½	Dry seasons without swelling or bleeding	Difficult to mate, worse to whelp, caesareans needed by up to 75 per cent of Boston bitches	4	2 to 3	6 to 8 oz	None	Swimmers, wry mouth, cleft palate, spina bifida, megaoesophagus
Bouvier des Flandres	75	Irregular oestrus		Up to 10	6 to 7	8 to 18 oz	Considerable colour change	Cleft palate

Table 12.1: Breeding table (cont.)

BREED	THE BITCH						THE PUPPIES		
	Weight in lb	Oestrus behaviour	Whelping and breeding characteristics	Number born	Kennel Club registration figures	Weight at birth	Coat colour change	Congenital faults often visible soon after birth and up to selling time.	
Boxer	62	First oestrus up to 15 months	Primary and secondary inertia and eclampsia common, slow whelpers	Up to 10	5 to 6	12 to 16 oz	Mouse colour clears to red, brindling hardly apparent at birth, noses blacken	Whites and checks, cleft lip or palate, cryptorchidism, megaoesophagus, hole-in-the-heart defect	
Briard	75		Easy whelpers	7 to 13	6 to 7	10 to 12 oz	Noses blacken	Yellow eyes	
Brittany Spaniel	35		Easy whelpers	Average 7	6	6 to 9 oz	None	Some born tailless	
Bulldog	50		Need constant help at whelping – 80 to 90 per cent need Caesars.	Average 5	3 to 4	10 to 14 oz	None	Nostrils obstructed, cleft palate, waterlogged puppies, deafness, eye conditions	
Bullmastiff	100	Irregular oestrus, dry seasons	Not easy to mate, slow whelpers, may need Ceasar	5 to 8		16 to 24 oz	None	Yellow eyes, cleft palate	
Bull Terrier	45	May have only one oestrus a year – begin at 7 to 11 months	Long whelping, may need veterinary assistance	5 to 7	4 to 5	11 to 13 oz	None	Umbilical hernia, deafness, cleft palate	

Table 12.1: Breeding table (cont.)

| BREED | THE BITCH | | | | THE PUPPIES | | | |
	Weight in lb	Oestrus behaviour	Whelping and breeding characteristics	Number born	Kennel Club registration figures	Weight at birth	Coat colour change	Congenital faults often visible soon after birth and up to selling time.
Cairn Terrier	14	Short oestrus	Easy whelpers	5 to 6	3 to 5	5 to 6 oz	None	Cryptorchidism
Canaan Dog	18		Easy whelpers	5 – 7		12 oz	None	Cleft palates
Cardigan Corgi	22		Some whelping difficulty possible	5 to 8	4	9 to 12 oz	None	
Cavalier King Charles Spaniel	18	First oestrus up to 9 months		4 to 5	3 to 4	5 to 8 oz	White areas tend to grow smaller. Blenheims may be born almost white all over	Under- or overshot mouths, heart problems, eye deformaties
Chihuahua	4		Caesarean common	2 to 5	2 to 3	Under 4 oz – unlikely to survive	None	Open fontanelle very undesirable, hydrocephalus
Chesapeake Bay Retriever	60	Irregular oestrus		7 to 10		12 to 16 oz	None	Soft coat
Chinese Crested	12		Easy whelpers, body temperature always higher than other dogs	3 to 4	2 to 3	2 to 4 oz	None, two coat types – with hair (the Powder Puff) and without	

Table 12.1: Breeding table (cont.)

BREED	THE BITCH				THE PUPPIES			
	Weight in lb	Oestrus behaviour	Whelping and breeding characteristics	Number born	Kennel Club registration figures	Weight at birth	Coat colour change	Congenital faults often visible soon after birth and up to selling time.
Chow Chow	55	Less than 6 monthly intervals	Difficult to mate, Caesarean not unknown	4 to 6	3 to 4	10 to 20 oz	Tongue pink at birth. Blue/black by 6 weeks	Short tail, pink tongue. Eye conditions
Clumber Spaniel	52½	Puberty up to 2 years. Irregular oestrus	Secondary uterine inertia	4 to 6	5 to 6	12 to 16 oz	None	Eye conditions
Cocker Spaniel (American)	28		Easy whelpers	4 to 5	4 to 6	6 oz	None	Hermaphrodites, water-logged puppies, cleft palate, eye conditions
Cocker Spaniel (English)	30		Short pregnancy – average 61 days	4	5	6 to 8 oz	None	Swimmers, cryptorchidism, Hermaphrodites, eye conditions
Collies (Rough and Smooth)	48½	Normal	Easy whelpers but not all pups survive	6 to 10	5	12 oz	None	Deafness, wall eyes, dwarfism, eye conditions
Corgi – see Cardigan Corgi and Pembroke Corgi								

Table 12.1: Breeding table (cont.)

BREED	THE BITCH				THE PUPPIES			
	Weight in lb	Oestrus behaviour	Whelping and breeding characteristics	Number born	Kennel Club registration	Weight at birth	Colour change	Congenital faults often visible soon after birth and up to selling time.
Curly-coated Retriever	75		Mating not always successful	6 to 9	6	8 to 14 oz	None	Coat not curly, light eyes
Dachshunds (Miniature)	under 11		Many false pregnancies. Inertia frequent, Caesars in Miniature Dachshunds	2 to 4	3 to 4	4 to 6 oz	None	Undershot and overshot mouths. Eye conditions, deafness, wall eyes, coat texture incorrect especially in Wires
Dachshunds (Standard)	19		Uterine Inertia frequent	5	4 to 5	5 oz	None	Undershot and overshot mouths. Eye conditions, deafness, wall eyes, coat texture incorrect especially in Wires
Dalmatian	55			Up to 13	6 to 7	11 to 15 oz	Born white with small pigmented spots on the skin. Dark hair appears at 2 weeks	Patched coats – tricolours or lemon spotted. Deafness
Dandie Dinmont Terrier	18		Pregnancy diagnosis difficult	4 to 6	3 to 4	8 to 10 oz	Colour Lightens	

Table 12.1: Breeding table (cont.)

BREED	THE BITCH			THE PUPPIES				
	Weight in lb	Oestrus behaviour	Whelping and breeding characteristics	Number born	Kennel Club registration figures	Weight at birth	Coat colour change	Congenital faults often visible soon after birth and up to selling time.
Deerhound	72½	First oestrus up to 16 months, thereafter a long cycle		8 to 9	6	16 to 32 oz	Pups are born black	
Dobermann	45		Easy whelps except when litter is very small	Average 8	6 to 7	16 oz	None	Demodectic mange
English Setter	59	Ovulation very irregular so whelping date variable	Pain sensitive	Up to 11	5	16 oz	Pups born white, ticking appears by 3 weeks	Deafness
English Springer Spaniel	42			7 to 3	5 to 6	9 to 14 oz	Nose pigment can take a long time to develop	Megaoesophagus, eye conditions
King Charles Spaniel	11	Puberty 12 to 14 months		2 to 5	2 to 3	5 to 10 oz	Pink noses blacken over later	White on black/tan and rubies
Field Spaniel	45	Irregular season often 2 year interval		6	5	Up to 16 oz	None	
Flat-coated Retriever	65	Normal	Easy whelpers	6 to 10	7 to 8	8 to 10 oz	None	

Table 12.1: Breeding table (cont.)

| BREED | THE BITCH | | | | THE PUPPIES | | | |
	Weight in lb	Oestrus behaviour	Whelping and breeding characteristics	Number born	Kennel Club registration figures	Weight at birth	Coat colour change	Congenital faults often visible soon after birth and up to selling time.
Fox Terrier (Smooth and Wire)	16	Normal		Up to 8	3 to 4	11 to 13 oz	None	Cerebellar hypoplasia, deafness, megaoesophagus
French Bulldog	24		Difficult to mate. Caesareans frequent. Cleft palate common in pup	4 to 5	2 to 3	6 to 8 oz	None	Cleft palate
German Shepherd Dog	65	Some 4 months cycels	Easy whelpers	8 to 15	6 to 7	12 to 20 oz	None	White, long coats, greys and livers. Megaoesophagus
German Short-haired Pointer	52½	Short anoestrus	Many false pregnancies	Up to 10	6 to 7	9 to 15	None	
German Wire Pointer	50		Easy Whelpers	Up to 10	7 to 9	9 to 15 oz	None	
Giant Schnauzer	90		Secondary uterine inertia common. Rapid growth of pups from 12 weeks	7 to 9	7 to 8	6 to 16 oz	None	
Golden Retriever	65	Oestrus 9 to 11 months	Short pregnancy, easy whelpers	6 to 8	6 to 7	16 to 24 oz	None	Mismarks. Cryptorchids, wry mouths

Table 12.1: Breeding table (cont.)

BREED	THE BITCH				THE PUPPIES			
	Weight in lb	Oestrus behaviour	Whelping and breeding characteristics	Number born	Kennel Club registration figures	Weight at birth	Coat colour change	Congenital faults often visible soon after birth and up to selling time.
Gordon Setter	56		Easy whelpers	8 to 12	6 to 7	12 to 16 oz	None	Red colouring or too much white
Great Dane	100		Phantom pregnancies, Overlaying of puppies common	up to 9	5 to 6	12 to 24 oz	None	Deafness, mismarks, wall eye, cryptorchidism
Greyhound	65	Long anoestrus	Foetal death rate high, difficult whelping	7 to 10	5	16 to 24 oz	None	Cryptorchidism
Griffon Bruxellois	8	Puberty up to 18 months	Breed from largest bitches only	4 to 5	3	5 to 6 oz	None	Hydrocephalus. Wry mouth. Cleft palate
Hungarian Viszla	65			6 to 8	6 to 7	10 to 14 oz	None	
Ibizan Hound	48	Anoestrus up to yearly intervals. First oestrus at 2 years old	Severe false pregnancies	6 to 12	5 to 6	14 oz	Pups colour darkens later	Cryptorchidism

Table 12.1: Breeding table (cont.)

BREED	THE BITCH				THE PUPPIES			
	Weight in lb	Oestrus behaviour	Whelping and breeding characteristics	Number born	Kennel Club registration figures	Weight at birth	Coat colour change	Congenital faults often visible soon after birth and up to selling time.
Irish Setter	57	Erractic cycles	Many false pregnancies. Secondary uterine inertia followed by hyperactive behaviour for a day or two after whelping	4 to 8	5	8 oz	None	Megaoesaphagus, kinked tail tip
Irish Terrier	25	Normal		4 to 8	5	8 oz	None	Soft coats
Irish Water Spaniel	53		Easy whelpers	8 to 10	6	12 to 16 oz	Pups eyes darken. White hairs disappear	Baldness
Irish Wolfhound	90	Late first oestrus at 18 to 24 months – cycle up to 9 months	Secondary uterine inertia. May overlay pups	5 to 6	6	20 to 24 oz	None	
Italian Greyhound	7	Puberty as late as 18 to 24 months	Easy whelpers	3 to 5	2 to 3	3 to 9 oz	Colour alters	
Italian Spinone	65		Easy whelpers	8 to 10	6 to 7	16 oz	None	

Table 12.1: Breeding table (cont.)

BREED	THE BITCH			THE PUPPIES				
	Weight in lb	Oestrus behaviour	Whelping and breeding characteristics	Number born	Kennel Club registration figures	Weight at birth	Coat colour change	Congenital faults often visible soon after birth and up to selling time.
Jack Russell Terrier – see Parson Jack Russell								
Japanese Chin	6		Caesareans sometimes necessary	3 to 5	2 to 3	3 to 4 oz	None	Wry mouths, cryptorchidism
Keeshond	40	First oestrus at 8 to 18 months	Easy whelpers	5 to 7	4 to 5	8 to 12 oz	A lot of colour change	
Kerry Blue Terrier	35		Short pregnancy	5	4 to 5	8 to 12 oz	Pups should be born black	Coat does not fade to blue
Komondor	110	8 months cycle, late ovulation	May need bottle feeding after birth as lactation is often delayed	7 to 8		12 to 18 oz	None	Light eyes
Labrador Retriever	62		Easy whelpers	7 to 8	6 to 7	12 to 16 oz	None	Mismarks, cryptorchids
Lakeland Terrier	15	12 to 15 month cycle common. First oestrus up to 2 years		4 to 5	3 to 4	8 oz	None	Hernias

Table 12.1: Breeding table (cont.)

BREED	THE BITCH			THE PUPPIES				
	Weight in lb	Oestrus behaviour	Whelping and breeding characteristics	Number born	Kennel Club registration figures	Weight at birth	Coat colour change	Congenital faults often visible soon after birth and up to selling time.
Lhasa Apsos	16		Help needed at whelping to sever cord	3 to 8	4 to 5	5 to 7 oz	None	
Lowchen	8	May cycle once a year	Easy whelpers	3 to 4	2 to 3	5 to 7 oz	None	
Maltese	12	Very short oestrus	False pregnancy common. Breed from largest bitch	2 to 4	2 to 3	3 to 6 oz	None	Lemon colour patches on paws
Manchester Terrier	15			3 to 6	3 to 4	5 to 6	Tan markings do not show until 3 to 4 weeks	
Maremma	85	First oestrus as late as 2 years	Irregular cycle – not easy to breed	8	5 to 6	17 to 30 oz	None	Screw tails
Mastiff	126	First oestrus 11 to 12 months old	Cycle irregular, many reabsorptions	5 to 10	5	16 to 24 oz	None	Eye conditions
Miniature Pinscher	8		Easy whelpers	1 to 6	3 to 4	4 to 6 oz	Considerable colour change	Lack of pigment
Miniature Bull Terrier	18		Easy whelpers	3 to 4		6 oz	None	

Table 12.1: Breeding table (cont.)

BREED	THE BITCH				THE PUPPIES			
	Weight in lb	Oestrus behaviour	Whelping and breeding characteristics	Number born	Kennel Club registration figures	Weight at birth	Coat colour change	Congenital faults often visible soon after birth and up to selling time.
Miniature Schnauzer	17			3 to 5	4 to 5	4 to 9 oz	None	
Neopolitan Mastiff	140		Easy whelpers	6 to 10		16 to 20 oz	None	Screw tails, cherry eye
Newfoundland	115		Long whelping	6	6	20 to 24 oz	None	Eye conditions
Norwegian Elkhound	43			7 to 8	6	10 to 12 oz	Pups born black	Cleft palate
Norwich/Norfolk Terrier	14			2 to 3	2 to 3	3 to 5 oz	None	Soft or long coat
Old English Sheepdog	65			8	5 to 6	10 to 16 oz	Pups are born black/white	Deafness
Otterhound	100		False pregnancies common	7 to 8	6	16 oz average	None	
Owczarer Nizinny (Polish Sheepdog)	40	8 month cycle	Easy whelpers	4 to 7	N/A	10 oz	None	Faded nose and eye pigment

Table 12.1: Breeding table (cont.)

BREED	THE BITCH				Kennel Club registration Figures	THE PUPPIES		
	Weight in lb	Oestrus behaviour	Whelping and breeding characteristics	Number born		Weight at birth	Coat colour change	Congenital faults often visible soon after birth and up to selling time.
Papillon	5½		Primary inertia or eclampsia common. Breed from larger bitches	2 to 4	2 to 3	4 to 5 oz	Considerable colour change	Mismarks
Parson Jack Russell	12		Easy whelpers. Not Kennel Club recognized	4 to 6		4 to 8 oz	None	
Pekingese	12		Caesarean frequent, need assistance at whelping	3 to 5	2 to 3	4 to 6 oz	None	Receding lower jaw
Pembroke Welsh Corgi	20		Need assistance at whelping	6 to 7	4 to 5	10 oz	Colour changes	White puppies, fluffy coats
Petit Basset Griffon Vendeen	40			Up to 10	5 to 6	14 to 16 oz	None	
Pharoah Hound	50	Late puberty	Easy whelpers	2 to 8	5 to 6	8 to 12 oz	Colour brightens	Too much white
Pointer	55		Easy whelpers	6 to 14	5 to 6	10 to 18 oz	None	Hernias
Pomeranian	5		Slow whelpers, do not rush into Caesarean. Not easy to rear	3	2	3 to 5 oz	None	Open fontanelle, cryptorchidism, hydrocephalus

Table 12.1: Breeding table (cont.)

BREED	THE BITCH			THE PUPPIES				
	Weight in lb	Oestrus behaviour	Whelping and breeding characteristics	Number born	Kennel Club registration figures	Weight at birth	Coat colour change	Congenital faults often visible soon after birth and up to selling time.
Poodle (Toy)	10			3 to 4	3 to 4	3 to 6 oz	None	Hydrocephalus, tear staining on face
Poodle (Miniature)	13½	Late puberty, up to 15 weeks		4 to 6	3 to 4	6 to 8 oz	None	Particolour coats, achondroplasia, eye problems, malformation of urinary system, urine dribbling
Poodle (Standard)	65			6 to 10	6 to 7	8 to 16 oz	Silvers are born black, nose often darkens after birth	Deafness, umbilical hernia, undershot/overshot mouths
Pug	16	Late puberty, up to 9 months	Short pregnancy	4 to 6	3 to 4	4 to 9 oz	Colour change on pups	Prolonged soft palate
Puli	29		Long pregnancy to 67 days	5 to 7	4 to 5	7 to 9 oz	Considerable colour change	
Pyrenean Mountain Dog	90	First oestrus at 12 months	Clumsy mothers	6 to 7	6	about 16 oz	Black spots fade	Swimmers, hernias, cleft palates
Rhodesian Ridgeback	70		Puppies can vary considerably in size	8 to 15	6 to 7	about 16 oz	None	Dermoid cyst, megaoesophagus

Table 12.1: Breeding table (cont.)

BREED	THE BITCH					THE PUPPIES		
	Weight in lb	Oestrus behaviour	Whelping and breeding characteristics	Number born	Kennel Club registration figures	Weight at birth	Coat colour change	Congenital faults often visible soon after birth and up to selling time.
Rottweiler	85	First oestrus 8 months	Pups of less than 7 oz unlikely to survive	7+	6	12 to 18 oz	None	No anus, cleft palate, deafness
Rough Collie – see Collie (Rough)								
St Bernard	150	First oestrus up to 15 months	A weight gain of 25 lb per month is expected	8 to 12	5	15 to 16 oz	None	Eye conditions
Saluki	42½	First oestrus up to 2 years, long cycle to be expected	Pregnancy does not show until late on	5 to 8	5	16 oz	Considerable colour changes in pups	Umbilical hernia
Samoyed	40	First oestrus up to one year plus	Short pregnancy	6 to 7	4 to 5	10 to 18 oz	Short white coat appears in first week	Blue eyes, eye conditions
Schipperke	18	First oestrus up to 2 years	Length of tail on pups varies widely	4 to 8	3	4 to 5 oz	None	Cleft palate, variable tail length, protruding incisors
Schnauzer – see Giant, Standard & Miniature								

Table 12.1: Breeding table (cont.)

BREED	THE BITCH			THE PUPPIES				
	Weight in lb	Oestrus behaviour	Whelping and breeding characteristics	Number born	Kennel Club registration figures	Weight at birth	Coat colour change	Congenital faults often visible soon after birth and up to selling time.
Scottish Terrier	21		Primary uterine inertia and some Caesareans	4 to 5	4	6 to 3oz	None	Deafness, swimmers, dwarf
Sealyham Terrier	18	Long cycle	Not easy to mate	4 to 5	4	6 to 8 oz	None	Deafness
Shar-Pei	45	Silent or false heats	Short pregnancy, may only be fertile in autumn	5	3 to 4	14 to 16 oz	None	Deafness, inguinal hernia, respiration difficulties, entropian, bowed legs
Shetland Sheepdog	20	Irregular cycles, first oestrus one year		4 to 6	3 to 4	4 to 10 oz	Colour alters at about 3 weeks	Cryptorchidism, eye conditions, deafness
Shih Tzu	15	Irregular cycles, not easy to mate	Slow whelpers	3 to 4	3 to 4	Average 6 oz	None	Unpigmented nose, eye rims
Siberian Husky	48		Diarrhoea during lactation, slow whelpers, long rest in middle of whelping	3 to 7	4 to 5	12 to 16 oz	None	Cleft lip and palate

Table 12.1: Breeding table (cont.)

BREED	THE BITCH				THE PUPPIES			
	Weight in lb	Oestrus behaviour	Whelping and breeding characteristics	Number born	Kennel Club registration figures	Weight at birth	Coat colour change	Congenital faults often visible soon after birth and up to selling time.
Skye Terrier	23			6	4	8 to 10 oz	None	Kinked tail tips, hydrocephalus, urine dribbling
Smooth Collie – see Collie (Smooth)								
Soft-coated Wheaten	40	Breed at 3rd season	Pregnancy hard to detect	5 to 7	5	7 to 11 oz	Considerable colour change, nose blackens	Yellow eyes, skin allergies
Staffordshire Bull Terrier	29		Some Caesareans to be expected	4 to 5	7	8 oz	None	Light eyes, harelip, cleft palate
Standard Schnauzer	35		Lactation problems	6 to 8	5 to 6	7 to 12 oz	Colour lightens in salt and peppers	Cleft lip and palate
Sussex Spaniel	40	May have only one oestrus a year	Low libido, poor maternal behaviour	2 to 8	5	4 to 6 oz	Growth in pups is slow, eyes may not open up to 21 days, coat colour lightens	Heart murmurs and enlarged hearts
Tibetan Spaniel	12	One oestrus a year common		3 to 4	3	4 to 5 oz	None	Umbilical hernia, undershot bites
Tibetan Terrier	27			5 to 6	4	4 to 5 oz	None	Slow to cut teeth
Weimaraner	50		Bitches tend to lose hair	6 to 9	6 to 7	10 to 16 oz	Striped colours at birth disappear	Cryptorchidism, hernias, eye problems

Table 12.1: Breeding table (cont.)

BREED	THE BITCH			THE PUPPIES				
	Weight in lb	Oestrus behaviour	Whelping and breeding characteristics	Number born	Kennel Club registration figures	Weight at birth	Coat colour change	Congenital faults often visible soon after birth and up to selling time.
Welsh Springer	37½	1st oestrus at one year	Easy whelpers	4 to 6	5	8 to 12 oz	Colour darkens	
Welsh Terrier	20		Easy whelpers	5 to 6	3 to 4	4 to 9 oz	Pups are born black	
West Highland White	17		Early slow whelpers	3 to 4		6 oz	None	Inguinal hernia, defects of central nervous system
Whippet	21½	First oestrus at 12 to 24 months	Early whelpers	4 to 8	4 to 5	8 to 12 oz	Colour lightens in some individuals	Light eyes, cryptorchidism, alopecia
Yorkshire Terrier	6½	First oestrus at 8 to 16 months	20 per cent require Caesarean	1 to 4	3 to 4	4 to 6 oz	Pups born black with small tan markings	Waterlogged puppies, inguinal hernias, hydrocephalus, hypoglycemia

Note: The difference between average number of puppies born, and the number registered at the Kennel Club is taken to represent the number of puppies which die before 21 days old or which are in some way substandard.

GLOSSARY OF FEMALE TERMS

What did the veterinary surgeon mean?

Often veterinary surgeons will use long or difficult words to describe various conditions or procedures relating to bitches. The glossary below is provided to help bitch owners understand what is meant. This glossary supplements the one that is provided in *The Doglopaedia* and should be used in conjunction with the general index, since some words that are adequately defined in the text, for example most of the anatomical names, are not included in this glossary.

Acromegaly a chronic condition in which there is increased tissue and bone growth as a result of over production of growth hormone. Snoring is a common and typical sign in affected bitches. See also page 147.

Afterbirth the membranes (placenta) expelled with the puppies during and after whelping.

Agalactia absence of milk.

Allantois the inner membrane surrounding the foetus in the uterus – part of the placenta.

Amnion the outer membrane surrounding the foetus in the uterus – part of the placenta.

Anaerobes bacteria which like to grow in the absence of air. They may occur in the uterus.

Anoestrus the period of sexual inactivity in the oestrous cycle.

Benign not malignant, recurring or spreading; usually applied to a tumour, e.g. of the mammary gland.

BHS beta-haemolytic streptococci – round shaped bacteria which may cause vaginitis and be involved with fading puppies.

Biopsy a minor operation to take part of an affected tissue to diagnose the cause of the lesion and give a prognosis.

Blastocyst a specific stage in the development of the foetus – a type of embryo.

Broken-down a lay term sometimes applied to greyhound bitches which have just come on heat.

219

Brucellosis	the disease caused by an infection with the bacterium *Brucella canis*.
Bursa	a sac or purse-like structure made usually of connective tissue. The ovary of the bitch is enclosed in a bursa.
Carcinogenic	cancer producing.
Carcinoma	a type of malignant tumour.
Cervical	related or pertaining to the cervix or the neck of the uterus.
Chorion	the outermost layer of the foetal membranes – part of the placenta.
Cilia	hair-like protrusions from the surface of cells which sweep the contents of hollow organs in one direction.
Coitus	sexual intercourse – copulation.
Colostrum	the first milk produced after giving birth.
Conceptus	offspring during development, an embryo, a foetus.
Congenital	present at birth.
Copulation	the act of mating – coitus.
Corpus luteum (pl. corpora lutea)	small 'bodies' which develop in the ovaries at the place from which an egg has been released. It produces the sex hormone progesterone.
Cytology	the study of cells.
Diapedesis	the passing of blood cells through the walls of intact blood vessels into the adjoining tissues.
Digital	use of the fingers.
Dys-	a prefix meaning painful or difficult.
Dystocia	difficult or abnormal birth.
Ecbolic	an agent which makes the uterus contract.
Ejaculation	expulsion of semen through the urethra to the outside.
Embryo	a developing progeny (puppy) in the uterus up to the time when the major organs have developed.
Endocrine glands	glands which secrete hormones into the blood to act as chemical messages.
Endometritis	inflammation of the lining of the womb.
Endometrium	the lining of the womb.
Episiotomy	incision of the vulva during parturition (whelping) to avoid excessive laceration and trauma to the genital tract.
Fertilization	the fusion between a spermatazoa and an egg.
Fits	episodes of involuntary muscle and nervous activity.
Foetus	a developing offspring (puppy) in the uterus from the time when the major organs have developed until birth.
Follicle	a developing egg in the ovary.
Follicle stimulating hormone	see FSH

FSH	follicle stimulating hormone – produced by the anterior pituitary gland in the brain; a gonadotrophin.
Gestation	period of development of the progeny in the womb from fertilization to birth.
Gonadotrophin releasing hormone	a hormone released by the hypothalamus (an area in the brain) which stimulates the anterior pituitary gland to produce the gonadotrophins FSH and LH.
Haematology	examination of the blood.
Haematoma	a mass of blood that has leaked from the blood vessels and become trapped under the skin or within a tissue.
Heat	a lay term used to describe the summation of pro-oestrus and oestrus.
Hepatitis	inflammation of the liver.
Heredity	the process of passing traits or characteristics from one generation to the next.
Hermaphrodite	an animal that is bisexual – it has one ovary and one testicle.
Histology	miscroscopic anatomy – looking at tissues with the aid of a microscope.
Hormone	a chemical messenger produced by an endocrine gland and transported in the blood to a target organ where it will exert its effect.
Hyper-	a prefix meaning excessive.
Hyperplasia	excessive growth of a tissue.
Hypertrophy	increase in size of an organ or tissue.
Hypo-	as a prefix means deficient, less than, e.g. hypothyroid – an underactive thyroid resulting in reduced levels of thyroid hormone in the blood.
Hypoplasia	incomplete development, e.g. vaginal hypoplasia.
Hypothalamus	an area in the brain near the pituitary gland which produces a releasing factor that stimulates the production of FSH and LH.
Hypothermia	lowered body temperature.
Hysterectomy	surgical removal of the uterus.
Iatrogenic	caused by medication.
Idiopathic	of unknown cause.
Implantation	attachment of the embryo to the uterus before the placenta is developed.
Insemination	the placement of semen in the vagina, naturally at coitus or artificially.
Intramuscular	into the body of a muscle viz. intramuscular injection.
Intravenous	into a vein viz. intravenous injection.
Intromission	the entrance of the penis into the vulva.
Involution	the decrease in size of an organ, e.g. the uterus after it has performed its function.

Larva (pl. larvae)	an immature stage in the development of some parasites viz *Toxocara canis*.
Lesion	a pathological change in a tissue.
LH	luteinizing hormone – a gonadotrophin produced by the anterior pituitary which brings about ovulation.
Lumen	the cavity in a hollow organ.
Luteinizing Hormone	see LH.
Malignant	severe, life-threatening, capable of spreading – applied to tumours.
Mastitis	inflammation of the mammary gland.
Melaena	passage of black faeces due to digested blood.
Metasteses	tumours resulting from malignant cells spreading to other parts of the body.
Metoestrus	that stage of the oestrous cycle which follows heat and precedes anoestrus.
Metritis	inflammation of the uterus.
Mismating	unintentional mating. Also called misalliance or mesalliance.
Monoestrus	relates to the oestrous cycle and is applied to animals that ovulate only once per breeding season.
Morula	an embryo which consists of undifferentiated cells, i.e. very early in its development.
Mucoid	applied to a discharge meaning that it is like mucus.
Mucus	a clear, slimy, often tenacious fluid produced by a mucous membrane, e.g. the lining of the vagina.
Necropsy	a post mortem or autopsy.
Necrosis	death of a tissue.
Neonatal	new-born.
Neoplasia	formation of a neoplasm or growth (tumour).
Oestrus	the period during heat during when the bitch will accept the male.
Ovariohysterectomy	surgical removal of the uterus and ovaries – to spay.
Ovulation	the release of an egg from the ovary.
Ovum	an egg.
Oxytocin	a hormone produced by the posterior pituitary gland which causes the uterus to contract during birth and which stimulates milk production. Often given as an injection to stimulate uterine regression after birth – see posterior pituitary injection.
Paediatrics	medicine related to young animals.
Palpation	examination by touch.
Parturition	the process of giving birth – whelping in the case of bitches.
Pathogenesis	the development of a disease process.
Perinatal	in the period around the time of birth.

Perineum	the area of the body around the anus and stretching to the vulva in bitches and the scrotum in dogs.
Physiology	the science dealing with the function of organs.
Pituitary gland	an endocrine gland that lies on the underside of the brain.
Placenta	afterbirth.
Poly-	a prefix meaning many or increased.
Polydypsia	increased thirst.
Polyuria	passing increased quantities of urine.
Prognosis	the expected outcome of a disease
Prolapse	protrusion, to the outside, of an abdominal organ, e.g. vagina.
Pro-oestrus	the first stage of heat, when a bitch first comes 'in season'.
Prophylaxis	prevention of a disease.
Pseudocyesis	synonomous with pseudo- or false pregnancy.
Puberty	the time of life when an animal becomes sexually mature.
Puerperal	pertaining to the period immediately after giving birth.
Pyrexia	raised body temperature – fever.
Season-in	a lay term to describe when a bitch is 'on heat'.
Spay (spey)	surgical sterilization of a female by removal of the uterus and ovaries – ovariohysterectomy.
Staphylococci	bacteria which commonly occur, particularly in association with skin disease.
Streptococci	commonly occurring bacteria which frequently affect dogs and may be associated, for example, with tonsillitis or vaginitis.
Subclinical	applied to a disease in which the signs are not obvious by clinical examination.
Subcutaneous	under the skin viz. subcutaneous injection.
Superficial	on the surface. Often applied to a wound.
Syndrome	a set of signs which occur together indicating a particular condition or disease.
Tenesmus	painful and ineffective straining – to pass faeces or urine.
Teratogenic	capable of producing abnormalities in puppies whilst they are in the womb, applied to a medicine, e.g. thalidomide.
Tie	the time during which the dog's penis is held in the vagina after ejaculation.
Tissue	an aggregation of similar cells in the body, e.g. a muscle.
Toxaemia	the spread of bacterial products (toxins) in the blood from a source of infection.
Transplacental	transfer across the placenta from mother to offspring, e.g. the passage of infection or antibodies.
Trauma	injury – wounding, shock.
Tumour	a growth, neoplasm.

Glossary

Umbilical cord the stalk of blood vessel and other tissues which join the developing foetus to the placenta.

Umbilicus the point on the abdominal wall where the umbilical cord emerged.

Uterus the womb.

Whelp a young puppy. To whelp – the process of a bitch giving birth to puppies.

Zoonosis a disease that can be transmitted from animals to man.

NAMES

TESSA   BUSTER

BELL   BUTCH

CARLA   SPANKY

PEBBLES

SUGAR

INDEX

For definitions and further entries, *see also* Glossary, pages 219–224

Index

Index

Index

179, 196 – during whelping, 87; morning sickness, 78

Vulva, 87–89, 128–129, 131, 134, 153, 157, 159, 160, 161, 170; – infantile, 155, 161, 173; licking of, 29, 144, 148, 149, 161, 162, 170, 177; swelling of, 29, 160–161, 171, 184

'Walrus puppies' (*see* Anasarca)

Water, 46, 51, 101, 115, 136, 148, 153–154, 170 (*see also* Feeding; Thirst); on the brain (*see* Hydrocephalus)

'Waterlogged puppies' (*see* Anasarca)

Weedkillers (*see* Teratogenic agents)

Weight 198–217 (*see also* Feeding); – birth, 102, 104, 106, 152, 195–217; gain, 32, 106, 152, 198–217; loss, 151; record, 193

Weaning, 116–118; – feeding during (*see* Feeding)

Whelping, 31, 79–80, 81, 83–99, 157, 192, 195–217 *passim*; –

bedding (*see* Bedding); bed-shredding during (*see* Bed-shredding); bitch care after, 118–119; box, 85–87, 97, 99, 152; contractions during, 88–89, 92; distress during, 96, 97–98; duration of, 86; feeding after, during (*see* Feeding); location, 60–61, 83–86, 152; panting during (*see* Panting); veterinary help during, 97–99; vomiting during (*see* Vomiting)

Whining, 145, 151

Womb (*see* Uterus)

Worming, 19, 25–26, 33, 152, 170; – during pregnancy, 82, 97; (*see also* Worms)

Worms, 162–165, 169; (*see also* Worming)

X-ray, 79

Yelping, 150

APPENDIX 1

METHODS FOR IDENTIFYING THE STAGES OF THE OESTROUS CYCLE

Essentially three methods of determining the stages of the cycle and thus the time of ovulation, are available to veterinary surgeons in practice: vaginal cytology, vaginoscopy and the measurement of hormone levels in the blood.

Vaginal cytology

Although this method can be used to detect pro-oestrus, oestrus and metoestrus, it is now recognised that it can in fact only be relied upon to detect the time of ovulation *after* the event. This is because the first day of metoestrus is the only stage of the cycle which can be pinpointed precisely by this technique. If the changes associated with the onset of metoestrus are seen it can be said with reasonable certainty that ovulation occurred approximately six days earlier. This, of course, is too late if the aim is to get the bitch in whelp.

Table 1: Vaginal smears in the bitch

Relative quantities of cells and debris present at each phase of the Oestrous Cycle

	Stage of Cycle					
	An-oestrus	Early Pro-oestrus	Late Pro-oestrus	Early Oestrus	Late Oestrus	Met-oestrus
Red Blood Cells		ООО	ОО	О		
Keratinized Cells		⬠	⬠⬠	⬠⬠⬠	⬠⬠	
Leucocytes	⬤⬤	⬤			⬤	⬤⬤⬤
Debris		+ +	+ + +	+ +	+	

The number of symbols represents the preponderance of cells and debris

Vaginoscopy

This technique involves the veterinary surgeon looking closely at the lining of the vagina using a special instrument called a vaginoscope. As one would expect the changes in the lining of the vagina as seen through a vaginoscope parallel those seen in vaginal smears. However, at the time of ovulation, the veterinary surgeon will note the onset of a wrinkling effect. The wrinkles become very obvious about four days after ovulation which is the most critical time for mating. Only vets with specialist expertise can provide this service and they will need to examine bitches at least every other day from 4-5 days after the onset of pro-oestrus if the method is to be used effectively.

Measurement of hormone levels

Progesterone levels start to rise at the end of pro-oestrus and increase further during oestrus and subsequently. They reach quite consistent and specific levels at the time of ovulation. A simple quick method of measuring progesterone levels in just a drop of plasma has been recently developed. This test, in kit form, is now available to veterinary surgeons commercially, and it enables clinicians to advise bitch owners when ovulation is about to occur or has just occurred so that mating can be timed to take place during the period of peak fertility.

For bitches which have been previously bred from successfully, a single sample taken 10-11 days after the onset of heat will normally suffice but the owner should be prepared to have the bitch mated within two days.

In the case of bitches which have failed to get in whelp previously it is recommended that sampling should start at the latest seven days after the onset of pro-oestrus and that samples should be taken subsequently at two day intervals. If a very high progesterone level is recorded at this point (day 7) there is a possibility that the bitch will have ovulated very early, maybe even 2-3 days after the onset of pro-oestrus. Mating immediately is necessary in these causes for a successful outcome.

In the majority of cases it is unlikely that there will be a need to test more than three samples unless the bitch is a late ovulator where in some cases testing may be necessary beyond 15 or 17 days after the beginning of pro-oestrus. If the progesterone level remains low for a prolonged period it is reasonably certain that the bitch will not have ovulated. However, understandably, owners may become restless and wish to mate their bitch anyway if she 'looks right'. However, in such cases it makes sense to return to the vet's surgery the day after mating for a retest. If the progesterone level is still low at this time it is most unlikely that the bitch will have conceived and owners should be prepared for testing at two day intervals to go on until progesterone levels indicate that ovulation has occurred. Bitches have been known to ovulate as late as 30 days after the onset of pro-oestrus!

If the progesterone level never rises, this is an indicator that the bitch has very real infertility problems. Luckily these cases are very rare but, if they occur, further in-depth examination is called for.

This new ability to determine the optimum mating time should prove to be extremely useful to dog breeders. Potentially it can save unnecessary costs and disappointment. Visiting a favoured stud dog can often mean travelling considerable distances and an overnight stay away from home; thus, it is important to ensure that the bitch is really 'ready' before setting out. If a bitch fails to conceive, valuable time is lost and potential puppy purchasers will inevitably be disappointed; failure to conceive will be much less likely if the time of ovulation is predicted in advance. Finally, the test will have an obvious application in bitches which have failed to conceive at previous matings; the assessment of progesterone levels is vital to the successful management of these 'problem' cases.